*Learning from
Real World Cases*

Lessons in
Leadership

D. D. Warrick & Jens Mueller

R■S
ROSSISMITH
ACADEMIC PUBLISHING

Warrick and Mueller collected an absolutely superb set of authors whose experiences run a broad gamete of organizations, nations, and cultures. They, in turn, present readers with a wide range of cases that collectively show almost every type of challenge a leader might face. The potential for discussing seems endless. Every student of leadership will benefit from this book.

– Jerry Porras – Lane Professor of Organization Behavior and Change Emeritus
  Stanford Graduate School of Business · Co-author with Jim Collins of *Built To Last*

This is a must read for individuals who would like to learn about multiple facets of leadersh In contrast to many books about leadership this one is grounded in powerful illustrative stories that will inspire you and help you learn from the practices of good leaders.

– Michael Beer
  Professor Emeritus - Harvard Business School · Co-author of *Higher Ambition: How Great Leaders Create Economic and Social Value* and author of *High Commitment/High Performance*

This is an exciting book. It links rich and outstanding cases with the critical leadership issu of our times. This is both a practical and visionary book – an excellent choice for leaders and students alike.

– Pam Shockley-Zalabak
  Chancellor, University of Colorado at Colorado Springs · Co-Author with Michael Hackman of
  Building The High Trust Organization

People love stories especially those that teach us something important. Warrick and Mueller have assembled a remarkable array of such stories. Most significant among this array is that although style and skills may differ, leadership is still leadership regardless of where in the world it may occur, that is, leadership is about influecing people to do something that they may n otherwise do. These stories beautifully convey that message.

– W. Warner Burke
  Edward Lee Thorndike Professor of Psychology and Education · Chair of Department of Organization and Leadership · Teachers College – Columbia University · Author of *Organization Change: Theory and Practice*

In today's turbulent economy, the imperative for strong leadership has never been greater. Organizations that possess a strong leadership culture will thrive in this environment and those that do not will be penalized by markets and/or their key stakeholders. Through insightful case studies, Lessons In Leadership is a powerful resource for organizations working to strengthen th leaders at all levels.

– Kevin Crockett, President/CEO and Principal Noel-Levitz

As a CEO of a bank and founder of a Leadership Institute, this book is a must read! Lessons In Leadership provides an excellent source for training executives and leaders at all levels. The authors offer "real case scenarios" that compel and impact those reaching for excellence in helping people reach their fullest potential. I highly recommend this book to those who are looking for a relevant, hands-on-approach to effective and influential leadership.

– Dan Heine, President and CEO The Bank of Oswego, Lake Oswego

A must-have, essential resource for both the class room and the training room! Lessons in Leadership offers our best and latest knowledge conveniently packaged in highly accessible, engaging, and easy to use leadership stories that make for excellent learning and practice in any leadership venue.

– Jim Barker, Professor Dalhousie University School of Business Administration, Halifax, Nova Scotia, Canad

Learning from Real World Cases
LESSONS in LEADERSHIP

D. D. Warrick & Jens Mueller

ROSSISMITH
ACADEMIC PUBLISHING

National Library of New Zealand Cataloguing-in-Publication Data

Warrick, D. D.
Lessons in leadership : learn from cases / Don Warrick & Jens Mueller.
Includes index.
ISBN 978-0-9864597-3-3
1. Leadership—Case studies. I. Mueller, Jens, 1956- II. Title.
658.4092—dc 22

©2011 RossiSmith Academic Publications Ltd., Oxford, UK
www.rossismith.com

Publisher: Triaxis Ltd., New Zeland,
www.publicationsales.com
Design and layout: TYPE+*grafik*, B Janitz

TABLE OF CONTENTS

Learning from Real World Cases
LESSONS in LEADERSHIP

CHAPTER ONE:
Inspirational Leaders Committed To Making A Difference

CHAPTER TWO:
The Need For Ethical Leaders Of Strong Character

CHAPTER THREE:
Leadership Styles And Their Consequences

CHAPTER FOUR:
Leading And Developing People

CHAPTER FIVE:
Leading And Developing Teams, Teamwork And Collaboration

CHAPTER SIX:
Leading Organizations To Excellence

CHAPTER SEVEN:
Leading Change

FOREWORD

It was our goal to produce a special book that was filled with interesting and relevant real world cases that cover the essentials of effective leadership, conclude with rich discussion options and summaries of leadership lessons, and can be used to develop present and future leaders into skilled leaders. In helping us reach this challenging goal, the authors, many of whom are well known experts in leadership, exceeded our expectations as the cases came from all over the globe and were filled with valuable leadership lessons. One interesting lesson that became evident in the cases is that regardless of where leaders lead, whether the US, China, Australia, Europe, or Guatemala, the principles of good leadership apply across the globe even though the application of those principles may differ.

The book is designed to present short to medium length cases and follows a logical flow for preparing leaders to lead. It begins with inspiring cases about leaders with a strong commitment to making a difference. This is followed with cases emphasizing the importance of ethics, character, and leadership style. The next cases show how leadership can be applied to working with people, building high performance teams and teamwork, and developing excellent organizations. The final chapter presents cases on how leaders can successfully lead change.

Chapter 1 begins with cases about **Inspirational Leaders Committed To Making A Difference.** You will read stories of a Physician who built an award winning medical center and a visionary woman from Northern Ireland who was the first woman to hold a number of high profile public sector leadership positions and who was skilled at uniting divided citizens to accomplish common goals. You will read of a Colonel who led a dangerous rescue mission for orphans, the first woman conductor of a major symphony, and a leader who led polar expeditions and utilized skills in entrepreneurship and developing leaders to promote environmental awareness and preserve Antarctica. These cases will hopefully inspire leaders at all levels to see that when leaders lead, great things are possible!

Chapter 2 forms an important foundation for leadership by addressing **The Need For Ethical Leaders Of Strong Character.** In this chapter you will see how a company has pioneered an impressive training program for developing ethical leaders, how Abraham Lincoln demonstrated ethical leadership, and how a company built an ethical culture. You will also be placed in the position of a Public Service Director who had to make an ethical decision that could significantly affect his career and the reputation and career of a governor and his staff and will need to decide what you would do as an Assistant Principle of a School who was faced with a difficult ethical decision that would affect the future of a student. There are leaders who try to lead with questionable ethics and weak character but they will never achieve the respect and positive influence of ethical leaders of exemplary character.

Chapter 3 addresses the importance of **Leadership Styles And Their Consequences.** As you will see in the cases, leadership style has a significant impact on the performance, motivation, and morale of people and the relationship leaders have with people. In this chapter you will read a fascinating and very moving case about the influence a leader's style has on Nicaraguan garment workers. This case should leave you with an unforgettable awareness of the importance of your leadership style. You will also see how two CEO's with different leadership styles affected whole companies with their styles. Another case will contrast the leadership styles of incident commanders responding to a simulated terrorist attack and the important consequences of the two styles. There is a case that points out how leadership styles can change, not always for the better, and the dangers of leaders jumping to conclusions and treating symptoms rather than the real issues. Finally, you will see how the leadership style of the founder of a Chinese-Australian family business enabled the business to grow and prosper. We are all leaders to some degree whether we occupy formal leadership positions or are simply influencing people and we all have a leadership style that is affecting people. These cases will help you understand your leadership style and the type of influence you are having.

Chapter 4 includes cases that focus on **Leading And Developing People.** It is a long time cliche' that "people are our greatest asset". While this is little more than talk in most organizations, it is a truism that the best organizations fully understand. You can duplicate facilities, technology, pay, and even resources but it takes a special commitment to develop leaders who have good people skills and understand how to lead, develop, and motivate people. In Chapter 4 you will begin with a case that clearly portrays the kind of demanding, busy, whitewater type of environment leaders must perform in today and the commitment it takes to know and work effectively with people without getting preoccupied with daily tasks. The next case shows a very novel approach to developing skilled, people oriented leaders. Then, readers are presented with a people problem to solve. How problems are approached will significantly influence the probability of achieving successful and lasting solutions. The final case in this chapter provides an opportunity for the reader to explore ways to motivate de-motivated and entrenched employees.

Chapter 5 is titled **Leading And Developing Teams, Teamwork, And Collaboration.** This is a very important chapter as it offers cases that emphasize the importance of teamwork and developing high performance teams and of encouraging collaboration within and between teams. It is common place to talk about the importance of teamwork but few organizations do anything to actually develop teamwork and few leaders know how to build high performance teams. This chapter starts off with an intriguing story about Robin Hood and how he skillfully built a remarkable team. You will read of his encounters with Little John, Friar Tuck, and others and how he surrounded himself with talented people and commended those who performed better than he did. You will then read a case about a talented leader who became the President of her alma mater and had to make difficult decisions regarding how to re-build a weak top leadership team. The next case presents an incredibly innovative approach to using large group meetings to quickly change the thinking and actions of leaders and build a culture of teamwork and collaboration. After studying these cases the reader should have a heightened understanding of the importance of teamwork and of purposely building high performance teams and developing teamwork and collaboration within and between teams.

Chapter 6 follows the progressions of leaders developing skills in working with people, teams, and organizations. It is titled **Leading Organizations To Excellence.** The chapter focuses on the importance and payoffs of pursing organization excellence. The cases in this chapter should educate the reader on the importance of building an excellent organization *that gets great results **and** is a great place to work*. Research on best run organizations consistently show that the best have skilled

FOREWORD

leaders who focus on both performance and people. The first case in this chapter shows how a Caucasian CEO was able to overcome cultural differences and build a failing Chinese bank into a successful bank and create a new, positive culture. Then we see how a leader transformed a Saudi Chamber of Commerce into an award winning organization and was named the **Corporate Management CEO of the Year** by the *Middle East Excellence Awards Institute*. The last case in this chapter tells the story of a plant manager in Ireland who has a passion for excellence that enabled her to achieve enviable results while overcoming many difficult challenges and setbacks. The case shows how effective leaders are willing to persevere in their pursuit of excellence even when faced with challenge after challenge.

Chapter 7 concludes the book with cases on **Leading Change**. Skills in leading change are often left to experts and yet in these times of dynamic, accelerated, non-stop, unpredictable change in organizations, this may be the most critical skill leaders need to learn. Few leaders are trained how to lead change and consequently research on change shows that most organization changes fail and that the lack of skills in leading change has far reaching consequences. The cases in this chapter begin with a case describing how leaders at a university in Australia were coached to effectively lead change. The second case describes a template of 19 success factors that leaders can be taught to increase their skills in leading change. The final case of the book describes a carefully planned large scale organization change and emphasizes the important role the Executive Leadership Team plays in leading successful changes.

It is our strong desire that this book will be a joy to read and will be used to significantly enhance the leadership skills of leaders in all sizes and types of organizations and undergraduate and graduate students preparing to be leaders. Leadership is an important skill that needs to be studied and continuously developed. Leaders can make a difference and we hope that you will use this book to increase your abilities to bring out the best in people, teams, and organizations.

In conclusion, we want to thank the many authors who made this book possible and who contributed such interesting and relevant cases filled with valuable leadership lessons. We also want to thank all who were involved in the production of the book and especially our wives who were so patient with us during the preparation of the book.

D.D. Warrick and Jens Mueller

BIOGRAPHY *D. D. Warrick*

Dr. Warrick is an award winning educator, consultant, and author
who specializes in developing high impact leaders, high performance
teams and organizations, and successfully managing change. He is a
Professor of Management and Organization Change at the University
of Colorado at Colorado Springs where he holds the title of President's
Teaching Scholar and has received the Chancellor's Award, the
university's highest award, as well as the Outstanding University
Teacher of the Year Award, and many teaching awards in the College
of Business. Dr. Warrick is also the President of the Warrick Agency
and has been a consultant to many large companies such as Allied
Signal, British Petroleum, Dow Corning, Harley-Davidson, Hewlett
Packard, IBM, and Whirlpool, as well as smaller and mid-sized companies, public
agencies, and numerous colleges and universities. He has received many awards for
his contributions including being named the Outstanding Organization Development
Practitioner of the Year, the Outstanding Human Resources Professional of the Year, and
the Outstanding Educator of the Year in Organization Behavior. He has also received
numerous awards from the Academy of Management and was recently named the Best
Professor in Organisational Development by the World HRD Congress.
Dr. Warrick received his BBA and MBA degrees from the University of Oklahoma and
doctorate from the University of Southern California.

D. D. Warrick
Professor of Management and Organization Change and President's Teaching Scholar
Graduate School of Business
Email: ddwarrick@aol.com

BIOGRAPHY *Jens Mueller*

Jens Muelloer is Associate Professor for Entrepreneurship
and Strategy at the Waikato Management School in Hamilton,
New Zealand, Triple Crown accredited business school and the
No 1 Research-Led Business School in New Zealand. Based on his
research work and more then 20 years of Chair/CEO experience
in global industries, Jens assists leaders of many organizations
worldwide to create effective strategies for sustainable growth.
Jens sits on several boards of companies and teaches MBA courses
at several prestigious universities internationally. He is a prolific
author and a very engaging presenter, frequently invited work with
the leadership teams of government departments, non-profit entities
and commercial enterprises. His details are at **www.muellerjens.com**

Jens Mueller
Waikato Management School, Hamilton, New Zealand
RossiSmith Academic Publishing, Editor
Email: mueller@rossismith.com

CHAPTER ONE

1

A Physician Turned Leader Commits To Building An Award Winning Organization

Susan Albers Mohrman & Arienne McCracken

Major Focus of the Case

Much leadership literature stresses the important role of the charismatic hero-leader. Yet in today's world of far-flung operations in diverse contexts where people throughout the organization have to deal with complexity and uncertainty, this model may not be possible or effective. Shared leadership, where there are many competent leaders spread throughout the organization at many levels, is an especially critical concept for any non-hierarchical organization in an environment characterized by the need to continually adapt and improve. (Lawler & Worley, 2006). Shared leadership occurs when practices are distributed and interdependent, and where leadership is a social process, occurring "in and through relationships and networks of influence." It leads ideally to outcomes of "mutual learning, greater shared understanding...and positive action" (Fletcher & Käufer, 2003, p. 23). Shared leadership does not naturally occur. In the case of Jeff Weisz, Executive Medical Director of the Southern California Permanente Medical Group, it reflects his and his team's understanding that today's world demands many leaders collaborating to lead an organization to greatness.

"I am a physician first, and my leadership is based on that premise." – Jeff Weisz

Introduction

Kaiser Permanente (KP) is both a health care delivery system and an insurance plan that provides comprehensive care to a defined population of members in exchange for a capitation premium paid by employers, individuals, Medicare, and MediCal (the State of California's Medicare program). It also provides charity care to uninsured patients. KP is comprised of the Kaiser Foundation Health Plan, the Kaiser Foundation Hospitals, and the Permanente Medical Groups. Nationally, KP's eight regions serve more than 8.6 million members, delivering care in 35 hospitals and 454 medical offices. 15,129 physicians and 164,098 technical, administrative, and care providers work in the Kaiser System (About Kaiser Permanente, 2010).

An independent Permanente Medical Group contracts with each region of Kaiser Permanente to provide comprehensive physician services to the member population. This case concerns the leadership of the Southern California Permanente Medical Group (SCPMG). The Southern California region has the largest membership of any of the regions KP serves, with 3,284,540 members as of 12/2009.

Dr. Jeffrey Weisz: A Physician Turned Leader

Jeffrey Weisz is a hematologist/oncologist who was elected as the Executive Medical Director of SCPMG in 2003. During his tenure, the Group has experienced a substantial culture change, a growing sense of pride in the doctors and staff, and world-class success in both patient outcomes and financial measures. His success, in a position that doesn't have a lot of hierarchical power, is due to his knowledge as a practicing physician, his knowledge of how the KP system works, and his ability to assemble a team of change agents to encourage, enable, incent, and align his fellow doctors throughout the organization. Jeff is quite humble about his role. One could take this as a kind of false modesty, a curious window dressing. But it is genuine. In fact, Jeff's humility is a sign that the accomplishments of the Southern California KP Region are, in fact, a triumph of shared leadership. The SCPMG demonstrates this capability repeatedly.

The SCPMG is a partnership of almost 4000 partner and 1500 associate physicians . The partners co-own and self-govern the group. They are accustomed to acting autonomously. They don't like being told what to do. As Dr. Jeffrey Selevan, Medical Director for Business Management, has noted, Weisz's "ability to directly manage the operations in our medical centers is tenuous at best, and mostly nonexistent." Add to this the fact that Weisz's position, per the bylaws of the partnership, is one elected by the Board of Directors, and requiring two-thirds of partners to affirm the Board of Director decision. One can see that the traditional definition of leadership, where an individual leader makes decisions that are pushed down into the organization, could not apply in this case.

Woodland Hills, California

Jeff Weisz always liked being a doctor and practicing medicine. He says it was a fluke that he first got into administration. Jeff started his leadership career by serving as the Woodland Hills Medical Center's elected representative to the SCPMG Board of Directors for 9 years; he then was selected as the Woodland Hills Medical Director. Woodland Hills is one of 11 Centers in the Southern California Region. His "platform" for the Woodland Hills Medical Director position consisted of six focuses that have remained constant throughout his leadership at SCPMG: 1) timely medical care, 2) service and compassion to patients, 3) leading in clinical strategic goals, 4) developing and promoting clinical best practices throughout the region, 5) valuing KP people, with competitive compensation, high morale, collaborative labor management partnership, mutual accountability, and cultural diversity, and 6) building on the integrated relationship with KP Foundation Health Plan and Hospitals by increasing collaboration and reducing duplication of work.

Woodland Hills had a history of never meeting its budget, and Weisz balanced the budget in his first year as medical director. He carefully, systematically, and deeply looked into the details of how the medical center was operating, which led him to examine the staffing patterns and other uses of resources in order to make changes that increased the quality and access. Weisz had personal relationships and trust with the doctors. He believes that one reason he was successful was because he was a doctor who still practiced – so he was "one of them." As Executive Medical Director of SCPMG, he has continued to articulate a three-fold mission: do what is good for patients, good for doctors, and good for the organization - always remembering that patients are first.

Dr. Weisz's Vision

In service of this mission, he began to formulate a belief that if Kaiser Permanente became the best in the world at Preventive Care, true greatness as a system would result. It was clear that healthcare expenses in the U.S. were becoming increasingly non-sustainable, consuming an ever-increasing percentage of the country's resources at a time when demographics and disease patterns suggested that demand would increase astronomically over the ensuing years. It was apparent to Jeff that high quality preventive health care would be a win for patients and their quality of life, for physicians whose primary motivation is delivering high quality care, and for payers who were struggling to cover the rapidly rising costs of healthcare. His tenure as Executive Medical Director for SCPMG has been a period during which the physicians throughout the region started to operate with this vision of greatness, and indeed moved toward "best in the country" in many areas, most notably in the areas of preventive care.

Shared Leadership in the Executive Team

As Weisz began in his role as SCPMG's Executive Medical Director in 2004, he assembled a small executive team. Included in that team were two physicians, Michael Kanter (Regional Medical Director of Quality and Clinical Analysis) and Paul Minardi (Regional Medical Director of Operations), who had sat with him at Paul's Cafe several years earlier "blue-skying" what Kaiser Permanente and American health care could become. As he did at Woodland Hills, Weisz, now with an executive team carefully chosen for energy, vision, and talent, would begin by closely scrutinizing the details in many areas of the SCPMG operation. They soon found significant inefficiencies in the system – where resources could be freed up to build a world-leading preventive system. As they chipped away at the inefficiencies, they were able to redirect resources to areas that made a positive difference in the lives of physicians and patients, and in costs. Other members of Weisz's executive team were Dr. Jeffrey Selevan as Medical Director of Business Management, Marilyn Owsley as Business Administrator of Finance, Systems, and Contracts, and Tom Williamson, Business Administrator of Operations. Together they explored ways to get resources more aligned with clinical and patient needs, and they found opportunities to dramatically improve clinical and administrative processes. They demonstrated to the physicians that through the smart practice of preventive medicine and through improving clinical and administrative processes throughout the system, resources could be freed up to provide greater support to physicians, hire more physicians, and provide better care to members. The change was couched as a way to provide the environment in which physicians could practice great medicine.

Weisz said he assembled his team by "pick[ing] people who are smarter than me," but more than just that, he assembled a team of co-leaders. Jeff may be the visionary – the person who puts a stake in the ground – but his team figures out what is needed and does the things to get it moving. Michael Kanter offered a perspective that is shared by the other members of the team: "Jeff articulated a vision of where we would go. He gave me and the others a lot of runway space. We're very cohesive, and none of us worry about who gets credit."

The executive team is composed of very independent, driven, high performers, who at the same time work closely together. Each member of the team has the power to make decisions. Weisz holds them accountable but doesn't micromanage. The team is small, and their responsibilities intentionally overlap, demanding a high degree of collaboration and cooperation among the team members for it to function. (By comparison, the executive team in Kaiser's Northern California region has at least 20 members.) "There is an extraordinary degree of cooperation among us," says Selevan. Kanter will "discover things as he works on quality and clinical analysis that affect me, and it gets handed over to me. And vice versa... So when we combine all these kinds of analysis, we collectively work synergistically with each other in a co-leader way," explains Minardi. The executive team members don't think alike and don't always agree amongst themselves or with Jeff. They feel free to challenge Jeff and each other, but always come together in the wake of a decision. The team members truly do not let egos get in the way when it comes to Kaiser, the doctors, and the patients.

Relationships and Networks

In the shared leadership model, we see movement, initiative, and change emanating from all parts of the organization, facilitated through SCPMG-wide relationships and networks, not just via Jeff Weisz and his executive team. Especially in a professional partnership, much has to come up from the bottom. Under Jeff's leadership, robust Region-wide networks have been built to share best practices, exchange knowledge, and innovate and improve processes. Medical Centers that previously ran quite independently have been connected through a web of cross-cutting relationships.

Regional chairs of the different medical specialties are a lateral type of leadership that cuts across the enterprise. Regional chairs in a particular medical specialty, such as gastroenterology (GI), build connections with the GI chiefs at the 13 medical centers in the region. Jeff has challenged each chair to work with the network to identify outcome areas where the Region will become the national leader. They meet regularly as a group to coordinate best practices, and the regional chair also meets individually with each medical center chief on a peer-to-peer basis. It's important for both learning and for developing personal relationships. Alexander Lee, the Regional Chair of Gastroenterology in Southern California, says that talking frequently is "very important because in an organization of this size it's easy for people to practice in a silo." Lee notes that this practice of sharing has grown beyond Southern California, so that now the nationwide network of Kaiser's GI regional chairs have conference calls bi-monthly and face-to-face meetings twice a year.

Similarly, each medical center has a physician champion for a particular chronic disease state, such as asthma. The champions are leaders for total health and preventive care, and they meet regularly to share best practices. If another medical center is having better outcomes than you are with your asthma patients, you'll hear about it here. It's a way to share learning, but it's not mandated from the top; instead, it is a "friendly competition that we take seriously," which is fueled by the extensive metrics collected from a variety of electronic databases, including KP's HealthConnect Electronic Medical Record (EMR), comments Julia Bae, the Area Medical Director of Kern County.

Jeff Weisz and his lateral counterpart, Dr. Ben Chu, the President of Kaiser Permanente Southern California (which encompasses the Kaiser Foundation Health Plan and the Kaiser Foundation Hospitals), share the vision of **great healthcare, work as a team, and trust each other.** They don't question each other's motivations, which was not necessarily how the heads of these separate pieces in the Kaiser system worked previously. This trust has been the foundation for many collaborative initiatives and for a flexibility in the application of resources to achieve region-wide objectives.

The Proactive Office Encounter (POE) concept has built on the capabilities of the system's Health Connect EMR to create a virtual system of care around each patient. No matter where in the system patients show up for care, they will be reminded of preventive measures and routine care that needs to be done, and staff will take responsibility for reaching out to patients when care is overdue. This system built on practices that were being introduced in the Orange County Medical Center. These were fine tuned by Kanter and Minardi and others, who worked with physicians and staff throughout the region to develop tools and protocols, and to define the roles for the various support staff. POE was rolled out to the entire Southern California region with measures, tools, consulting, training, and other forms of support being provided from the Region.

Minardi points out that much change emanates from the Centers, and that the executive team gets "involved in the [ideas] that can be scaled up and make a difference across the system." POE, for example, emphasizes proactive care and prevention. Two-thirds of visits by patients needing a mammogram are with specialists, not primary care physicians, so it made sense, for example, that if a patient came in to see a dermatologist, but hadn't had a mammogram, the dermatologist could alert the patient, order the exam, and get her scheduled right then and there. It made sense – but initially violated long-standing norms of practice and divisions between primary and specialty care. Together, Weisz, Kanter, Minardi, and other leaders built a data-based business case that demonstrated the clinical and financial benefits, and provided the support to physicians and other medical staff in changing roles, relationships, and processes and in achieving aggressive new targets for preventive medicine. The POE was one innovation that led to SCPMG now leading the nation in breast cancer screening among women ages 52-69 and having similar national leadership outcomes in other areas of prevention.

Challenges Of A Proactive Leader

Although leadership is disbursed throughout the system, Jeff Weisz is a lightning rod, because he sticks his neck out and advocates for his vision, which can sometimes involve unpopular measures. The many changes that were effected during Jeff's first term led to him losing reelection as Executive Medical Director. Weisz frankly blames this on the fact that he asked physicians for a much higher level of performance within a defined amount of resources. Jeff and his team had to find ways to free up resources to address the truly important challenges and raise performance levels. They also were tasked with having to energize partners (the owners of the group practice) who were dispersed through a huge geographical area in medical centers and area structures with their own elected leaders and cultures. Weisz didn't give up, however – he reran for the position and was successfully reelected, without compromising his values and vision.

HealthConnect, KP's national EMR, was introduced during Weisz's first term, and it was a huge sticking point. "HealthConnect killed me for three years," Weisz wryly noted. Many physicians felt completely overloaded trying to practice medicine and learn the new system of record keeping (in some cases, learning to type!) and accepting a new level of measurement and transparency to their practice. Many of them simply hated it at first. Although Weisz at one point scaled back the pace of the roll out, he continued to be dedicated to it, because he knew that an EMR would increase patient outcomes and bring greater transparency and accountability to how doctors practiced, and to the quality of care by the SCPMG.

How They Succeeded

How does an agenda that is basically values and performance based get implemented in a far-flung organization of professionals who value autonomy and medical centers used to managing themselves? Weisz and his team kept in their minds the best vision of what a physician can and should be – continually learning, striving for the best outcomes, always focused on the patient. To effect their agenda, they asked more of the whole health team, worked to encourage connections at all levels, created an environment of bubble up of ideas from below and enabled broad dissemination from above, as well as introducing transparent and accountable management.

The HealthConnect EMR was a critical component in the changes that occurred in the SCPMG because it allows about 130 very detailed metrics to be taken on a regular basis, which permits real-time research into effective care. From all these metrics, the Vital Signs report is issued monthly, in which all the medical centers are ranked according to quality, financial, and service measures. People have a bit of a love-hate relationship with metrics. "Without the metrics, everyone thought they were doing great," commented Selevan. The transparency about data, care, and outcomes had a real impact on the physicians, and drove increasingly greater levels of system performance.

In addition, the measures generated in the Vital Signs report – a monthly report on a slew of measures of elements relating to quality, prevention, cost, and patient satisfaction and outcomes – feed into the incentive pay system that Weisz and his team developed. Someone hitting identified clinical strategic goals receives additional incentive pay, over and above his/her base salary. Under Weisz's tenure, base pay has gone up every year for physicians across the board, and the incentive pay program has helped in driving desired changes. Although the amount of incentive pay is not large, Lee noted that it is useful because it gives physicians "a goal to focus on.... Physicians in general are self-motivated and a little bit competitive."

Conclusion

Keeping a vision of doing what is good for patients, doctors, and the organization alive in the minds of their colleagues, Jeff Weisz and his team have demonstrated, encouraged and enabled shared leadership throughout the Southern California Permanente Medical Group. They have worked to align incentives, develop pride in achievement, and have called upon the competitive urge of doctors to effect lasting change. The Southern California Region of KP is ranked #1 in the U.S. in a number of metrics, and is listed in the Top 8 on U.S. News and World Report's ranking of Health Plans for Medicare members (Best Health Plans Search, 2010). The Economist wrote that Kaiser Permanente as a whole is a possible model for healthcare worldwide (Anonymous, 2010).

Discussion

1. Describe the leadership style of Jeff Weisz using examples to support your conclusions and then discuss your understanding of shared leadership.
2. Dr. Weisz practiced medicine in the Kaiser Permanente system for 25 years before he became the executive medical director of the SCPMG.
   Is experience and knowledge important in being an effective leader?
3. What are some things Jeff Weisz did to build a highly effective top leadership team?
4. What are some things Jeff Weisz did as a leader to help build a world class organization?

Key Leadership Lessons

1. Having an effective leadership style is key to motivating people to excel and change.
2. Visionary leaders create clear and compelling visions for people to pursue and make clear what it takes to achieve the visions.
3. Although innovation and change within a non-hierarchical system are difficult, they can be done.
4. The literature shows that shared leadership is extremely difficult to accomplish, especially in executive teams, which are often teams in name only. Yet, carefully chosen teams with clear mutual expectations can greatly leverage their impact through collaboration and shared vision.
5. Shared leadership extends down into the organization, both vertically and horizontally, with the networks in the organization providing the knowledge sharing and cohesion required to move a complex system forward.

References

About Kaiser Permanente. (2010). *Fast facts about Kaiser Permanente.* Retrieved September 3, 2010 from http://xnet.kp.org/newscenter/aboutkp/fastfacts.html.

Anonymous. (2010, May 1). Business: Another American way; Controlling health-care costs. *The Economist, 395*(8680), 67.

Best Health Plans Search. (2010). Search best health insurance plans 2009-10: Medicare. *U.S. News & World Report.* Retrieved September 15, 2010 from http://health.usnews.com/directories/health-plans/index_html/plan_cat+medicare/

Fletcher, J. K., & Käufer, K. (2003). Shared leadership: Paradox and possibility. In C. L. Pearce & J. A. Conger (Eds.), *Shared leadership: Reframing the hows and whys of leadership.* Thousand Oaks, CA: Sage Publications.

Lawler, E. E., & Worley, C. G. (2006). *Built to change: How to achieve sustained organizational effectiveness.* San Francisco: Jossey-Bass.

BIOGRAPHY

Susan Albers Mohrman (Ph.D., Northwestern University) is senior research scientist at USC's Center for Effective Organizations (CEO) in the Marshall School of Business. She is co-author of Self-Designing Organizations, Designing Team-Based Organizations, and editor of The Handbook of Collaborative Research and Useful Research: Advancing Theory and Practice.
She is co-faculty director of CEO's program in organization design and of its Sustainability Program, a program based on collaborative research and the creation of an international learning community involving practitioners and academics. She lives in Altadena, California.

Susan Albers Mohrman
Center for Effective Organizations
Marshall School of Business
University of Southern California
3415 South Figueroa Street, DCC 200, Los Angeles, CA 90089-0871, United States.
Tel: +1 213 740 9814.
Email: smohrman@marshall.usc.edu.

Arienne McCracken is program manager and research associate for the Sustainability Program at USC's Center for Effective Organizations (CEO) in the Marshall School of Business. She lives in Los Angeles.

Arienne McCracken
Center for Effective Organizations
Marshall School of Business
University of Southern California
3415 South Figueroa Street, DCC 200, Los Angeles, CA 90089-0871, United States.
Tel: +1 213 740 9814.
Email: amccracken@marshall.usc.edu

2

Visionary Leadership From Northern Ireland:
A Woman Of Many Firsts

Sandra Janoff & Marvin Weisbord

Major Focus of the Case

Aideen McGinley has been the first woman in Northern Ireland in each of her leadership positions – CEO of County Fermangh, Permanent Secretary of Culture Arts and Leisure for the new joint government, Permanent Secretary for Employment and Learning and CEO of Ilex Regeneration Company. As a civil servant during and after the decades of violence, she brought a new norm of behavior to her organizations and to the communities they served – that of being completely human despite the hierarchical and political setting. As a result, people moved closer to that behavior. McGinley's story, in the face of economic stress, political upheaval and social conflict, is one of classic good leadership.

Introduction

Aideen McGinley, Chief Executive of Fermanagh District Council, had made a decision to have the first comprehensive, integrated development plan in Northern Ireland. The year was 1998, just before the April 10 Good Friday Agreement on the principle of shared government between Unionists and Nationalists. McGinley's single-minded focus was on strategic planning for County Fermanagh. "People have to have a hand in creating their future," she said in a phone call to us. "I want to involve the community across all sectors, backgrounds and viewpoints." That may not strike you as a radical position for a local leader. McGinley, however, was no ordinary executive. She was the first woman in Northern Ireland's history to be CEO of a local government district. Involving the whole community in planning was not something local leaders had experience doing at that time.

Fermanagh is a rural county of 54,000 people in the southwest corner of Northern Ireland, adjacent to the Irish Republic. In the 1990's it had a vulnerable economy with a small manufacturing sector and sharply declining agriculture. Farming jobs had fallen 48% over three decades. Young people were leaving the county to pursue higher education or get jobs elsewhere. Some people, who had no option to leave, were starting their own businesses. McGinley imagined an inclusive planning process that would integrate people's needs from across the spectrum of business and the community. More, she saw this issue as a way to unite local people in dialogue across many ideological boundaries. Rather than the traditional top-down economic planning, she was determined to bring in people from education, business, health care, the arts and other sectors to complement and inform a total plan.

Fermanagh in 1999 did not have the most fertile soil for growing the seeds of cooperation. The county had known decades of religious and political tensions. Eleven years earlier an IRA bomb had exploded during a Remembrance Day service in Enniskillen, the seat of local government, killing 11 people and injuring 63. Ten years later 29 people were killed in a widely-publicized bombing in the neighboring town of Omagh. Community relations was not a job to take lightly. Strategic planning was usually commissioned by the 23-member Council to consultants. The usual practice in NI was to have experts write the plan, then engage citizens to accept it. In proposing to involve people across the political, religious, economic and community spectrum, McGinley would face two significant hurdles. One was convincing the Council to support her plan. Another was convincing citizens that they had a right to be involved. She kept going, she would say later, because of her profound belief in dialogue and democracy.

"The Troubles"

McGinley was not a stranger to Fermanagh. Years earlier she had been Fermanagh's first Community Services Officer, a post she later filled for 13 years in Strabane, a town 50 miles away. McGinley's years in Strabane came during the height of "the troubles" between Unionists and Nationalists. The Strabane Council was largely Nationalist. It was politically-sensitive work, McGinley recalled. She was supporting women's groups, rural development and community adult education programs. Her duties took her to places where bombs and bullets were frequent and unpredictable. She became a great believer in discovering common interests with people in her district, regardless of differences and worked hard to develop rapport across party and religious lines. She became known as someone who could be trusted. She recalled an incident when meeting with government officials from Belfast and Derry in a community centre in the heart of a heavily Nationalist area. During the meeting a series of explosions were heard outside. Protestors, who were supporting the hunger strikers at the time, many naked except for blankets over their shoulders, had set off paint bombs. When she went out to the car park, McGinley found that hers was the only car untouched by paint. Someone had covered it with a blanket.

In the early 1990's McGinley returned to Fermanagh to a post working with the chief executive on strategic policy issues. She then became the county's first Director of Development, consolidating community services, economic development, tourism, European Union issues and community relations under one umbrella. The Fermanagh Council was a diverse and finely balanced political body. McGinley had support across the political spectrum. In February 1995, when she was 40 years old, McGinley's boss retired. She was appointed in an unprecedented cross party vote as his replacement.

The Fermanagh Future Search

By the time McGinley became CEO in Fermanagh, many communities in the United Kingdom had adopted forms of citizen participation. "Consultation" was a much used – some would say over-used – word, referring to paper exercises or local meetings in which public officials took citizen questions on draft plans prepared by experts. McGinley proposed turning this practice upside down. She would involve citizens, including the experts, from the start in dialogue on the underlying values and policies for an integrated economic and social development plan. The experts would then join a local team to work out the technicalities. Her hope was that the whole community would support the plan and its implementation, as success would depend on ownership.

McGinley also believed – more heresy – that to be successful, the plan had to go beyond economics. "From where I stood," she said, "I could see lights shining in the darkness where people were doing good things in education, tourism, health care, and the arts. To plan it all at once would be good for the county because of the synergy we would gain and the resources we could realize." The first challenge was her own Council. She had recently participated in a strategic planning meeting – a "Future Search" –for the woman's sector in Northern Ireland which was attended by women from around the country (See Figure 1 for a description of the Future Search Process). The meeting had resulted in an agreed-upon process for women's involvement in local legislative decision-making recently mandated by the government. McGinley was struck by the great release of energy into action planning. Future Search was new to her but she was certain that this form of planning fit her vision of community. She imagined Future Search as step one in comprehensive planning that might go on indefinitely, involving more and more citizens.

McGinley was not surprised when some Council members were quite skeptical and had to be convinced that it did not erode their role as elected members. They were used to doing things from the top down. "I don't see how that can possibly work here," one member said, a sentiment echoed by a number of others. McGinley was not deterred. She wanted this form of planning for her county and had visualized the whole thing: diverse citizens finding common ground; new economic initiatives; cooperative planning that included all interests. "Persistent" and "persuasive" were two words we heard people use repeatedly to describe McGinley. Both qualities were evident in her interactions with the Council. "It was a challenge," she said later. Basically, I was asking them to delegate their democratic mandate to the electorate. After several meetings, she prevailed, proving the trust she had built up across party lines after years in public life. The council agreed to a participative planning meeting.

The next challenge was getting a cross section of the community to come together for a three-day meeting. Most had no concept of "strategic planning," nor could they imagine they had a right to do it for themselves. She had to convince people from all walks of life that their hopes and dreams counted too. She called people on the phone. "I'm asking you personally," she said. "Will you do this?" In letters of invitation, she wrote, "This is about you and it's important to the county." Above all she had faith, "I knew it would work. I just had to get the people there and it would work." Enthusiasticaly, people signed up, ordinary citizens and prominent officials together.

McGinley invited (co-author) Sandra Janoff and Ruth McCambridge to help her plan and run the Fermanagh Future Search. She had learned early in her career the benefits of meeting on a "social island," where people could separate from daily concerns. So, on a bitter cold January day in 1999, people found themselves on a flat bottom boat chugging across Lough Erne in a sleet storm. They were headed for a real island, Lusty Beg, site of a remote conference center. McGinley's persuasive recruiting had paid off. More than 100 Fermanagh residents had carved three days out of their busy lives and braved the elements to participate. "Metaphorically, as well as literally, she was pushing out the boat," recalled Eamonn Cox, then Chief Executive of Fermanagh Business Initiative.

The diversity, for a remote, rural community, was astounding – farmers, educators, environmentalists, economic developers, nongovernmental organizations, youth, artists, health care and community workers, business people, and seven Council members from all political shades, Catholics and Protestants alike – Sinn Fein, Social Democrats and Labor Party, Ulster Unionists, Democratic Unionists, and Independents. McGinley was standing on the pier as they arrived, greeting everyone with her warm laugh, joking that even if you wanted to go back, you probably couldn't, because the weather was surely getting worse.

Over the next three days, the group put together a comprehensive look at County Fermanagh's past and present in light of trends both local and global. Each person had a small piece of a large puzzle, a story of complexity and opportunity that none had quite seen before. "We genuinely built a whole picture of life in our community," said McGinley, "and no longer were we working on aspects of life in Fermanagh in isolation from each other." People organized nine working groups: arts and culture; agriculture and rural development; education; environment; equal opportunities; health; jobs, employment and training; tourism; voluntary and community sector.

After the meeting, people used workshops, seminars, surveys, and interviews with experts to flesh out action plans, adding along the way infrastructure, community relations, technology and sport, recreation and leisure. They put together a comprehensive strategy for Fermanagh's future.

Some 30,000 Fermanagh households received an outline of the first draft with a request for ideas and opinions that were made part of the final document.

Implementing the Plan

By mid-year 1999, more than 1000 residents had attended 150 meetings, tackling hundreds of action agenda items. (A local student did a master's thesis on the planning process, finding that although 79% of participants had never heard of Future Search before, 89% now believed it could be used elsewhere in Northern Ireland, a data point that McGinley would take to heart in years to come.) In a 128-page, full color report to the community, replete with charts, graphs, names, dates, and action agendas, Fermanagh noted more than 100 local organizations actively supporting its development plan. "In particular," said the document, "we have focused on achievable outputs and outcomes, both quantitative and qualitative." The report included a full description of each goal, where the County was now, who was working on what, and goals stretching over two, five, and ten-year time frames.

Aideen McGinley, after riding a roller coaster, got her integrated development plan for County Fermanagh. There were 370 documented action steps in 45 priority areas, the most comprehensive plan any Northern Ireland county had ever published. By the end of year one, 24 action plans had been completed, 256 were well along, and another 107 had been categorized long term. "The report has since been upheld as a model of good practice and used as a template for similar plans throughout Ireland and much further afield," said Eamonn Cox. In 2010 McGinley told us, "We ultimately involved over 1500 people. We secured hospital services that were under threat, we improved roads and infrastructure, we increased tourism, we developed creative crafts industries, we promoted local culture. There were hundreds of action plans, and even after I moved on, over 90% of them were achieved."

Postscript

In November 1999, while working on plans after Lusty Beg, McGinley became the Permanent Secretary of Culture, Arts and Leisure in the new joint government of Northern Ireland, the first and only woman and external appointment to secure such a post. She promptly organized a Future Search in Belfast, "Face to Face: A Vision for Arts and Culture." Participants were flabbergasted by the ease and assurance with which she handed the task over to them. "Despite unusual diversity," said Shona McCarthy, now chief executive of the British Council in Northern Ireland, "people worked with enormous energy, generosity and humor to lay the framework for cultural development in Northern Ireland." McGinley went on to sponsor eight Future Searches in the next 10 years. They covered topics as diverse as a soccer strategy for Northern Ireland, a geographic information system, a library strategy, a new system for archives, and a plan for the future of the Ulster Scots Language and Culture.

In 2006, McGinley was moved to the post of Permanent Secretary of the Department of Employment and Learning. In 2008, she suggested a Future Search to the Derry-Londonderry city leaders, a city whose citizens face enormous challenges of social and economic inequality and underperformance. She was instrumental in planning the meeting and in February 2009, 120 citizens met and, despite decades of divisiveness, agreed on a common ground vision for the city. The agenda they built has become the basis of Derry-Londonderry's Regeneration Plan and, to date, over 1000 citizens have been involved in its development. In mid-2009, she was seconded to Ilex Regeneration Company as CEO and now oversees the implementation of the plan, including the development of two former military sites and the building of the new Peace Bridge across the Foyle River. In spring, 2010 McGinley spearheaded a city-wide initiative to apply for the first-ever

UK City of Culture. On July 15, 2010, Derry-Londonderry won the honor and in 2013 will host a year-long programme of culture events. All are invited! On June 25, 2011, McGinley, the Ilex Team and over 40,000 Derry-Londonderry citizens celebrated the opening of the Peace Bridge – a walking bridge connecting two sides of a once-divided city and now symbolizing reconciliation, peace and regeneration.

How does she do it? "I can only say I believe in dialogue," said McGinley. " As leaders we can't be totally risk averse if we want to be needs driven. We have to get the genuine voice, of what people want to see and what they value, heard. That's why I consider it so important to have my staff and stakeholders with me in whatever we do. Human beings naturally gravitate toward the norm because that's where our comfort zone is, but to me that's the biggest danger and the hardest part of leading anything is keeping my energy up so that I'm not afraid to continue standing for what I believe in."

THE FUTURE SEARCH PROCESS

Future Search is a planning meeting that enables a community or organization to:

(1) Develop and/or confirm a vision and strategy	(2) Make an implementation plan	(3) Start action planning with goal clarity and high commitment, all in less than three days.

The meeting's success derives from four principles:

(1) Get "the whole system" in the room, meaning people who collectively have authority, resources, expertise, information and need	(2) Explore the whole from every perspective before seeking to fix any part	(3) Focus on common ground and the future, treating problems and conflicts as information, not action items.	(4) Enable people to take responsibility for their own views, analyses, and decisions

Discussion

1. Aideen McGinley is a courageous, visionary leader. What did you learn about good visionary leadership from her story?

2. Aideen McGinley used a collaborative approach to accomplish great things. What did you learn about the value of collaboration and involvement?

3. What did Aideen McGinley do after the initial three day meetings to sustain and keep change going?

4. Study Figure 1 and discuss the Future Search process and principles and the potential risks and payoffs of large group meetings.

Key Leadership Lessons

1. Aideen McGinley sees four challenges for leaders:
1) to have courage, 2) to spread joy, 3) to care about the outcome, processes and people and, 4) to clear the way. From her point of view, having courage means to speak your mind, listen to your own gut feelings and to have integrity. To spread joy means encouraging, believing, having hope and inspiring others. To care about product, process and people means to pay attention to what you are doing and who's doing it. It also means understanding the integration of people, economics and technology. To clear the way is to identify the obstacles and deal with them, to be the negotiator and cut through the red tape.

2. McGinley's perspective on stakeholder engagement is that it's an essential element in leading for whole systems change. If you don't include stakeholder's perspectives in your thinking, you might as well be operating in a vacuum. Leaders can't respond unless they know the needs, capabilities and aspirations of all those who have a stake in the issue. McGinley sees it as the only way she can get to the root issues and deliver meaningful and implemental actions. Otherwise, she adds, it becomes a meaningless effort.

3. It is McGinley's experience that when you are trying to influence a governmental system, you will need a very intense and robust process of analysis on which to base your bid for resources or action.

4. Be true to yourself. Be grounded in your principles. You have to believe in what you are doing because your reputation and integrity can be at stake!

5. Celebrate your successes. It's a journey of discovery. Have enough fun and exciting challenge to stay motivated and strong.

BIOGRAPHY

Sandra Janoff along with Marvin Weisbord is Co-Director of Future Search Network, Co-author of *Future Search: Getting the Whole System in the Room for Vision, Commitment, and Action* (Berrett-Koehler, 3rd ed., 2010). She is an international consultant and psychologist, has worked with corporations, government, regions and communities worldwide on issues of globalization, sustainability, economic development and humane practices. Her research on relationships among organizational structure, behavior, and gender, "The Influence of Legal Education on Moral Reasoning," was published in the *Minnesota Law Review and in Feminist Jurisprudence: Taking Women Seriously – Cases and Materials.*

Sandra Janoff, PhD, Co-Director, Future Search Network

Sandra Janoff
409 Arthurs Round Table, Wynnewood PA 19096
Tel. +1 610 909 0640
Email: sjanoff@futuresearch.net

Marvin Weisbord along with Sandra Janoff is Co-Director of Future Search Network, Co-author of *Future Search: Getting the Whole System in the Room for Vision, Commitment, and Action* (Berrett-Koehler, 3rd ed., 2010). He is an international consultant. He received a Lifetime Achievement Award in 2004 from the Organization Development Network which voted *Productive Workplaces* one of the most influential books of the previous 40 years. Marv has written dozens of articles on organizational change and is the author of *Productive Workplaces Revisited* (2004), *Discovering Common Ground* (1992), and *Organizational Diagnosis* (1978).

Marvin Weisbord
Marvin Weisbord, Co-Director, Future Search Network
530 Wynlyn Road, Wynnewood PA 19096
Tel. +1 610 896 7035,
Email: mweisbord@futuresearch.net

3

Colonel Russell Blaisdell:
A Case of Spontaneous Leadership

Dr. Thomas N. Duening
El Pomar Chair of Business & Entrepreneurship

Major Focus

Anybody can be a leader, but not everybody. What this means is that some of us must be loyal followers, at least some of the time, for leadership to exist at all. Unfortunately, the scholarly and popular literature on leadership rarely acknowledges the need for loyal followers, or the relatively ephemeral nature of leadership itself. Leadership winks in and out of the world at an astonishing rate, even if one tracks the singular life of exemplary historical figures who are regarded as paragons of leadership. Human to the core, these individuals have invariably intermixed courageous leadership with desultory bouts of personal failings (O'Malley, 2010). Contrary to popular notions that would have us believe that we can all become leaders now and forever by willing it to be so, leadership in reality, is often context-dependent (Thomas & Carnall, 2008).

Introduction

Popular books on leadership abound in the business section of most major bookstores. Books on leadership are often among the top sellers both in the nonfiction and business book categories (Pagel & Westerfelhaus, 2005). The most popular titles seem to be those that promise to reveal the specific "Habits", "Immutable Laws", or "Secrets" of leadership.[1] Each of these suggests that by reading the book and discovering the habits, laws, and/or secrets of leadership anyone can become a leader.

In addition to the hundreds of books on leadership, corporate spending on leadership development continues to spiral upward (Van Buren & Erskine, 2002). The topic is of immense importance and concerns not only the imperative to produce leaders, but also the manner of creating them – which generally focuses on proper training and career development. What is often neglected in the popular literature is that leadership emerges from a combination of self-making intent and contingent and uncontrollable context (Hannah, et al., 2009). As we will see in this case, Colonel Russell Blaisdell was a self-described "average pastor" who became a leader of the highest caliber when the time and circumstance called for leadership. Blaisdell's story is one of courage and determination. It illustrates that anyone can be a leader, and that spontaneous leadership is a product not simply of "habits" and/or "secrets", but also of one's response to unexpected circumstances.

---

1 For example, Stephen Covey's "Seven Habits of Highly Effective People" has been a best-seller since its publication in 1989, with over 15 million sold; John Maxwell is another highly successful popular writer on leadership, with his book "The 21 Irrefutable Laws of Leadership" also a perennial best seller; finally, a more recent publishing phenomenon has been Rhonda Byrnes's "The Secret" which purports to help people become fulfilled by revealing a little known (secretive) law of the universe.

In Blaisdell's case the circumstances that called for and produced leadership were unexpected. Although the case concerns the extraordinary circumstances of wartime, the extrapolation to daily life and its unexpected events is not difficult. Our rapidly changing global economy has become highly unpredictable (Ireland & Hitt, 2005). In fact, there is as much a need for "spontaneous leadership" as there is for the kind of leadership that emerges from carefully crafted careers. We clearly do need traditional leaders who work and study their way up the proverbial "corporate ladder". But we also need those who have no aspirations to lead, but who heed the call to lead when spontaneous events require it. Colonel Blaisdell's story of spontaneous leadership is an example of how the ability to lead may lie dormant until called, and then emerge in as great a force as any corporate ladder climber would be able to conjure.

War Provides Many Opportunities For Spontaneous Leadership

This case is about a little known leader in the Korean war who never fully realized his leadership potential until a situation brought the best out in him as a leader. Today's air wars with their precision bombs and laser-guided missiles sometimes distract us from seeing the horrors and tragedies of war (Greenfield, 1998). The Korean war (officially deemed a "conflict") was a different kind of war. It was a war waged between North and South Korea between the years 1950-1953. The United States military was involved as part of the United Nation's "peacekeeping" efforts. Eventually, the Chinese were drawn into the conflict to the aid of their ally North Korea. The war technically continues to the present day as no treaty has been signed between the warring parties. The Korean War is dubiously characterized by its brutality, barbarity, horrendous weather, civilian death toll and suffering, and wanton destruction (Varhola, 2000). More than 39,000 U.S. troops, 400,000 some South Korean soldiers, and more than two-and-a-half million South Korean civilians lost their lives. The number of North Korean and Chinese military deaths, and North Korean civilian deaths no doubt exceeded those numbers, although no official figures are available.

Leadership in wartime is usually relegated to well-trained and battle-tested professional leaders. The chain of command is an integral part of the prosecution of war, and is an indispensable element of well-trained armed forces. And yet, most military commanders fully agree with the bromide: "All plans are valid until they meet the enemy". In other words, the chaos of war often calls for quick thinking, context based alterations of plans, innovation, and, not least, spontaneous acts of leadership. Spontaneous acts of leadership are antithetical to classical military training, but are practiced daily by officers, foot soldiers, airmen, and seamen alike as the "fog of war" presents surprises, unprecedented obstacles, and life or death consequences to moment-by-moment decisions. Most people would shrink in the face of the spontaneous leadership challenges that are presented during wartime. One individual, Colonel Russell Blaisdell, rose to an incredible challenge during the height of the Korean War, presenting an example of spontaneous leadership that is instructive for individuals unexpectedly called to lead in nearly any walk of life.

The Situation That Motivated Colonel Blaisdell
To Rise To A New Level Of Leadership

Blaisdell's story is surprisingly unknown to most Americans despite its near made-for-Hollywood storyline. Blaisdell was a self-described "average pastor" who had been interested in foreign missions prior to his deployment to the war zone in Korea. For the most part, Blaisdell served out his term in Korea with little distinction. He performed his duties as pastor under horrendous conditions, to be sure. Cold, wet, hunger and other privations were commonplace, even for the comparatively well-funded and well-fed members of America's fighting forces. Working along the 38th parallel he ministered to civilians and soldiers alike, including many North Korean refugees who had been led to the relative calm of the region by their spiritual guides.

Despite the hardships that he endured in the dark and frigid winter months along the border between the North and South, nothing that he saw during that time prepared him for the abundant horrors he witnessed when he re-entered Seoul late in 1950. As he described it, he and his colleagues "found buildings bombed and leveled to the ground. We saw families digging in the rubble with their fingers, seeking for bits of charcoal or other usable material. We heard through the streets and in the compounds the wailing of little children, babies, some too weak to make a loud sound. Their bodies were bloated and emaciated from a lack of food, covered with vermin. A number of them were resigned to death and lay quietly awaiting the end" (Blaisdell, 1950).

Blaisdell estimated that there were 4,000 to 6,000 orphaned children on the streets of Seoul that cold winter of 1950. Something had to be done to relieve their suffering, but the usual organizations for taking charge of the situation were non-functioning. Outside relief agencies also were not equipped to enter an active war zone to render aid. He was alone with the problem, and he had to act.

How Colonel Blaisdell Responded To A Heart Breaking And Difficult Situation

With assistance from others, Blaisdell set up a Seoul Orphan center to provide food, clothing and a warm place for the children to sleep. However, soon after opening the center in an abandoned building it was flooded with children. Despite the demand there was capacity enough to take in only 50 per day; well below what was necessary to alleviate the problem.

This small effort to relieve the suffering of the orphans was interrupted violently in December 1950 when the Chinese Army began to advance rapidly from the north. It was decided that the children had to be evacuated to escape the wrath of the approaching Red Army. Blaisdell realized there was no one to turn to for the leadership that was required. "No one was going to stick around to see what would happen," Blaisdell said. City officials had already decided to abandon the orphanage and leave the children to fend for themselves. There was no time to lose.

Blaisdell arranged to transport nearly 1,000 orphans to the city of Inchon, more than 20 miles to the south of Seoul. He was told there would be a South Korean ship at the Inchon harbor that could take the orphans to Cheju Island off the coast of Korea and out of harm's way. Blaisdell had a single truck at his disposal, and he used it over the course of five days to ferry the children from Seoul to Inchon. In Inchon, the children were temporarily housed in an abandoned school building, where they waited for their opportunity to board the promised boat to safety. As they waited, many of the children contracted whooping cough or measles and eight of them died.

After he had successfully transported the orphans from Seoul to Inchon, Blaisdell decided to drive down to the harbor to see if the promised ship was waiting. When he got to the docks in Inchon his worst suspicions were confirmed: The ship was an old scow that he wouldn't recommend to the enemy. Worse, the captain of the ship had no knowledge of the orphans or of the promised evacuation to Cheju Island. Blaisdell was devastated. Not only could he not get the children to safety on the ship as he had promised, but he had few provisions left for them in Inchon. The situation was bleak.

Blaisdell had not slept much in five days as he drove back into Inchon, wondering how he was going to save the children. When he reached the city he went to see his friend Brigadier General T.C. Rogers. Rogers asked him why he looked so terrible. Blaisdell told him about his lack of sleep, about his efforts to transfer the children to Inchon, and about the "ship" that was supposed to take them to safety. Rogers was moved by Blaisdell's efforts to rescue the children. He informed Blaisdell that he had a squadron of C-54 aircraft on the ground at Kimpo airfield, and that the squadron was looking for a mission. Rogers told him that if he could get the children to Kimpo the next day, he would have the squadron airlift them to Cheju Island.

Blaisdell was elated by this change of fortune. The only problem was, Kimpo airfield was another 20 miles from Inchon, and Blaisdell had only the single truck to use as transport. It had already taken him five days to transport the children the 20 miles from Seoul to Inchon. How, he wondered, could he get them all to Kimpo by the next afternoon?

Blaisdell left Rogers' office with no idea how he was going to get the children to Kimpo, but he was determined to find a way. As he was driving back to the makeshift orphanage, he spotted some Marines unloading a truck into an ammunition warehouse. Blaisdell, in a spontaneous act of leadership didn't hesitate to take charge. He drove over to the area and told the Marine truck driver that he was supposed to report to a certain Sergeant for duty. When the driver refused, Blaisdell pulled out his lieutenant colonel badge and told the driver he wasn't asking, he was giving an order. It was the first order Blaisdell had given, but it wouldn't be his last. The Marine obeyed the order, putting Blaisdell in charge of a second truck. But two trucks wouldn't be enough, he needed more if he was going to be able to get the children to Kimpo by the next afternoon. Thus, each time another truck arrived at the ammunition shed, Blaisdell would pull rank on the driver to acquire it for his cause. Soon enough, he had four trucks, enough to make it if he and his assistants worked through the night. When they had successfully transported the orphans to Kimpo, the promised planes were waiting.

On December 20, 1950, the C-54 airplanes carrying more than 950 orphan children arrived on Cheju Island. When they arrived U.S. and Korean officials greeted the children. Blaisdell said, "They gave us a building at the Agricultural School for Boys in Cheju City to use as an orphanage." Mrs. On Soon Whang was appointed director of the new orphanage. In short order, this quiet, firm woman whose husband and son were both killed in the fighting was providing the children with food, clothing, and a warm, safe place to sleep.

Follow-Up On The Difference Committed Spontaneous Leaders Can Make

In 2001 a reunion was held between the then 90-year old Colonel Blaisdell and survivors among the original group of orphans. Many of the surviving orphans were provoked to tears as they recounted how they had been saved through Blaisdell's act of spontaneous leadership. Some of the articles written about Blaisdell's spontaneous leadership refer to him as the "Schindler of Korea". The latter reference of course is to Oscar Schindler, the Austrian businessman responsible for rescuing hundreds of Jews during World War II by employing them in his factories.

Conclusion

Leadership is arguably the most captivating of traits among people in nearly all walks of life. Regally deployed, leadership has beautifully illustrated the glories of human nature, the power of commitment to higher purposes, and the incredible achievements that can be derived from mortal beings striving to make a difference against the odds. On this exalted plain leadership has chosen to express itself in individuals diverse and unequally gifted. There are exemplars among this group about whom few would quibble: George Washington, Abraham Lincoln, Winston Churchill, Mohandas Gandhi, Martin Luther King, Jr., and Mother Teresa. Individuals each, possessed of gifts unavailable to the naked eye, and evocative of values and dispositions we regard as ideals to which all people might aspire.

On the other side of the leadership equation we are reminded of how strongly human nature can be corrupted by power. Brutal, dictatorial leadership that rises through the liberal administration of fear is only too common. Historical figures that have "led" under such conditions are legion. In more modern times, society has witnessed the unfortunate effects of the human desire to follow in the popular elevation of such figures as Adolf Hitler, Benito Mussolini, and Saddam

Hussein. These figures illustrate how leadership can emerge from the basest elements of our common nature.

A review of the scholarly and popular literature on leadership and its development supports the idea that becoming a leader requires a decision to place oneself into the fray, but it takes so much more. The interplay between individual will and contingent circumstance is a crucial element of what has been referred to here as "spontaneous leadership". Most people can decide to point their personal or career development toward a leadership role, but not all will have the opportunity to lead. One can imagine cubicles full of unrequited leaders who absorbed the popular belief that they could will themselves into becoming a leader. Unfavored by their current circumstances, their disappointment saps their energy and reduces their ability to be productive non-leaders.

By way of contrast, understanding that leadership combines intent with unpredictable circumstance can spare unrequited leaders their frustrations. By accepting that the present context has not selected one for leadership can enable one to perform loyal follower duties until conditions change. Further, knowledge that leadership is often a spontaneous event can motivate personal growth in preparation for circumstances and events that may call for spontaneous leadership.

As the story of Colonel Russell Blaisdell illustrates, leadership often calls the most unassuming to perform spontaneously as leaders. As the case revealed, even an unassuming "average pastor" can lead, and lead heroically, in crucial times. This gives a new hope to those unrequited leaders who are seeking a context where the lessons they've learned from the self-help and leadership "gurus" can be put into action. Spontaneous acts of leadership are required every day, in nearly every context.

References

Blaisdell, R.L. 1950. Orphan Care and Evacuation, Korea, December 1950. Unpublished memoir available at: http://www.nas.com/creche/docs/Blaisdell.htm.

Greenfield, M. 1998. "The Armchair Air War", *Newsweek*, 131(8): 78.

Hannah, S., M. Uhl-Bien, B.J. Avolio, & F.L. Cavaretta. 2009. A Framework for Examining Leadership in Extreme Contexts", *Leadership Quarterly*, 20(6): 897-919.

Ireland, D.R., & M.A. Hitt. 2005. "Achieving and Maintaining Strategic Competitiveness in the 21st Century: The Role of Strategic Leadership", *Academy of Management Executive*, 19(4): 63-77.

O'Malley, M. 2010. "Leadership Imperfections", *Leadership Excellence*, 27(8): 6.

Pagel, S., and R. Westerfelhaus. 2005. "Charting Managerial Reading Preferences in Relation to Popular Management Theory Books", *Journal of Business Communication*, 42(4): 420-448.

Thomas, H., & C. Carnall. 2008. "Leadership Development: Integration in Context", *Strategic Change*, 17(5/6): 193-206.

Van Buren, M.E., & W. Erskine. 2002. "State of the Industry: ASTD's Annual Review of Trends in Employer-Provided Training in the United States," American Society of Training & Development, Report 2002.

Varhola, M.J. 2000. Fire and Ice: The Korean War 1950-1953. Cambridge, MA: De Capo Press.

Discussion

1. What is meant by the term "spontaneous leadership"? Is spontaneous leadership a chance situation or is it more of a case of preparation meeting opportunity?

2. Do you think that leaders are born, made, or both? If possible use examples to support your position.

3. Describe the situation Colonel Blaisdell found, how he responded as a leader, how he persevered in spite of many obstacles, and the difference his efforts made.

4. Discuss possible situations at work and outside of work that could present opportunities for spontaneous leadership.

5. What prevents people from responding to opportunities for spontaneous leadership and what is the difference in people like Colonel Blaisdell who do respond?

Key Leadership Lessons

1. Leadership can be cultivated via training and development programs, but it also is contingent on environmental circumstances.

2. Anyone may be presented with opportunities to lead at some time or another in their life or even during an average day. It is how they respond that determines their willingness to lead.

3. Spontaneous leadership may require you to do things that you have never done before or that you have not been trained to do but it allows you to learn and grow at an accelerated rate.

4. You can prepare to some degree to be a spontaneous leader. The best prepared who are looking for opportunities to lead or have prepared themselves to lead are more likely to be presented with opportunities for spontaneous leadership.

5. Spontaneous leadership does not require fancy titles, corner offices, or big rewards. It does Require a determination to do the right thing and the willingness to face reality, innovate on the fly, and overcome obstacles until the final goal is reached.

BIOGRAPHY

Thomas Duening is the El Pomar Chair in Business & Entrepreneurship at the University of Colorado at Colorado Springs. Dr. Duening earned his MA and PhD degrees from the University of Minnesota. He was previously the director of the Entrepreneurial Programs Office in the Fulton School of Engineering at Arizona State University and assistant dean of the C.T. Bauer College of Business at the University of Houston. Duening is the founder of numerous ventures, including U.S. Learning Systems, InfoLabs, and Businesses2Learn. Duening is the author of numerous journal articles and 12 books on business, management, and entrepreneurship. His most recent book: "Technology Entrepreneurship: Value Creation, Protection, and Capture" was published by Elsevier in October 2009.

Thomas Duening PhD
El Pomar Chair in Business & Entrepreneurship
Associate Professor of Management
College of Business
University of Colorado at Colorado Springs

4

The First Woman Conductor Of
The Baltimore Symphony Orchestra

Katherine Farquhar & David W. Jamieson

Major Focus of the Case

This is the inspiring story of a courageous leader who became the first to do what she did. In addition to the usual vital dimensions that all leadership textbooks cover – such as traits, skills, behaviors, style, experience, education, and organizational context – gender can also be a major factor if it is a situation where gender is unique in a leadership role. When a CEO or other top executive differs from the mainstream image of the top leaders, all impressions and actions flow through that filter of visibility. On top of the anticipated workload in a traditional organization's adjustment to a new leader is added the necessity to resolve potential disturbance posed by stereotypes, expectations, and emotional responses to reach acceptance of the diversity element. The most critical aspects of these elements fall under the heading of the organization's culture.

This case is about the experience of Marin Alsop, the first woman Music Director of the Baltimore Symphony Orchestra (BSO: www.bsomusic.org) and the first to conduct one of the USA's 17 top major orchestras. Maestra Alsop publicly debuted in the position in September 2007. Under her artistic leadership, the BSO has greatly expanded its visibility and programming, including early steps into electronic media and deeper engagement with the community.[1]

Introduction

The Marin Alsop case focuses on the metaphor of the orchestra conductor for two purposes: to highlight the context of a woman leader in a profession that is nearly exclusively male (Eagly & Carli, 2007; Rhode, 2003), and to examine the importance to leadership of focusing an organization's culture (Schein, 2004).

Begin the case by watching the 2007 PBS televised interview with Alsop http://www.youtube.com/watch?v = nFzxMhU3Qi8&feature = related[2] You thenread the case, focusing on challenges that faced Alsop as she entered, and considering the choices she made in managing these, as well as the emergence of her leadership of the orchestra. You are invited to discuss several points where gender disparity within the ranks of world-class orchestra conductors may have required unique skills and behaviors from Maestra Alsop **and** the orchestra members. You will also explore how her talents and passion for the organization's core business may have eased the transition of a minority leader into a majority culture. How does her case inform the considerations, choices, and actions that face a leader and organization in similar circumstances?

----

1 Note that gender has been chosen in this case as a surrogate for numerous forms of diversity.
2 PBS News 10/17/2007: http://www.youtube.com/watch?v = nFzxMhU3Qi8&feature = related

Finally, what broader message can be derived from studying the metaphor of a new conductor and her resistant orchestra?[3] What lessons about effective executive leadership do you take away from this example?

Background

For a moment, put yourself in the shoes of Marin Alsop, then a 48-year old violinist and a renowned conductor mentored by the late Leonard Bernstein. The BSO Board just invited you to take the baton as their Music Director. This orchestra is no stranger; you've been a guest conductor here seven times. Say "Yes," and you are the Orchestra's first woman conductor – and the first female conductor of an elite cluster of top symphony orchestras in the USA. Say "Yes," and you have joined a fraternity of distinguished male conductors. You will conduct a Baltimore Symphony Orchestra where the largely male orchestra has worked only with male conductors.

You break the mold and you challenge the culture, simply by being who you are. From the moment you walk into a room, you affect the dynamics among those present. Not surprisingly, Marin Alsop is frequently queried about being a "first." She reflects:

The first thing that I have noticed…is that women in the audience seem to have a different concert-going experience when a woman is leading the orchestra. Frequently women tell me that they feel empowered and can relate very directly with a woman conducting. At the BSO's opening gala a female journalist told me that the woman seated next to her, dressed in a formal gown, stood up and high-fived her at the end of the concert…

…all questions about discrimination are very difficult to answer because so much of anyone's interpretation of events is based on personal attitude and personal experience. Becoming a conductor is an extremely competitive ambition to begin with; but I would attribute some of my success to the fact that I never interpreted any rejections as gender based, even if I could have done so! This enabled me to use each rejection as an opportunity to improve myself by working harder, listening to criticism, and developing even more perseverance. I personally feel that accepting the role of powerless victim can become a self-fulfilling prophecy and I am unwilling to even entertain that concept! (http://www.marinalsop.com/mediafaq.php)

ENTRY: Checkpoint 1

Maestra Alsop accepted. She entered an unusually hostile work environment. Just before her appointment was announced by the BSO Board in 2005, the pending decision was leaked to the press. Immediately, the player-members of the search committee balked and went public with their concerns. In a press release, the players said:

The musicians of the Baltimore Symphony are asking Philip English, chairman of the Board of Directors, to postpone any vote on the appointment of a new Music Director…

The Artistic Advisory Committee, seven musicians who represent the whole orchestra, has carefully surveyed the entire active membership. Approximately ninety percent of the orchestra musicians believe that ending the search process now, before we are sure the best candidate has been found, would be a disservice to the patrons of the BSO and all music lovers in Maryland. If the Board of Directors makes a decision opposed by the vast majority of the orchestra, all confidence in the current leadership of the orchestra would be lost. (Page, 2005).

---

3 See also DVD: The music paradigm: A seminar in business management (2005) featuring Maestro Roger Nierenberg teaching executives while he conducts the BBC Concert Orchestra. Princeton: Films for the Humanities & Sciences (www.films.com)

Despite the controversy, the BSO Board offered the job to Alsop. Reflecting on the situation, she said, "It was a trying and stressful experience in many ways. To be perfectly honest, my initial reaction, when it all started, was to run. 'Gosh, who needs this?'" (Wakin, 2005).

She did not sign on until she had confronted the situation with the players directly. In a private meeting with the orchestra, she "told the players she needed to get over her own hard feelings. 'Obviously, you do too, and we need to meet in the middle.'" (Wakin, 2005). She referenced the orchestra's "large debt and poor attendance," and she "praised the players as part of a gifted and deeply musical orchestra."

"I also told them that I didn't think they knew who I was." (Wakin,2005).

ADJUSTMENT: Checkpoint 2

Alsop's appointment in 2005 started the quiet phase of her onboarding. It wouldn't be until fall of 2007 that she publicly conducted her first concert as BSO Music Director. There was enormous press coverage of her hiring, and great anticipation of her debut. Much of the coverage emphasized "first's":

> *...pioneer (she is the first female music director of a major American orchestra); protégée (she is a disciple of Leonard Bernstein); great communicator (she is a master speaker from the stage and charming with donors); and most recently 'genius' (she is a recipient of a 2005 MacArthur Fellowship).* (Wakin, 2005)

Back in the rehearsal hall, before her debut concert in September 2007, Alsop faced a key challenge: her conducting style sharply contrasted with that of her predecessor, Yuri Temirkanov.
... the differences were immediately obvious. As the first woman to lead a major American orchestra, Alsop was, of course, shorter than her predecessor, but her stocky frame and brusque energy, bundled up in a simple white blouse and black slacks, suggested an athleticism in contrast to the ailing, elegant Russian who is 18 years older. (Himes, 2007)

Maestro Temirkanov had led the orchestra for 6 years in a heavily classical repertoire. Alsop, by contrast, favors contemporary and American music blended with the classics. Thus, the orchestra was challenged to change its culture: accepting a new conducting style and an unfamiliar playlist. Concertmaster and violinist Jonathan Carney spoke of adjustments required from players:

> *You need to have different kinds of conductors to revitalize an orchestra...The last thing you want is an orchestra that's on autopilot, repeating the same habits they acquired from the last music director.* (Himes, 2007)

Maestra Alsop has a specific philosophy about this:

> *Music directors come and go, but the musicians remain and they have their own influence as well. Musicians can't play a phrase that's devoid of their personality, so the essence of who they are comes through. An orchestra feels these influences, but it also retains its own style.* (Himes, 2007)

ALIGNMENT: Checkpoint 3

Beyond developing the musical repertoire and conducting the orchestra, Alsop was now a top leader in an organization with a complex history: success, hard times, labor unrest. The BSO was founded in 1916 as part of Baltimore's municipal government and went private in 1942. In subsequent years, the Orchestra built a multi-million dollar endowment and earned critical acclaim worldwide. Economic downturns caused severe financial damage over the years and deficits mounted. Despite these difficulties, the BSO remains in the elite group of 17 surviving 52-week orchestras in the USA.

When Maestra Alsop joined the BSO, the organization had recently withdrawn $22 million from the endowment to cover accumulated debt. There were disputes between labor and management. Shortly after she arrived to conduct a dispirited orchestra, the BSO's finances plummeted. In early 2009 the BSO's President and CEO announced a $1M budget cut. Later in 2009 there was a 12.5% pay cut and a furlough for musicians. At the end of 2009, there was more bad news: further wage reductions, longer furloughs (now at 5 weeks), and a freeze on filling vacant orchestra seats.

During these difficulties, the players' union took unusual steps to support the BSO, including the offer to forgo planned raises and other benefits if donors would match the dollars "given back" by the players. Although this campaign raised over $650K, the BSO 's financial troubles continued. A new round of pay cuts, salary freezes and reduced benefits was announced in 2010. At this point the orchestra was frozen at 85 of the full complement of 96 seats, and some top musicians began to look elsewhere as salary gaps widened and fears grew that the BSO would lose standing in the music world.

Alsop called the situation "really heartbreaking. I could cry...But...I'm proud that this is a collaborative effort. This speaks of the amazing and admirable commitment of our musicians to retain a full-time major orchestra in this city." (Smith, 2010b). BSO French Horn player Jane Marvine said:

> In the last decade, two times we had great contracts that were unfulfilled. This sets us back a decade. We have everything going for us... we have a music director committed to expanding the orchestra as a resource for the community. We have a collaborative spirit. So it seems impossible to us that we have not been able to thrive as a major American orchestra in one of the wealthiest states...There have been a lot of broken promises, but there is no reason why this orchestra can't succeed here. (Smith, 2010a)

And Now:

In this context, Maestra Alsop now seeks to provide leadership to inspire and motivate a shrunken orchestra that has worked with her for nearly 5 years. She asks your advice: what leadership strategies and personal competencies can she bring to this situation to continue the BSO's standing among the USA's "major orchestras," retain players, and earn critical acclaim for the orchestra's musical pursuits?

Discussion Questions

1. What were the major challenges and obstacles that Marin Alsop faced in becoming and then being the conductor of the Baltimore Symphony Orchestra?

2. As inspiring as Marin Alsop is, like all leaders she has strengths and weaknesses. Evaluate what you consider to be her major strengths and weaknesses as a leader.

3. What personal traits, skills, and behaviors did Marin Alsop need to use and cultivate in order to develop a strong leader-follower relationship? In what ways is her gender a factor and why?

4. What aspects of the BSO's culture did Marin Alsop need to change in order to ensure its survival and growth and how did she cause the changes?

5. What leadership strategies and personal competencies could Marin Alsop bring to her present situation to continue the BSO's standing, retain players, and earn critical acclaim for the orchestra?

6. What can leaders learn from the metaphor of leading an orchestra?

Key Leadership Lessons

1. Diversity matters in leadership dynamics. Being a "first," regardless of the way that you differ from the prototypic leader in the field, directly or indirectly occupies a significant piece of the leader's time and informal role, and requires that organization members engage in the emotional and cognitive work to accept the unfamiliar and the leader to be a strong example.

2. The ability to communicate passion about his or her vision and craft is a powerful tool of any leader. This goes beyond technical expertise (whether you are an engineer, a violinist, or a doctor) to take this passion to a level that inspires and motivates others.

3. Skilled leaders have an ability to turn difficulties, such as the many difficulties facing the BSO, into opportunities to unite and focus people, make needed changes, and involve people in finding solutions.

4. Effective leadership, especially in unique situations such as presented in this case, requires self-awareness, self-reflection, a willingness to accept feedback, and the discernment to seek wise counsel.

References

Alsop, M. (http://www.marinalsop.com/mediafaq.php)

Alsop, M. (2007). Appearance on PBS Nightly News, October 17. http://www.youtube.com/watch?v=nF zxMhU3Qi8&feature=related

Eagly, A. H. and Carli, L.L. (2007). *Through the labyrinth: The truth about how women become leaders.* Boston: Harvard Business School Press.

Films for the Humanities & Sciences. (2005). *The music paradigm: A seminar in business management.* Princeton: Films for the Humanities & Sciences (www.films.com)

Himes, G. (2007). (Re)Making the band: Marin Alsop conducts the BSO into the 21st century. *Baltimore City Paper.* November 21. (accessed online: http://www2.citypaper.com/news/story. asp?id=14843)

Page, T. (2005). Musicians balk at choice of Baltimore conductor. *Washington Post,* July 18. (accessed online: http://www.washingtonpost.com/wp-dyn/content/article/2005/07/17/AR2005071701267. html)

Rhode, D.L. (Ed.) (2003). *The difference 'difference' makes: Women and leadership.* Stanford, CA: Stanford University Press.

Schein, E.H. (2004). *Organizational culture and leadership.* (3rd Ed.). San Francisco: Jossey-Bass.

Smith, T. (2010a). Musicians accept pay cut to help struggling BSO. *Baltimore Sun.* March 25. Purchased March 29 2010 from www.Baltimoresun.com.

Smith, T. (2010b). BSO salaries hit sour note once again: Players 'devastated' by pay freeze and future 16.6% cut. *Baltimore Sun.* March 26. Purchased March 29 2010 from www.Baltimoresun.com.

Wakin, D. (2005). Best wishes on your job. Now get out. *New York Times.* October 9. (accessed online: http://www.nytimes.com/2005/10/09/arts/music/09waki.html).

BIOGRAPHY

Dr. Katherine Farquhar is Director of the AU/NTL Master of Science in Organization Development at American University in Washington DC and an Associate Professor of Public Administration and Policy in AU's School of Public Affairs. She is a member of the NTL Institute for Applied Behavioral Science. She has taught leadership in the School of Public Affairs for more than two decades, and has received the School's awards for Excellence in Teaching and Excellence in Service. Her publications focus on the organizational impact of nonroutine executive departure, the dynamics of short-term/ interim leadership, and on the 21st century practice of Organization Development. She created and runs an International Residency program within the MSOD curriculum where nearly three dozen teams of graduate students have completed OD consultations with local leaders from all sectors, in client systems outside the USA. Dr. Farquhar earned her BA from Wellesley College, an MAT from Harvard University, and the Ph.D. in Social Psychology from Boston University.

Katherine Farquhar (Lead Author)
Director, AU/NTL MSOD Program School of Public Affairs
Watkins Building, American University, 4400 Massachusetts Avenue NW,Washington DC 20016, 202 885 6206
Email: kfarq@american.edu

Dr. David Jamieson is Associate Professor & Department Chair, Organization Learning & Development, College of Applied Professional Studies at the University of St. Thomas. He is also President of the Jamieson Consulting Group, Inc., Practicum Director in the M.S. in Organization Development Program at American University/NTL and a Distinguished Visiting Scholar in Benedictine's Ph. D. in OD Program. He has 40 years of experience consulting to organizations on leadership, change, strategy, design and human resource issues. He is a Past National President of the American Society for Training and Development (1984), Past Chair of the Management Consultation Division and Practice Theme Committee of the Academy of Management and currently serves as Education Liaison for the OD Network. Dave is co-author of *Managing Workforce 2000: Gaining the Diversity Advantage* (Jossey-Bass, 1991), co-author of *The Facilitator's Fieldbook, 2ⁿᵈ Edition* (AMACOM, 2006) and co-author of *Consultation for Organizational Change* (IAP, 2010). In addition he has published 11 chapters and numerous articles in journals and newsletters. He serves as Editor of *Practicing OD*, an OD Network on-line journal; Associate Editor for the Reflections on Experience Section of the *Journal of Management Inquiry* and on the Editorial Boards for the *Journal of Organization Change Management and The Organization Development Practitioner.*

David W. Jamieson (Co-Author)
Department Chair, Organization Learning & Development
College of Applied Professional Studies, University of St Thomas
1000 LaSalle Ave. Minneapolis, MN 55403, 651-962-4387 · Email: djamieson@stthomas.edu

5

Robert Swan:
From Polar Expeditions To Entrepreneurial
Environmental Leadership

Jireh Hooi-Inn Seow

The Major Focus of the Case

Robert Swan's leadership in polar expeditions, in generating public awareness on environmental issues, and in preserving Antarctica as the last true pristine wilderness on earth, highlights a number of leadership lessons. His story speaks of a motivating inspiration, a worthy vision, dogged determination, action leadership, authentic leadership, entrepreneurial leadership, global leadership, and team building.

Introduction

It was sheer madness. Robert Swan, Antarctic expedition leader of In the Footsteps of Scott and his team members, Roger Mear and Gareth Wood, had not taken a bath or shower for a year; this was extreme even for Englishmen. Less than forty-eight hours earlier, they were standing at the South Pole after living for a year in the coldest and windiest place on earth and after walking unassisted for seventy days to the South Pole. Then right after landing on London's Healthrow Airport, they faced a camera crew for a surprise and live TV-news show, and what was the world itching to know? The first question from the interviewer:

"Was it cold, Robert?"

Robert Swan, knighted an Officer of the British Empire (OBE) in 1995 by Her Majesty Queen Elizabeth II, is the first person in history to have walked to both the South Pole and the North Pole unaided by radio communication or back-up support. He often thinks about madness. "About half of the world's population starve while the other half struggle to lose weight" he once pointed out in a speech, showing another madness of the present world. Yet the greatest folly of this century may very well be how man has been treating Mother Nature and human consumption of fossil-fuel energy. As such, Robert Swan has dedicated his life to increasing awareness of environmental issues and the prudent use of energy. The 21st Century may see the human race face multiple global crises for the first time in history. Among these crises, global environmental issues may turn out to be among the most important. However, Robert Swan is a leader in believing and acting on the proposition that if we work together we can meet the challenges we face.

From Polar Explorer To Environmental And Entrepreneurial Leader

Robert Swan is among the very few polar explorers and climate leaders who use entrepreneurship to create public awareness of Antarctica, global environmental issues, and renewable energy. This is exercising environmental leadership through entrepreneurship. Through practising action leadership, authentic leadership, that is leadership by example, and entrepreneurial leadership, he passionately promotes the use of renewable energy and behavioural and social change in energy consumption as solutions to addressing environmental challenges, protecting Antarctica as the last true wilderness on earth, and sustaining economic development.

Robert Swan's story began when, at the age of eleven, he was inspired by the film Scott of the Antarctic, a heroic story of Robert Falcon Scott and his expedition to the South Pole. Even though Antarctica is the coldest, windiest, driest, and highest continent with the size of about two Australias, this inspirational leadership story of Robert Scott sustained his motivation, determination, and focus all the way from the years of fund-raising from individuals and organisations to the actual walk to the South Pole. To fulfil his inspired vision, he set goals and made plans; he then implemented the plans in incremental steps. For five years, beginning from 1979 to 1984, Robert Swan planned the expedition, procured funds (about five million US Dollars) from about two thousand sponsors, procured a ship (which he christened the Southern Quest), and overtime, networked with and motivated twenty-five people to give up three years of their lives to bring his dream into reality. His Antarctic expedition was also known as In the Footsteps of Scott. On January 11, 1986, Robert Swan led the team (Roger Mear and Gareth Wood were his two other team mates) to reach the South Pole, after seventy days of walking and hauling 160kg sledges (Swan 2009a).

The Icewalk Expedition

Three years after the Antarctic expedition, Robert Swan formed and led an international team of eight members of various demographic backgrounds and expertise from seven countries to walk to the North Pole in an expedition dubbed Icewalk. The base camp of Icewalk consisted of twenty-two representatives from fifteen countries; this Arctic expedition also produced numerous educational films and helped the removal of rubbish surrounding the Arctic area. Although Robert Swan succeeded in leading his international team to reach the North Pole on May 14, 1989, the whole team almost perish from drowning due to unexpected early melting and break-up of Arctic ice – another effect of increasing global temperature.

Efforts To Bring Business, Industry, And Young People Together To Address Environmental Issues

As protecting Antarctica and fighting against global environmental damage are complementary, Robert Swan joined individuals such as Robert F. Kennedy and organisations such as the World Wildlife Fund in a global common effort to make the public aware of these crucial environmental issues. As a result, the United Nations (UN) invited Robert Swan in 1992 to be the first keynote speaker in Rio de Janeiro, Brazil, for the first Earth Summit for Sustainable Development. As a leader responding to the world's leaders to "think global, act local", Robert Swan made a commitment to bring together business, industry, and young people to address environmental issues both globally and locally.

The Mission Antarctica Expedition

In relation to both this commitment and his personal promise to preserve Antarctica (Swan and Reavil 2009), Robert Swan led thirty-five young people from twenty-five countries in 1996 to remove and recycle 1,500 tons of waste and metal scraps, from decades of scientific research, in the Russian Bellinghausen Station in King George Island, Antarctica. This Mission Antarctica took him and his team mates about eight years to raise the fund, and to plan and execute the actions. When it was finally cleared, the penguins of Antarctica reclaimed that piece of their beach for the first time in forty-seven years. This was leadership by action; this was leadership by example. In addition, there was a bonus achievement: global leadership was realised in the process. Friendships were forged among members of feuding nations. Bosnians chose to bunk with Croatians and Palestinians made friends with Israelis. The "enemies" developed a closer relationship with each other than with those from other countries (Swan and Reavil 2009).

Entrepreneurial Endeavours To Promote Environmental Awareness

In his leadership journey to protect Antarctica and the earth's environment, Robert Swan set up a for-profit social enterprise called 2041. This organisation is named after the year 2041 when the moratorium on drilling and mining the resources of Antarctica will be up for review. Presently, Antarctica is still protected by the Antarctic Treaty and is reserved only for scientific research, expeditions, and responsible tourism. However, comes the year 2041, the Protocol on Environmental Protection of the Antarctic Treaty will expire and it will be hard to keep countries hungry for fossil fuels at bay. Therefore, Robert Swan and 2041 realized that the only practical way to protect Antarctic after the year 2041 is through worldwide adoption of renewable energy.

In efforts to showcase and inspire people to use renewable energy, Robert Swan built and developed the "E-base" in King George Island, Antarctica. Back when Robert Swan and his team were clearing the rubbish at Bellinghausen, he noticed a small discarded scientists' station. He remodelled and recycled this station into the first education station in the world in Antarctica and christened it "E-base". E-base is powered entirely by renewable energy, via a wind turbine and photo-voltaic panels. In March 2008, Robert Swan and a small team lived and broadcasted from the E-base via the internet for two weeks. For the first time in history, a group of people relied entirely on renewable energy to survive in Antarctica. Through this example of authentic leadership, he sent a message to the world that if they could survive on renewable energy in a place such as Antarctica, the world could run on renewable energy.

Re-Fitting A Yacht

In 1998, to publicise his endeavours in preserving Antarctica and the earth's environment, to raise funds, and to advertise for speaking engagements with corporations worldwide, Robert Swan and his team members re-fitted a sixty-seven-foot racing yacht, donated by a group of Dutch businessmen, into a floating and globe-trotting advertisement billboard running totally on renewable energy. The lean and green yacht, re-christened the 2041, has been running on wind turbines, polyethylene terephthalate (PET) sails made from recycled Coca-Cola PET bottles (later layered with thin-film solar panels), and biofuel-powered engines. Over the years, Robert Swan made use of the yacht to carry out his entrepreneurial and environmental leadership to:

- ferry volunteers for the Antarctic clean-up at Bellinghausen,
- generate enormous public attention for environmental and health care (AIDS) issues through out South Africa and in the 2002 (Second) Earth Summit in Johannesburg,
- compete in the Cape Town to Rio de Janeiro Yacht Race in 2003 (to gain publicity),
- circumnavigate the whole African continent and stopping at key ports to carry out clean-up projects and promote environmental and health care issues,
- compete in the famously brutal Sydney-Hobart Yacht Race in 2004 (again, for publicity purposes), and
- bring about public awareness on environmental issues in the five economies contribute the most to global environmental damages (the United States, the European Union, China, Russia, and India) through Voyage for Cleaner Energy.

Voyage for Cleaner Energy began in 2008 and it will culminate in the 2012 (Third) Earth Summit on Sustainable Development.

Entrepreneurial Environmental Leadership

Traditionally, environmental advocacy and entities associated with it are seen as those on the political left who are antagonistic to entrepreneurial and business endeavours while people on the political right tend to be supportive of economic growth, entrepreneurial ventures, and corporate business. Robert Swan is an environmental advocate who also believes in entrepreneurial endeavours. He is well-paid for his speaking engagements, which increases as he and his for-profit international company, 2041, become more and more globally renowned for environmental leadership just as he becomes more and more recognised as a motivational speaker. Business corporations invite him to inspire and motivate their executives. Thus, he makes use of his fame and the responsibilities entrusted to him by world leaders to be an entrepreneurial motivational speaker on leadership. These speaking tours on leadership also give Robert Swan the opportunities to promote environment protection, the preservation of Antarctica, and issues of renewable energy (Swan 2009c).

Moreover, his speaking engagements to these business organisations open the way for back-end sales, thus increasing the revenue of 2041 and the amount of funds available for subsequent environmental projects. To prove what he says is true, to further inspire the participants of his seminars, and to make a lasting impact on the lives of the corporate professionals, he and his company bring leaders and managers of these organisations from all over the world to visit Antarctica in the form of responsible adventure tourism called Inspire Antarctic Expeditions. In addition, the revenue from business corporations who send their executives on the expeditions would help subsidise the cost of students that Robert Swan would select and take along on the same expeditions (Swan 2009c). The networking between corporate executives and students would thus be another significant beneficial impact of Inspire Antarctic Expeditions.

During the trip across the Drake Passage (one of the most tumultuous seas) from the Argentinean picturesque city of Ushuaia (the southernmost city in the world) to the Antarctic Peninsula, Robert Swan would give lectures and advices on leadership. Furthermore, as a bonus to public awareness, these Antarctic expeditions would carve deep impressions on the present and future corporate leaders as they personally witness the beauty of Antarctica and the effect of increasing global average temperature on the continent (Swan 2009b). As they come face to face with the beauty and purity of nature, these students and corporate professionals, who make or will make consequential decisions, would be emotionally connected to nature and inspired to love and preserve the natural environment. They would thus return with the desire to preserve Antarctica as the last true wilderness on earth and to take steps to practically reduce their fossil-fuel energy consumption in their own personal and professional lives.

From the first business corporate expedition to Antarctica in 2003 to the present expeditions, Robert Swan and his company have been operating the Inspire Antarctic Expeditions in the form through the vehicle of a for-profit social enterprise. As Robert Swan tasks these leaders during the expeditions to incorporate sustainability into their respective operations and to even become environmental leaders themselves in their respective endeavours, he moves towards his vision of making people across the globe more environmentally aware.

Conclusion

Just as Robert Swan's life story would be about facing disasters and challenges, it would also be about leadership. It is a story about a twenty-plus nobody who raised millions of dollars to walk to the South Pole and did something larger with it. It is a story of an English chap who motivated numerous people and organisations worldwide to help him in his endeavours, and most did so altruistically. It is also a story about an ordinary man who inspired people to risk their lives to follow him in his expeditions, persuaded people to open their wallets and purses to support his projects, and kept on going at it to sustain his environmental leadership. Robert Swan's practice of authentic leadership in environmental issues through social entrepreneurship turns out to be one of the most inspirational and motivational ways for people to love and protect the earth. The leaders and future leaders who return with their stories, photographs, and video recordings of their personal encounter with Antarctica and their first-hand experience of the captivating beauty of pristine nature have a new love for nature and a new environmental awareness that affects their lives and those they influence. Much can be learned from Robert Swan's approach to entrepreneurial environmental leadership.

References

SWAN, R. AND REAVIL, G. (2009). *Antarctica 2041: My Quest to Save the Earth's Last Wilderness.* Broadway Books, New York.

SWAN, R. (2009a). Seminar and trainings by Robert Swan. *BP Antarctic Expedition.*

SWAN, R. (2009b). Personal conversation with Robert Swan. *BP Antarctic Expedition.*

SWAN, R. (2009c). An interview with Robert Swan. *BP Antarctic Expedition.*

Discussion

1. What inspired Robert Swan to invest his time, energy, and financial resources, and even risk his life to walk to the South Pole and engage in other high risk endeavours? In looking at the example of Robert Swan and other visionary leaders, what sets them apart from other leaders?

2. Discuss the specific leadership skills you see Robert Swan using in this case through the many examples of his accomplishments.

3. How do leaders like Robert Swan tend to face difficulties, disappointments, and challenges?

4. How does the idea of thinking both global and local apply to being an effective leader?

5. If you could only take away three valuable leadership lessons from this case, what would they be?

6. What inspires you to make a difference?

Key Leadership Lessons

1. Leadership often begins with a genuine inspiration. It is difficult for a leader to inspire followers if he or she has no inspiration. Vision governs and sustains leadership. People follow a leader with an inspiring vision.

2. Leadership requires determination. One of Robert Swan's supporters and backers was Lord Edward Shackleton, the son of the renowned Antarctic explorer Ernest Shackleton. Initially sceptical, Lord Shackleton was later impressed by Robert Swan's dogged determination.   Robert Swan's Leadership Rule Number One: if you say you are going to do something, do it; no excuses, no dodges.

3. Think and act global and local. Leadership, including environmental leadership, requires thinking and acting globally and locally. Environmental leadership requires the teamwork of many people and organisations worldwide. In the Footsteps of Scott, Icewalk, Mission Antarctica, the Second Earth Summit for Sustainable Development in Johannesburg, E-Base, and the Voyage for Cleaner Energy are all the results of both global-cum-local leadership.

4. Leadership also requires the ability to recruit the right people and build a formidable team. Another of Robert Swan's leadership advice says: "all true leaders know that putting together a team is a crucial step in any successful endeavour" (Swan and Reavil 2009 p.62). For all his expeditions and in all his endeavours, he was able to partner with people who know things that he does not and joint-venture with experts who know a little more than he does about the tasks and challenges at hand. Therefore, recruiting people and building a team also involves controlling one's ego and desire for power. Moreover, these projects that require global teamwork are not just thought leadership; they are action leadership.

BIOGRAPHY

Jireh Hooi-Inn Seow resides in Scotland and is a doctoral researcher of Aberdeen Business School, Robert Gordon University. His research interests include leadership and management development, entrepreneurship, environmental issues, and renewable energy. In 2009, he was selected from a pool of over 1,700 applicants worldwide to be among the 50 university students in the BP Antarctic Expedition under the leadership of Robert Swan, OBE. Together with globally renowned researchers in environmental science, renewable energy, organisational behaviour and studies, and social change, Robert Swan inspired these high-calibre students be future leaders that will make an impact in global environmental issues.

Jireh Hooi-Inn Seow
Aberdeen Business School
Robert Gordon University
Garthdee Road, Aberdeen AB10 7QE
Email: theanthropos@yahoo.com
Tel. +44 [0]1224263973
Tel. +44 [0]7949048289

CHAPTER TWO

1

Ecolab Inc.:
How A Company Encourages Ethical Leadership

Tracy L. Gonzalez-Padron

Major Focus of the Case

Global salespeople are notorious for unethical practices due to pressures to close a sale or address legal and cultural differences. Leaders set the tone for an ethical culture for an organization, which may require special considerations for global sales organizations. This case highlights the importance of tone at the top, tools for ethics training, and a culture that encourages responsible business practices in a company with aggressive targets for sales and international growth. Ecolab Inc. is the global leader in cleaning, sanitizing, food safety and infection prevention products and services with sales of $6 billion. The scenario examined is an actual situation where a major potential customer pressured the salesperson to engage in deceitful practices.

Introduction

Ethics in sales is part of a larger dialogue on the ethics of business that began centuries ago with a focus on the relationship of ethical practices and profit. Marketing, and in particular sales, is the business function responsible for interacting most directly with consumers. When there is a conflict of management goals of profit and customer goals of cost savings, there is pressure for salespeople to engage in unethical practices to make a sale. This greater pressure for performance combines with an increasing amount and speed of information in a complex business environment, making ethical mishaps more likely (Toor and Ofori 2009). In addition, work locations for salespeople are scattered across the globe, isolated from direct supervision and oversight from the company headquarters. A 1997 study of 200 sales managers indicated that

- 49 Percent of surveyed managers say their reps have lied on a sales call.
- 34 Percent say they have heard reps make unrealistic promises on a sales call.
- 22 Percent say their reps have sold products their customers did not need.
- 30 Percent say customers have demanded a kickback for buying their product or service.
- 54 Percent say the drive to meet sales goals does a disservice to customers.

(Marchetti 1997: p. 30)

The prevalence of unethical sales behaviors is alarming since sales relationships depend on consumer trust for continuation of sales. Studies of consumers show that a salesperson's ethical sales behavior effects customer loyalty through customer trust (Chen and Mau 2009, Whalen et al. 1991). There are differences, however, in what consumers consider unethical sales practices such as exaggerations about the features and benefits of his/her products/services, lies about availability in order to make a sale, selling products/services people do not need, selling dangerous or hazardous products and accepting favors from customers. For example, a recent study in the United States finds that younger age groups consider a variety of sales tactics as less unethical than do their older counterparts (Ramsey et al. 2007). Further research illustrates that while females tend to reach ethical judgments about sales tactics with more concern for feelings and relationships than men, the gender difference narrows with age and experience (Dawson 1997). Cross-cultural researchers have found that national culture affects salespeople's ethical decision-making, adherence to organizational processes, negotiation and teamwork (Dubinsky et al. 2004, Zarkada-Fraser and Fraser 2001).

Managerial attention to the ethics in a sales organization is essential, given the importance of the sales function, the complexity of legal and cultural considerations in global sales, and the prevalence of unethical sales behavior. Ferrell, Ingram, and LaForge (2000) provide seven guidelines to enhance ethical and legal behavior for sales organizations around the globe:

1. **Establish Specific Standards of Conduct for the Sales Organization**
   Statements within the code of conduct related to customer interaction, competitive intelligence and sales activities.

2. **Appoint a Sales Manager as a Compliance Officer**
   Having a key ethics person within the sales organization communicates the importance of ethical behavior to everyone in the sales organization.

3. **Address Ethical Propensity in the Sales Organization Hiring Process**
   A global sales organization requires strong, principled individuals that bring ethical values and behaviors to the group.

4. **Provide Ethics Training to Salespeople and Sales Managers**
   Training includes awareness of ethical issues and accepted behaviors in a global business environment.

5. **Monitor Behavior of Salespeople and Sales Managers**
   Incorporate checks and balances in the sales performance system, while ensuring no retaliation for reporting misconduct.

6. **Enforce Sales Organization's Ethical Standards**
   Communicate situations where unethical behavior was punished, as well as success stories of ethical actions.

7. **Develop Ethical Culture Within the Sales Organization**
   The ethical culture of the organization determines what constitutes ethical behavior in the workplace, resulting in lower role conflict and role ambiguity, which increases job performance of sales professionals. Employees perceive the ethical culture of an organization through experiences with their superiors, stressing that leader's actions are particularly important in defining the ethical climate of the organization (Mulki et al. 2009).

Ecolab Inc.

A chemical company providing products and services to the food preparation industry would have many opportunities for ethical misconduct, especially when sales occur in over 160 countries. This is the case for Ecolab Inc., the global leader in cleaning, sanitizing, food safety and infection prevention products and services. With more than 14,000 direct sales and service staff, Ecolab assists customers worldwide in the foodservice, food and beverage processing, hospitality, healthcare, government and education, retail, textile care, commercial facilities, and vehicle wash industries.

Started as Economics Laboratory in 1923, Ecolab has a long history of serving customers for more than 80 years. The original name reflected how the company would be "economic" by helping customers save time, labor and costs and offer innovative products through "laboratory" research. The company motto in the early years was "Saving Time –Lightening Labor – Reducing Costs to Those We Serve." Even though the range of products and customers expanded, the focus on serving the customer is a dominant feature in the "Circle the Customer – Circle the Globe" strategy adopted in mid-1980. "Our strategy is to surround our existing customers with a variety of services, so that all they have to do is look to Ecolab for all their cleaning and sanitizing needs" (1989 Al Schuman, Ecolab Services Group and next CEO).

Ecolab admits to being an aggressive competitor in the industrial cleaning industry, even including a section in their Culture Statement saying, "Ambitious and aggressive, driven and determined, enthusiastic and energetic, we cultivate the opportunity to compete." International sales have been a part of Ecolab's growth since their entry into Canada in 1955 and Swedish subsidiary in 1956, with customer service capabilities in 160 countries today. Growth throughout the years also came from acquisitions of companies around the globe, requiring the blending of diverse organizational and national cultures.

Ethical Dilemma in Sales

An example of pressure for a salesperson to make a sale by engaging in unethical practices occurred at Ecolab. A new customer developed a relationship with the Ecolab sales representative in the U.S. The account was substantial and could greatly enhance the company's revenues and the salesperson's compensation. With a signed purchasing contract in hand, the deal closed. Shortly thereafter, the client approached the salesperson requesting a letter with some specific sales information. "It's a standard procedure for purchases," was the customer's explanation. The salesperson contacted the headquarters' legal department, as a side agreement was not an expected practice of Ecolab. After much scrutiny, legal staff informed the salesperson that Ecolab Inc. could not provide the requested letter, as it could be perceived as accounting fraud. Months later, another vendor that had supplied that customer with a similar side agreement was implicated in an accounting scandal. Ecolab Inc. averted an ethical misconduct disaster due to the culture of their sales staff to do the right thing.

Ecolab Ethical Leadership

"We are extremely proud to receive this award once again," said Douglas M. Baker, Jr., Chairman, President and Chief Executive Officer of Ecolab after receiving an award for ethical practices. "We value and expect good business results - and we also value how we achieve those results. We believe our focus on ethical leadership and corporate social responsibility, which are fundamental factors in how we conduct business at Ecolab, are why we are able to successfully, sustainably and profitably grow our business." ('Ecolab Named among the World's Most Ethical Companies for Fourth Consecutive Year' Mar 22, 2010)

Ecolab joins other reputable companies such as General Electric, Starbucks, American Express, Google, Nike, Time Warner and PepsiCo for four consecutive years of recognition as a leader in promoting ethical business standards. As Doug Baker highlights in his comments, ethical leadership is fundamental to the business at Ecolab. Ethical leadership refers to management throughout the company that role model ethical behavior; communicate about matters of right and wrong; and reinforce ethical conduct among the employees. Ecolab instills a climate that is conducive to ethical actions in the sales force through establishing an industry expectation of honesty, integrity, and commitment to serving customers. This commitment is reflected in the corporate Quest for Excellence where it states:

"We work closely with our customers, tell them the truth and earn their business every day. Superior service built this company and continues to be our central policy and philosophy. We are a vigorous, tough, ethical competitor."

An ethical culture that permeates throughout an organization must begin at the top – characterized by the phrase "tone at the top." Often, employees will look to the CEO for guidance on strategic priorities, communicated through internal and public venues. Douglas Baker, current CEO of Ecolab stresses his personal ethics when saying "living by my personal moral code is one of the key reasons I have this job"(Lennick and Kiel 2005: p. 4) and the organizational ethics when speeches include language such as:

".... Because our teams and our customers are counting on us to do real things for them, not theoretical things, and to make a difference where it counts, and it's our people that do it. Now, importantly, our people are tied together by a culture. And it's an inherited culture, and it's really the strength of the company, and why I get to stand here today, and it's a legacy that goes back a long way."(Baker 2007)

Interviews of employees at Ecolab showed a sense of pride in the company ethical culture. As one manager with twenty years at the company stated, "I am thankful that I am at a company that I don't have to 'go there' (meaning compromise his/her ethics) – I'm fortunate enough that I don't have to make those decisions. It is something that the company is very proud of."

This tone from the top cascades down the organization throughout the leadership with global responsibilities, who carry the message to the country managers around the globe. Managers are provided tools, training, and monitoring to foster an ethical culture. For example, in order to communicate the tone from the top internally, a letter from Doug Baker is provided to all employees. The message reinforces ethical conduct is an Ecolab philosophy, regardless of where business is conducted. As one manager interviewed stated, "People want to be known to senior management for the right reasons. They are afraid of being the one that got the company in trouble and their name would be known to senior management for all the wrong reasons." The culture encourages sales people to include their manager and the Legal Department if an ethical issue arises. While Ecolab is very customer focused, losing a customer for the right reason (price, ethics) is encouraged, knowing from experience that customers return when they realize the quality of Ecolab's service.

A new employee receives a copy of the Code of Conduct during orientation, and the employee signs the document. There is also an annual code certification process for top management globally. The code of conduct includes guidelines for making decisions to avoid conflict of interests and disciplinary actions for failure to comply. It includes the following opening direction:

Ultimately, the responsibility for proper conduct rests with each of us.

There is no substitute for personal integrity and good judgment.

When faced with a difficult situation, consider these questions:

- Is my action or decision the right thing to do?
- Could my action or decision withstand public review?
- Will my action or decision protect Ecolab's reputation as an ethical company?

If the answer to each question is "yes," the action or decision is probably the correct one.

Topics in the code of conduct include working with Customers, Working with Suppliers, Agents and Consultants, Contact with Competitors, Working with Government Officials, Working with Each Other, and Accounting/Financial and Corporate Information. See the Excerpts from the Ecolab Code of Conduct for specific entries regarding customer interaction and competitive relations. While country managers typically speak and understand English, the Ecolab Code of Conduct is available in more than 25 languages to allow all employees to access the guidelines for ethical behavior.

Conducting Ecolab Business

Conducting the business of Ecolab means that we deal with a variety of people and organizations including customers, suppliers, competitors, community and government representatives, and other employees. These relationships will be based on honesty and fairness. We will be truthful in representing Ecolab.

Working with Customers

The company that fails its customers fails! We will stay close to our customers, tell them the truth and earn their business every day. There will be no bribes, illegal payments or pricing practices. We will only promise what we can deliver. Our services, products and systems will be truthfully represented and ethically sold.

Contact with Competitors

General

The basic policy is for Ecolab employees to have no inappropriate contacts with our competitors. That way, we comply with the law and also maintain full independence and freedom to act. Any business activity which involves repeated or unusual contact with competitors - whether at meetings, in telephone calls or by correspondence - must be approved by your supervisor and the Law Department.

Also avoid unfair acts against competitors. Prohibited activities include:

- Threats and harassment, physical abuse, and equipment tampering directed against a competitor;
- Unlawfully interfering with an existing contractual relationship between a competitor and its customer; and
- Raiding key employees with the intent to drive a competitor out of business.

Comparisons with Competition

Ecolab sells its services and systems on merit - not by making false or misleading comparisons with the competition. Specifically, in comparing Ecolab to the competition, we will not intentionally:

- Misappropriate or misuse the trade names or trademarks of a competitor;
- Make false or misleading statements about a competitor or its products, business practices, financial status or reliability; or
- Engage in false or misleading advertising.

Gathering Competitor Information

Ecolab keeps up with competitive developments and reviews all pertinent public information concerning competitors. Information about competitors is collected from a variety of legitimate sources to help evaluate our products, services and marketing methods. Proper sources include information from customers or which is published or in the public domain, or information or product samples lawfully received from the owner or from an authorized third party.

Ecolab respects the trade secrets of others. There are limits to the ways that information can be ethically acquired and used. Espionage, burglary, wire tapping and stealing are wrong. But so is hiring a competitor's employees solely to get confidential information. So is gaining unauthorized access to electronic mail or other confidential competitor communications.

If possession is gained of competitor information that is marked confidential, or which is believed to be confidential, consult with the Law Department immediately.

Training for new hires includes instruction about recognizing an ethical issue, and knowing when to elevate the issue to management or the legal department. New hires sometimes come from competitors, requiring coaching (by human resources and legal staff) that focuses on the unethical use of their former employers' confidential information to win customers. Training also includes instruction on looking for "red flags," such as side agreements for a corporate account. Other training includes procedures for reviewing written sales contracts with the legal department. While some customers may not have written contracts, salespeople are trained to consider whether a sale is good for the company – in other words, whether it makes financial sense.

Ecolab has developed procedures to monitor sales performance to prevent opportunities for misconduct. For example, customer service staff follows up on submitted service and sales reports. There are systems for reporting misconduct, including a help line available 24/7 in 150 languages. A non-retaliatory policy encourages reporting, and anonymous reports are permitted. The General Counsel gives an annual accounting of incidents to the Audit Committee of Board of Directors. Reported misconduct or incidents are handled by the legal department, and depending on the nature of the claim would require collaboration with human resources, internal audit, or other functional departments. One manager admitted, "Problems happen, but we work to detect them early and we address them." As situations arise, there is a continuous improvement focus. Documentation of lessons learned and reflection on how to prevent a repeat incident are part of the process.

Even though Ecolab salespeople work in a very aggressive culture, at the same time, they strive to do things the right way because it makes good business sense. It is all about relationships and accountability – and that is when ethics comes to play. When a salesperson at Ecolab says they are going to do something, they need to deliver on the promise. By being honest, fair and following through on promises, the salesperson maintains the trust of the customer for repeated sales.

References
Baker, Douglas 2007. 'Keynote Speech.' Presented at CRO Conference. May 10, 2007.

Chen, M. & Mau, L. 2009. 'The impacts of ethical sales behaviour on customer loyalty in the life insurance industry.' *The Service Industries Journal*, 29:1, 1.

Dawson, Leslie M. 1997. 'Ethical Differences Between Men and Women in The Sales Profession.' *Journal of Business Ethics*, 16:11, 1143-52.

Dubinsky, Alan J., Nataraajan, Rajan & Huang, Wen-Yeh 2004. 'The Influence of Moral Philosophy on Retail Salespeople's Ethical Perceptions.' *The Journal of Consumer Affairs*, 38:2, 297.

'Ecolab Named among the World's Most Ethical Companies for Fourth Consecutive Year.' Mar 22, 2010 investor.ecolab.com: BUSINESS WIRE:

Ferrell, O. C., Ingram, Thomas N. & LaForge, Raymond W. 2000. 'Initiating Structure for Legal and Ethical Decisions in a Global Sales Organization.' *Industrial Marketing Management*, 29:6, 555-64.

Lennick, Doug & Kiel, Fred 2005. *Moral Intelligence: Enhancing Business Performance and Leadership Success* New Jersey: Wharton School Publishing.

Marchetti, Michele 1997. 'Whatever it takes.' *Sales and Marketing Management*, 149:13, 28.

Mulki, Jay, Jaramillo, Jorge & Locander, William 2009. 'Critical Role of Leadership on Ethical Climate and Salesperson Behaviors.' *Journal of Business Ethics*, 86:2, 125-41.

Ramsey, Rosemary P., Marshall, Greg W., Johnston, Mark W. & Deeter-Schmelz, Dawn R. 2007. 'Ethical Ideologies and Older Consumer Perceptions of Unethical Sales Tactics.' *Journal of Business Ethics*, 70:2, 191.

Toor, Shamas-ur-Rehman & Ofori, George 2009. 'Ethical Leadership: Examining the Relationships with Full Range Leadership Model, Employee Outcomes, and Organizational Culture.' *Journal of Business Ethics*, 90, 533-47.

Whalen, Joel, Pitts, Robert E. & Wong, John K. 1991. 'Exploring the Structure of Ethical Attributions as a Component of the Consumer Decision Model: The Vicarious Versus Personal Perspective.' *Journal of Business Ethics*, 10:4, 285.

Zarkada-Fraser, Anna & Fraser, Campbell 2001. 'Moral decision making in international sales negotiations.' *Journal of Business & Industrial Marketing*, 16:4, 274.

Discussion

1. In what ways does a strong company ethical position affect the conduct and culture of an organization?

2. What are some of the possible consequences internally and externally of not taking a strong ethical position?

3. What are some things Ecolab does to encourage ethical conduct?

4. How does the tone at the top influence responses to ethical dilemmas, especially in light of CEO successions over the years?

5. What are the characteristics of an ethical leader? How can they influence responsible behavior in an organization?

Key Leadership Lessons

1. Leaders play a critical role in creating the ethical climate of the organization that determines what constitutes ethical behavior in the workplace. Employees perceive the ethical climate of an organization through experiences with their superiors.

2. Ethical challenges and opportunities evolve as business becomes more complex, rapidly changing, and global. Sales organizations in particular are confronted with many ethical dilemmas.

3. Tone cascades down the organization from the top leadership. An ethical organizational culture can transcend CEO succession when the core philosophy is embedded throughout the business.

4. Comprehensive ethical programs that include leadership, tools, and training can minimize ethical and legal dilemmas for global salespeople.

BIOGRAPHY

Tracy L. Gonzalez-Padron is the Director of the College of Business Ethics Initiative and an Assistant Professor of Marketing at the University of Colorado at Colorado Springs. She received her Ph.D. in marketing and international business from Michigan State University. Her research interests include marketing strategy, global marketing, and corporate social responsibility. She has published research in Industrial Marketing Management, Journal of International Business Studies, Journal of Macromarketing, Journal of Public Policy & Marketing, Journal of Personal Selling & Sales Management, British Journal of Management, and presented at international conferences. She has considerable managerial business experience relating to new business development in North America, Europe, Latin America, India, and China.

Tracy Gonzalez-Padron, PhD
Director, Ethics Initiative
Assistant Professor, Marketing & International Business
College of Business and Administration
University of Colorado at Colorado Springs
1420 Austin Bluffs Parkway, Colorado Springs, Colorado 80918
Tel. 719-255-3794, Fax: 719-255-3494 · Email: tgonzale@uccs.edu

2

Abraham Lincoln And The Reaper Case: On Forgiveness, Trust-building And Mutual Respect

Mark L. McConkie

Major Focus:

No segment of the leadership formula is more important, or more powerful, than the character component. Very often, it is also the most difficult to build and manage. Feelings, perceptions, preferences and personal ambitions easily get in the way of the nobler virtues of trust building, showing deference and respect, and of forgiving others. When high-trust relationships exist, every other positive interpersonal skill and aptitude is positively affected, and people not only have the freedom to give of their best selves – or rely on "the better angels of our nature" as Lincoln once expressed it – but also to exploit their own talent and inner reserves so as to produce at the highest levels. High trust produces high performance. This case details the events surrounding a court case in which the young attorney Abraham Lincoln was deliberately scorned and embarrassed, his equally deliberate decision to forgive those who had embarrassed him, his priority of placing task accomplishment above grudge-bearing, his manifesting high-trust behaviors, and consequently his ability to make a friend of a former foe – all while engaged in the process of "getting the job done."

Introduction:

Just as high-trust facilitates positive interpersonal growth and interaction, grudge-bearing, it's opposite, hinders that growth and interaction. Leadership, then, is about trust-building. It is   true that low trust leadership models can produce results, sometimes even high performance rates. The lives of tyrants, dictators, and mafia chieftains so attest – and that is part of the point: leaders can force followers to achieve, but those achievements endure only so long as the coercion is in force. High trust relationships and leadership styles produce results which endure beyond the moment of accomplishment. Few are the continued disciples of Genghis Kahn, Adolph Hitler and Joseph Stalin (low trust building leaders); many are the continued disciples of George Washington, Abraham Lincoln and   Gandhi (high-trust building leaders), for example. Trust-building takes time, self-discipline and commitment. But it is at the heart of effective leadership.

The "Reaper Case":

OPPOSING COUNSEL IN MCCORMICK VS. MANNY	
Counsel for the Prosecution: (McCormick)	Counsel for the Defense: (Manny)
• Edward M. Dickenson • Reverdy Johnson	• George Harding • Edwin M. Stanton • Peter Watson • Abraham Lincoln

The year was 1834. Cyrus H. McCormick, of Lexington, Virginia, invented a reaping machine, which dramatically increased his capacity to harvest crops. Sensing both the power of the machine to increase farmer productivity, and the business opportunity this new reaper represented, it took only a few years for McCormick and his brothers to go to Chicago to manufacture and sell the new reaper. Business was good: in 1854 McCormick sold 1,558 farm machines, and by 1855 expected to sell 3000 – mostly reapers.[1] Over time McCormick made mechanical improvements and secured patents. Others, seeing McCormick's success, began to imitate his product, and it was not long until the market hosted multiple variations of the reaping machine.

A partnership headed by John H. Manny, located a factory at Rockford, Illinois, and began to produce what McCormick considered to be a variant of his original machine. He therefore sued Manny and his associates for infringement of patents. The case was to be presented before the United States Court for the Northern District of Illinois, presided over by Judge Thomas Drummond. Rival reaper manufacturers in the eastern part of the United States joined Manny in his defense against McCormick. As both sides considered the McCormick-Manny suit a test case, the stage was set for high legal drama, and the "reaper combination" in particular raised large sums of money to protect what they considered to be their right to build and manufacture reapers of their own.

Not surprisingly, the case attracted the most competent patent lawyers in the United States – Edward M. Dickerson of New York represented McCormick and George Harding of Philadelphia spoke for the defense. Dickerson chose former Attorney General Reverdy Johnson, a leader in the American bar, to join his prosecution team, and Harding chose Edwin M. Stanton and the relatively unknown Abraham Lincoln to join his defense team. The choice of Lincoln was neither easy nor automatic, as he had but a regional reputation and was inexperienced in patent law. Still, Lincoln had previously practiced before Judge Drummond, was well known by the judge, knew the Judge and his judicial temperament, understood the local setting, and had a reputation for honesty. Harding however, had little confidence in the unknown and inexperienced Lincoln. He first tried to obtain the services of Isaac N. Arnold, but failing, settled on Lincoln as a second choice. In making that decision, Harding commissioned one of his associates, Peter Watson, to go to Springfield, Illinois, and interview Lincoln, and then hire him if he deemed it appropriate. When Watson arrived in Springfield he found Lincoln's office closed, and so he went to Lincoln's home, which was "a small frame structure, not such as would indicate that its occupant was a lawyer of such standing" as his defense team desired. Still, he knocked on the door.

Mary Todd Lincoln, Lincoln's wife, stuck her head out of an upper window and asked "Who is there?" Watson introduced himself, saying he was looking for Abraham Lincoln.

"Business or politics?" she asked.

"Business" said the impatient Watson.

"Abe, here is a man who wants to see you on business."

Watson was unimpressed with Lincoln's appearance, and thought that the plain, simple home he lived in suggested Lincoln's professional success represented only moderate achievement at best. After talking with Lincoln for some time, Watson concluded that Lincoln "might be rather effective in that community." Moreover, it would be better to have Lincoln on retainer, than to gamble on the possibility that he might be employed by the prosecution. Surprising Lincoln, Watson paid him a cash retailer, promised him a substantial fee at the end of the trial, and left. Lincoln understood the arrangement to mean that he should be prepared to argue before the Court. He later wrote, requesting all the material on the case that could be had, and went to Rockford, Illinois, where he spent a day and a half examining Manny's machine.

Watson, for his part, reported to Harding, who concluded, based on Watson's report, that it would be unwise to have Lincoln participate in the argument before the court. Moreover, as the case had been moved to Cincinnati, the need for Lincoln's awareness of the Chicago political and legal environment was no longer as important a consideration. With their minds set on winning the case, the senior partners failed to advise the young Lincoln that they intended to use neither he nor his arguments in court. Thus, in September 1855, Lincoln arrived in Cincinnati with the brief he had prepared. Harding and Stanton, already in Cincinnati, felt justified in excluding Lincoln when they saw him: he looked like "a tall, rawly boned, ungainly backwoodsman, with coarse, ill-fitting clothing, his trousers hardly reaching his ankles, holding in his hands a blue cotton umbrella with a ball on the end of the handle." Lincoln was introduced to Harding and Stanton, who barely spoke to him. "Let's go up in a gang," said Lincoln, and in an aside which Lincoln did not hear, Stanton said to Harding, "Let that fellow go up with his gang. We'll walk up together" – which they did. Stanton further demanded to know of Harding, "Why did you bring that that long armed Ape here... he does not know anything and can do you no good."

When the Court opened session, McCormick's two lawyers, Dickerson and Johnson, sought to take advantage of Lincoln's inexperience and strange appearance. Johnson addressed the Judge:"We perceive that defendants are represented by three Counsel. We are quite willing that they shall be fully heard: and shall waive objection to there being more than two arguments on a side, merely asking that Mr. Dickerson be permitted to speak twice, if we so desire."

Harding and Stanton immediately saw the trap, and, determined that Lincoln not be positioned in such a way as to embarrass their case, Stanton told the Court that they expected Lincoln to resign from the case, which he immediately did, to his shame and embarrassment. In spite of this humiliation in front of his legal peers, and the reports that went to an interested public, Lincoln stayed in Cincinnati and watched the legal proceedings. The embarrassments, however, were only increased: Stanton and Harding never even read Lincoln's brief, and although they stayed at the same hotel, they never conferred or dined with him, even though he was on retainer. When Justice McLean invited Counsel on both sides to a dinner at his home, Lincoln was not invited. When the hearing was over, Stanton and Harding left Cincinnati without speaking a word to Lincoln. It was the perfect snub; Lincoln had been rejected personally, professionally, and socially. And it was all deliberate.

Just before leaving Cincinnati, Lincoln went to visit William Dickson, one of the few people who had shown him kindness. He revealed his hurt, and said to Dickson's wife: "you have made my stay here most agreeable, and I am a thousand times obliged to you, but in reply to your request for me to come again I must say to you I never expect to be in Cincinnati again. I have nothing against the city, but things have so happened here as to make it undesirable for me ever to return here."[2]

Years later, Ralph Emerson, one of Manny's partners and a co-defendant in the McCormick Case, recalled that in spite of Lincoln's multiple rejections, he attended the entire proceedings, paid strict attention to all that Stanton and Harding said and did, considering himself a student of attorneys who were better trained and better prepared. Lincoln repeatedly said, following this uncomfortable tutorial, "I am going home to study law! I am going home to study law!" Talking with Lincoln as they walked out of the Courtroom, Emerson told Lincoln that he had been studying law. "No," Lincoln replied, "not as these college bred men study it. I have learned my lesson. These college bred fellows have reached Ohio, they will soon be in Illinois, and when they come, Emerson, I will be ready for them."[3]

Within a few short years Lincoln was elected President. Harding and Stanton, nonetheless, stood firm in their anti-Lincoln prejudices. "When Lincoln was named for President," said Harding, "by the party to which I belonged, my disgust was such that I felt I could not vote for him and I did not intend to, but the situation had become so ominous by election day that I finally took a Lincoln and Hamlin ballot, closed my eyes, and with great reluctance dropped it in the box."

Stanton, for his part, was a Democrat, and Lincoln a Republican. He thus opposed Lincoln on party grounds. In addition, Stanton attacked Lincoln with extraordinary energy, saying Lincoln lacked sense, manners and character. In short, the image shaped in the "Reaper Case" was more deeply and negatively etched with the passage of time.

Six years after the Cincinnati trial, Lincoln, as President of the United States, appointed Harding to be United States Commissioner of Patents, and Stanton to be Secretary of War. During the Civil War years – the burden of Lincoln's Presidency – he interacted much more frequently with Stanton than with Harding. Lincoln leaned on Stanton's advice, but was never afraid to overrule him. Their styles were different: in crisis Stanton was frantic, hurried, quick and decisive in judgment; Lincoln, for his part, was equally decisive, but calm, pensive and not afraid of humor, even during the same crisis. Stanton was studied, detailed and well-thought out; Lincoln, equally well-studied, was reflective, pensive and meditative. Stanton seemed to carry many goals in his head at once, and Lincoln had the greater ability to focus on long term goals with singleness of purpose. Stanton was more formal in his interactions with others; Lincoln more relaxed, even "folksy." Stanton was more likely to try to control in a situation, Lincoln more adaptive and flexible.

Lincoln, however, did not let differences in style interfere with his focus on the task, or with his ability to depend upon and build a high trust relationship with Stanton. Lincoln initiated the trust building: he was always honest in his assessments and in his interactions with Stanton; he sought out Stanton's advice and counsel; he always defined the goals and objectives, and was honest in his praise and acknowledgement of Stanton for what he accomplished; he was always respectful and courteous to Stanton, even when he had cause to be condescending – Lincoln, for instance, often walked over to the War Department when as President he might have demanded that Stanton come to him. The respect Lincoln showed Stanton was correctly interpreted by Stanton to mean he was trusted, and that trust was a medicine that healed the wounded feelings Stanton had carried for years. One night, for example. Lincoln was up late signing military commissions. His aide, a man named Carpenter, noted that Lincoln did not read all the documents he was signing. Lincoln explained his actions by saying, "I do not, as you see, pretend to read over these documents. I see that Stanton has signed them, so I conclude that are all right."[4] Stanton knew of such trust and respect, and it caused him not only to change his feelings toward Lincoln, but to become one of his most vigorous defenders and loyal supporters.

By the time Lincoln died, on April 15, 1865, Stanton felt he had lost his best friend.

Discussion

1. What are some valuable lessons about effective and ineffective leadership that can be learned from the case?

2. How important is character to leadership and what were some character traits of Lincoln that made him such an effective leader?

3. What does Lincoln's willingness to give such high posts in his administration to two men who had publicly affronted and embarrassed him tell us about Lincoln? What does it suggest about effective leadership?

4. Much of Lincoln's interaction with Stanton took place in the public sector. Are public sector examples and cases relevant to students of the private sector, and are private sector interactions relevant and applicable to students in the public sector?

5. The "Stanton team" was initially worried by and fearful of Lincoln's appearance and interaction style. To what degree is leadership capacity related to and influenced by the way one dresses and interacts with others?

Key Leadership Lessons

The Harding-Stanton-Lincoln interactions over the years suggests the existence of enduring leadership principles which transcend time and culture. This means the study of history is a valuable source of insight and leadership instruction, and that many if not all of leadership questions we ask of living leaders might also be asked about dead leaders. It was such awareness that led Harvard historian Georges Santayana to write that those unfamiliar with the lessons of history are doomed to repeat them.

The existence of enduring or fixed principles of leadership suggests that public, private and not-for-profit sector leaders have much to learn from each other, and that some of that learning takes place in asking the simple question: "Does what they do there, work here?" Peter F. Drucker, for instance, regarded by many as the foremost management theorist of the twentieth century,[5] was fond of using public sector illustrations such as General George C. Marshall in his writings to the business sector.[6]

Appearance and speech patterns are a tricky issue: sometimes they are important, and sometimes they can be overlooked. This means leadership requires discernment and judgment and the ability to decide who should wear what and when. In the military, for example, a well-pressed and neatly worn uniform has come to represent discipline and self-respect, both desired traits, which affect how military men and women see themselves as well as how others see them. The same might be said of others – airplane pilots, nurses, police officers, and some clergy, for example. Many business people share the expectations that men wear suits and women wear "appropriate business attire" which in differentially defined in different settings. Artists, many blue-collar workers, and others are typically much more casual and relaxed in appearance. The local TV newsroom, to illustrate, is very professional, very skilled, but like a team of engineers, less likely to be attired in shirts or ties. Speech patterns, accents, language use and general verbal skills are similarly judged differently in different settings, and leadership requires appropriate discernment in these particular environments.

Lincoln's ability to learn from others, even those who mistreated him, such as Harding and Stanton, demonstrates an important self-awareness and humility that enabled him to learn, adapt, progress and grow. The leader who cannot learn from others, even in unpleasant environments, will inevitably be unable to influence those environments, and hence to lead. Lincoln saw his own weakness, and set out to make it a strength – leading self is an important dimension of preparing to lead others.

Lincoln's ability to forgive Harding and Stanton showcases an important moral dimension of leadership. Grudge-bearing turns the grudge-bearer into the prisoner of the one against whom the grudge is leveled. It is a Trojan horse filled with many negatives: it obscures personal judgment, it interferes with the ability to listen, to communicate accurately, and to trust another, for instance. Lincoln's ability to forgive enabled him to focus on the task, and to hire people of exceptional talent, who were able to do much that he himself could not. It enabled him to ask important leadership questions like "What can this man contribute?" and "How can we utilize this man's talent, skills and abilities?" He was unslowed by any thought of "this man hurt me, therefore I will ignore him" or any "you lost your chance" mindset. Lincoln was able to focus on what Harding and Stanton could do, rather than on wrongs they had done.

References

----

1 Carl Sandberg, *Abraham Lincoln: The Prairie Years and the War Years, One Volume Edition.* New York: Harcourt, Brace, Jovanovich, 1966, p. 116.

2 Doris Kearns Goodwin, *Team of Rivals: The Political Genius of Abraham Lincoln.* New York: Simon and Schuster, 2005, p. 175.

3 Albert J. Beveridge, *Abraham Lincoln 1809-1858,* New York: Houghton-Mifflin Co., 1928, Vol. 1, pp. 574-583.

4 Sandberg, p. 597.

5 A. Bedeian & D. A. Wren, "Most Influential Management Books of the 20th Century," *Organizational Dynamics,* 2001, 29 (3), p. 222; see also L. Prusak & T. H. Davenport, "Who are the Gurus' Gurus?" *Harvard Business Review,* 2003, 81 (12), pp. 14-16.

6 See, e.g. Peter F. Drucker, *The Effective Executive.* New York: Harper and Row, 1967.

BIOGRAPHY

Dr. McConkie specializes in organization behavior, management development and ethics. He is a Professor of Public Administration in the School of Public Affairs at the University of Colorado at Colorado Springs. He has consulted, lectured and taught in 49 of the 50 states, and in over 30 nations. He has consulted widely with organizations in the public, private and not-for-profit sectors, and has over 100 scholarly publications or presentations

Mark McConkie
Professor of Public Administration
School of Public Administration
University of Colorado at Colorado Springs
1420 Austin Bluffs Parkway, PO Box 7150, Colorado Springs, Colorado 80933-7150
Tel. 719/255-4011 · Email: mmcconki@uccs.edu

3

Cultural Leadership:
Building An Ethical Organizational Culture

Achilles Armenakis, Steven Brown & Anju Mehta

Major Focus

This brief case summarizes a more detailed manuscript (Armenakis, Brown, & Mehta, in press) describing the development of a strong ethical culture over 30 years by Jim Pursell, CEO of the Pursell Family Corporation (PFC). The culture labeled the Christian culture was initiated by Jim Pursell, the cultural leader, and diffused throughout the company by managers and non-managers. The company patented, produced, and distributed the most technologically sophisticated lawn and garden product useful to homeowners, golf courses, and plant nurseries. Patented under the trademark POLYON, the product is described as a controlled-release product, which consists of small beads comprising multiple coatings of a water soluble material. Sandwiched between the coatings is fertilizer, herbicides, or insecticides. Water dissolves the coatings and the product between the coatings is released. We recently conducted an organizational audit of PFC. The first author has served as a process consultant to PFC since 1981.

Introduction

The company was established in 1904 as an agricultural fertilizer company (Canyon Publications, 2001). Jim Pursell, married Christine Parker, granddaughter of the founder and was employed as a salesman after being discharged from the Air Force at the end of the Korean Conflict. In 1964, Jim Pursell was named CEO after the death of his father-in-law, Howard Parker. Under the leadership of Jim Pursell the strategy of the company expanded to include domestic consumer and professional (i.e., nursery and golf course) fertilizers.

DEFINING MOMENT ONE: Amnesty for Fertilizer Thieves

In 1970, a contract was executed with the Pinkerton Investigation Agency. Agents were placed throughout the company as new employees. Soon, as suspected, a theft ring was uncovered. The fertilizer was being sold illegally by some truck drivers to a distributor who, in turn, apparently sold the fertilizer to retailers. Some of the drivers involved were prosecuted and some recompense was made by the distributor. However, some drivers, who had worked with the company for many years, and who were involved in a minor way, were given a second chance with the company.

DEFINING MOMENT TWO: The 1976 Announcement

In the fall of 1976, Jim Pursell called all of his employees together and announced that from that day on the company would be managed according to Christian principles. He admitted to us during our audit that he did not know what it meant but that he felt like it was the right thing to do. He felt he should dedicate his 72 year old business to the Lord. At the time he had never heard of anyone else dedicating a business to the Lord and hoped that mixing religion with business would not ruin the business. For years afterward, company employees described his decision and his determination to manage according to Christian principles as brave and that it was an excellent re-direction of the company.

DEFINING MOMENT THREE: 1981 Organizational Assessment

In 1981 Jim Pursell contacted the first author, who at the time was the director of the Auburn Technical Assistance Center that offered management assistance to businesses. Jim Pursell's primary goal was to establish a growth plan for PFC. The project, described in Armenakis and Burdg (1986), included (a) personal interviews with managers and non-managers to gather information regarding strengths and weaknesses of the company and (b) numerous team building workshops to develop improved management practices. One workshop was devoted exclusively to formalizing a mission statement and company goals and objectives focused on Christian principles.

2006: Organizational Ethical Practices Audit

PFC was sold to Agrium International in 2006. Soon afterward, we conducted an organizational ethical practices audit of PFC. We developed our audit questions by analyzing the summary reports of the Baldrige National Quality Program Award (NIST, 2008) recipients from 1988-2006. Of the 70 recipients, 28 described 135 ethical practices. We content analyzed the award summaries and developed our Organizational Ethical Practices Audit (OEPA) containing 28 open-ended questions (Armenakis, Brown & Mehta, in press). We interviewed nine individuals. Seven were former members of the top management team (TMT), while two had formal business relations with the company. The interviews were digitally recorded and transcribed into 277 pages of double-spaced typescript. Our first content analysis of the interviewee responses to our OEPA questions were grouped into two broad categories, namely human resources management practices (HRMP) and stakeholder relations (SR). Our objective in gathering information on HRMP was to identify practices that contributed to employee behavior that supported an ethical culture. Table 1 provides the summary findings.

The Organizational Culture

A second content analysis of the transcripts revealed Schein's (2004) framework, comprised of cultural artifacts (e.g., observable documents, and rituals/ceremonies), espoused beliefs and values (e.g., the importance of conducting business ethically), and underlying assumptions (e.g., unconscious thoughts, theories, and expectations), was appropriate for classifying the content. For example, an artifact of an ethical culture might be a formal code of ethics, based on an espoused belief/value of "we conduct business honestly," which is an expression of the underlying assumption "if we cannot be ethical in conducting our business, we should not exist."

This company had a reputation for being an ethically managed company. Its Christian orientation was well known and its products were recognized as being the most scientifically advanced on the market. It is important to point out that our analysis of the Baldrige award summaries revealed that the recipients relied extensively on human resource management practices to communicate to employees the importance placed on ethical behavior. As professors of management we teach these practices to our students as the ideal way to manage organizations. However, in the case of PFC no formal periodic performance appraisal was performed, no compensation incentive was provided to employees, and no ethics training was offered to employees. However, a conscientious effort was made to select employees that fit the culture. Further analysis of the information in Table 1 reveals the company was attentive to stakeholder relations.

Artifacts and espoused beliefs can be identified easily by observing organizational conditions and interviewing employees. In addition to the information summarized in Table 1, two important cultural artifacts are important in describing the culture. About twice a month a voluntary devotional was held in the corporate headquarters. It is important that it be understood that this devotional was considered voluntary. In fact, one TMT executive stated in one of our interviews that he never attended a devotional and never felt pressured to do so. Another important artifact was that Bibles were on several employees desks (presented to them by Jim Pursell). Furthermore, we were told that the guiding belief and value that the managers followed was to manage by the Golden Rule, i.e., do unto others as you would have them do unto you.

Schein (2004) states that one way to identify unconscious underlying assumptions is through in-depth discussions with groups of employees. This can be accomplished by presenting to groups of employees the artifacts and espoused beliefs and values and then challenging them to discover and articulate the underlying assumptions. Our familiarity with PFC executives and our analysis of the interview transcripts allowed us to infer unconscious underlying assumptions, the primary one being that the Bible is the word of God.

Requirements for Cultural Formation

We summarize five requirements for cultural formation to take place.

1: Authentic Leadership: The Foundation for Culture

The formation of organizational culture begins at the top of the organization. An authentic ethical leader is one who is acutely aware of his/her and others' moral character, values, and perspectives and acts in accordance with his/her own beliefs. The authentic leader identifies the desired culture and is a role model and through his/her behavior establishes the foundation for the culture and solicits buy-in from others, especially the cultural carriers.

2: Cultural Carriers: Agents of Cultural Diffusion

As important as authentic leadership is in establishing an organizational culture, diffusing the culture throughout the organization is required and is facilitated through cultural carriers. These are senior-level leaders who walk the talk and serve as extensions of the authentic leader. Through their actions they mimic the behavior of the authentic leader and reinforce the cultural elements.

3: Establishing the Organizational Culture

The culture impacts the behaviors of all organizational members. The cultural leader and cultural carriers must establish the cultural elements by incorporating them into the ways they perform their jobs. For example, during group meetings, discussions could overtly include the espoused beliefs and values, even serving as criteria for decision making. The artifacts that we identified (e.g., Bibles), the espoused beliefs and values (e.g., acting in accordance with the Golden Rule) and underlying assumptions (e.g., the Bible is the word of God) are clearly Christian and certainly ethical. Furthermore, they identify the culture. Any culture can be described using these three elements and an unethical culture can be transformed to an ethical one by changing these elements.

4: Important Formal and Informal Practices

A living code of ethics (Verbos et al., 2007) has been described as ethics embedded within leadership, attraction-selection-attrition, socialization, decision making, reward systems, and organizational learning. From Table 1, it is apparent that, with the exception of a specific ethical reward procedure, all were evident in PFC. PFC employees learned through their daily interactions that they were expected to be ethical. The Christian influence was obvious but certainly not mandatory.

5: Cultural Internalization

Cultural internalization occurs when employees internalize the meaning of the artifacts, espoused beliefs and values and underlying assumptions. The presence of co-ethicists is a powerful dynamic who finalize the internalization of culture. For those individuals who feel uncomfortable in the culture they will ultimately face a decision regarding their continued employment with the organization and likely separate from the company.

The Role Of Leaders In Shaping Culture

The importance of leadership and organizational culture cannot be taken for granted. There are numerous lessons that can be emphasized from this brief case. However, the most striking are summarized below:

1. *Be* honest, *behave* with integrity (leaders are supposed be role models), and expect those who you interact with to be similar. The expectations of the leader will be obvious to others. Those who do not subscribe to the values will sense the lack of fit.
2. Be committed to develop and maintain an organizational culture that is congruent with your values. A leader must feel comfortable with his/her values.
3. *Lead* (i.e., pull do not push) according to the cultural elements.
4. Select cultural carriers carefully. A leader cannot expect to develop and maintain the culture alone. Cultural carriers are necessary to diffuse the culture.
5. Organizational culture influences the behaviors of organization members. Organizational culture can compensate for some organizational practices that are not executed.
6. Simply attempting to execute some practices does not develop and maintain a culture. Cultural internalization must occur.

Epilogue

In 2006, company sales were approximately 50 times greater than in 1981. Jim Pursell stated that he felt the success of PFC was due to the decision he made in 1976 to manage according to Christian principles. Agrium International purchased PFC in 2006.

References

Armenakis, A., Brown, S., & Mehta, A. (2011). Organization Culture: Assessment and transformation. *Journal Of Change Management.*

Armenakis, A. & Burdg, H. (1986). Planning for growth. *Long Range Planning,* 19(3), 93-102.

Canyon Communications. (2001). *A Growing Legacy: The History of Pursell Technologies Incorporated 1904-2001.* Chandler, AZ: Five Star Publications, Inc.

National Institute of Standards and Technology (NIST; 2008). *Overview of the Award Process Review Cycle. Baldrige National Quality Program.* Retrieved December 28, 2008. Website: http://www.quality.nist.gov/Overview.htm

Schein, E. (2004). *Organizational culture and leadership, 3rd edition.* San Francisco, CA: Jossey-Bass.

Verbos, A., Gerard, J., Forshey, P., Harding, C., & Miller, J. (2007). The positive ethical organization: Enacting a living code of ethics and ethical organizational identity. *Journal of Business Ethics,* 76(1), 17–33.

Discussion

1. Discuss the primary shapers of organization culture and how culture influences behavior.

2. What did Jim Pursell do to articulate and shape the organization's culture?

3. Describe the symbolic meaning of each defining moment. In terms of Schein's (2004) three cultural elements, what artifacts, espoused beliefs and values, and underlying assumptions explain the success of PFC in building a strong and ethical culture?

4. Discuss and try to understand each of the five steps in the cultural formation process.

5. What insights can be gained from studying the leaders role in shaping culture?

6. It takes time to build a healthy culture but cultures can erode or be destroyed fairly quickly. Discuss things that can cause organizations to lose their cultures that leaders should pay attention to.

Key Leadership Lessons

1. Leaders are the primary shapers of culture whether it is a whole company, department, team, or family.

2. Cultures happen by default or design. It is important for leaders to know what kind of culture they want to build and then think about what they are doing or not doing to shape the desired culture.

3. In today's environment where so many organizations are affected and sometimes destroyed by ethical scandals, it is essential for leaders to have a plan for building and maintaining an ethical culture.

4. Leaders who do not understand the importance of organization culture can make decisions that undermine cultures without being aware of the affects.

Table 1

SUMMARY OF ETHICAL PRACTICES

Practice	Description
HRMP: Personnel Selection	PFC managers devoted significant time to the steps in personnel selection in order to select employees who were a good fit with the organizational culture.
HRMP: Performance Appraisal	No formal periodic performance appraisals were conducted. Rather, if an employee was observed engaging in some act that was not consistent with the culture, the manager who observed the act would discretely meet with the employee and provide feedback.
HRMP: Compensation	No formal incentive system existed to reward and to recognize employees for ethical behavior. Ethical behavior was considered the norm. A bonus pool was established annually based on the performance of the company. Each person's contributions were discussed and those who contributed more received higher bonuses. Equity analyses based on industry data for geographical location and company size were conducted and adjustments were made for anyone found to be inequitably compensated.
HRMP: Training	No ethics training programs were provided.
SR: Employee Safety	PFC followed industry best practices
SR: Consumer Protection and Product Quality	Multiple coatings of the product protected consumers and employees from hazardous effects of pesticides, herbicides, and fertilizers. Strict quality control procedures were followed to maximize product quality.
SR: Social Responsibility	Controlled release nature of the products (Polyon) produced minimizes potential pollution of underground water, water tables, and surface water, like rivers, lakes, and seas. Jim Pursell helped found (and served on the board of directors of) the Fellowship of Companies for Christ. Jim Pursell served on Alabama's State Ethics Commission. Jim Pursell served on Alabama's Certificate of Need Commission to regulate unnecessary health care expansion.
SR: Generosity	PFC donated 10% or more of corporate profits to 28 charities.

BIOGRAPHY

Achilles Armenakis (DBA) is the J. T. Pursell, Sr. Eminent Scholar of Management Ethics at Auburn University. He has served as a member of the faculty as well as in several administrative positions at Auburn since 1973. Currently, he is the director of the Auburn University Center for Ethical Organizational Cultures.

Achilles Armenakis
Auburn University

Steven Brown (Ph.D.) is Assistant Professor of Management at Columbus State University. He is a former entrepreneur with over 20 years of experience owning and managing businesses. His research interests include organizational hypocrisy, ethical organizational culture, opinion leadership, and technology acceptance.

Steven Brown
Columbus State University

Anju Mehta (Ph.D.) is Assistant Professor of Management at the University of Northern Iowa. She has over 10 years of experience in teaching business students, both in India and the US. She is engaged in cross-cultural research in the areas of leader-member exchange, team management, organizational change, management, and business ethics.

Anju Mehta
University of Northern Iowa
April 22, 2011

4

To Act Or Not To Act:
This Is John's Dilemma

Lisa Catherine Ehrich, Megan Kimber & Neil Cranston

Major Focus of the Case

The case proposes an ethical dilemma that a Public Service Director faces that could affect his career, the career of his boss, and the career of the governor of a state. There is a strong need for ethical leaders in this changing global organization world where the headlines are filled with stories of private sector and public sector leaders who have made serious ethical and moral compromises. It is easy to follow ethical leaders who you can count on to do what is right and difficult to follow those who will do what is expedient or personally beneficial. However, ethical leadership is not always black and white as this case will portray. Difficult decisions must be made where it may not always be clear what to do. The names in the case have been changed although the situation is a real one.

Introduction

John is a senior public servant who works in the Department of the Public Service in a midwestern state in the United States. He has been employed by various public service departments over a 25 year period. For the last two years, he has held the position of Executive Director. Prior to his time in the public service, John worked as a chartered accountant. Although John's current role is more administrative/managerial than accountancy focused, he continues to pay his membership fees to the American Institute of Certified Public Accountants, a peak body that represents accountants, because of his commitment to and interest in his previous field of accountancy. John is married to Ellen, a primary school teacher, and together they are supporting financially their two children, who are both studying law at Harvard University.

The Ethical Dilemma That John Faces

In the course of performing his duties as Executive Director in the department, John accidently becomes aware that public revenue is being used inappropriately. While he is not directly responsible for the operationalisation of this aspect of the budget, he raises his concerns with Bill, his supervisor, about what seems to be the channelling of small, but regular sums of money to the Governor. Bill's position is Commissioner of the Department and his role involves him working closely with the Governor. Because John has a good working relationship with Bill, he feels he can talk openly and honestly to him. Much to John's surprise and disappointment, he learns that not only is Bill fully aware of this practice, but he condones it. Bill tells him that this type of practice has been going on for years and he has learned to accept it. Indeed, given that the Governor is rather poorly paid, Bill suggests this is a way to top up the Governor's salary to a more reasonable standard.

Not long after their encounter, the Governor summons John and Bill to a meeting to discuss this issue as he has become aware that John now knows what is happening. In preparation for the meeting, John develops a succinct yet comprehensive paper that outlines his understandings and concerns. He presents the paper to both of them and talks through the major issues and some actions he believes need to occur to stop the practice.

Due to the politically sensitive nature of the issue, John is told by both the Governor and Bill that the matter is out of his jurisdiction and he should 'keep his nose out of it'. This advice is based on the fact that if the matter becomes public, the Governor and government will not only face questions about how it puts its budget together but also it potentially faces a scandal. The Governor is up for re-election the following year.

What Should John Do?

John is torn between his own strong values of honesty and integrity and the explicit wishes of his immediate supervisors to keep quiet about the situation. While John has a genuine desire to do what is right and to serve his country and to be loyal to his organization and his leaders, he is acutely aware that if he speaks out he could lose his job, affect the careers of others, and create a public scandal. What should John do?

Discussion

1. Some would say that if you are a good leader doing a good job, ideals such as character, morals, and a strong sense of ethics should not matter. Do you agree or disagree and why?
2. In this case what is the ethical dilemma John faces and what are the possible consequences of his choices?
3. What would be some possible alternatives for how John could approach this ethical dilemma in a positive and helpful way?
4. If it was you in this situation instead of John, what would you do?

Key Leadership Lessons

1. Leaders need to be clear on their values, beliefs, convictions and sense of ethics as their behavior and choices can affect many people.
2. Leaders who have a strong sense of ethics are easy to follow and trust.
3. The ethical choices leaders make shapes the ethical environment of the organizations (whole organization, department, or team) they lead.
4. Ethical leadership is particularly important in today's fast moving, highly competitive work environment.

BIOGRAPHY

Lisa C. Ehrich is an Associate Professor in the School of Learning and Professional Studies at Queensland University of Technology. She has taught and researched in the field of leadership for over 15 years. In 2009, she co-edited a book with Neil Cranston entitled, *Australian School Leadership Today*, published by Australian Academic Press.

Lisa Catherine Ehrich Associate Professor
School of Learning & Professional Studies
Queensland University of Technology
Victoria Park Road, Kelvin Grove, Queensland 4059, Australia
Tel. +61 07 3138 3038; Email: l.ehrich@qut.edu.au

Megan Kimber is a Senior Researcher in the School of Learning and Professional Studies at the Queensland University of Technology. Her research traverses Australian politics, administration, and ethics, and she has taught Australian politics and education policy.

Dr Megan Kimber
Research Officer
School of Learning & Professional Studies
Queensland University of Technology
Victoria Park Road, Kelvin Grove, Queensland 4059, Australia
Tel. +61 07 3138 5922; Email: m.kimber@qut.edu.au

Neil Cranston is Professor in Educational Leadership and Curriculum in the Faculty of Education, University of Tasmania. He teaches, researches and supervises postgraduate students in leadership and has recently co-authored/edited two books with Lisa Ehrich, *What is this thing called leadership: Prominent Australians tell their stories* (2007) and *Australian School Leadership Today* (2009).

Professor Neil Cranston
Educational Leadership & Curriculum
Private Bag of Education
University of Tasmania
Private Bag 66, Hobart, Tasmania 7001, Australia
Tel. +61 03 6226 7404; Email: Neil.Cranston@utas.edu.au

5

The Challenges Of Ethical Decision Making In An Australian School

Neil Cranston, Lisa Catherine Ehrich & Megan Kimber

Major Focus of the case

The focus of this case study concerns Peter Davies, one of three Assistant Principals in a large Australian secondary school, who faces an ethical dilemma regarding a student discipline issue. It is an important case because it underscores the point that ethical decision-making for leaders is fraught with complexity and whatever decision is made, there will be implications for all parties concerned.

Introduction

Firm but Fair State High School (FFSHS) is a large well-established secondary school in the leafy suburbs of Brisbane, Australia. It has a long tradition of strong student discipline. For many parents, this is the prime reason for sending their children to the school. Peter Davies is one of three Assistant Principals in the school. Peter arrived two years ago and this was his first appointment as Assistant Principal. He still feels like the 'new boy' as the Principal, Kevin Jakes, and the two female Assistant Principals have been at the school for over ten years. These other three get on well together, seem to have very similar views about things and often socialise together. To date, Peter hasn't been invited to any of their social functions.

The school's discipline policy has been in place for many years, and works on the basis that students are allowed two reasonably significant misdemeanours; then they are expelled. In effect, this is a 'two strikes and you're out policy'. The exception here is when drugs are concerned as there are no second chances. From semester one this year, Peter has inherited the role as school-wide coordinator of the discipline policy. He is replacing one of the female assistant principals who usually looks after such matters, as she is on maternity leave for the semester. Peter is quite uncomfortable about the black and white nature of the school's discipline policy. At his previous school, there were a large number of students who presented very challenging behaviours but the school managed to accommodate these with a more considerate discipline approach than the one at FFSHS.

The Ethical Dilemma Peter Is Faced With

Yesterday, one of the teachers reported that Tony, one of the mature-aged students, had been caught with a very small amount of marijuana in his possession. The School's administration team has never been happy about enrolling older students but it has been a useful strategy to keep numbers up. Peter understands that the school discipline policy requires an immediate suspension of Tony, with the likelihood that he will be expelled as quickly as possible under the drug zero tolerance regime of the school. Peter does some checking with Tony's form .

teacher and learns from this teacher that Tony, who is 19, has been under considerable pressure in recent months. His father has left home, resulting in Tony having to assume 'head of the house' responsibilities. Tony's mother is unemployed and has been seriously ill for some time. Tony has two younger siblings at the local primary school and he has been taking greater responsibility for their care of late. He also works two part-time jobs, as he is trying to support the family as well as save up enough money to attend a Catering College next year when he finishes school. He wants desperately to be a chef. Having wasted his first chance at school, he knows he must be successful this time or his life will be a mess.

Peter starts to prepare the paperwork for Tony' suspension for the principal's signature, knowing Kevin's response will be to get Tony out of Firm but Fair SHS as quickly as possible. Peter has a restless weekend reflecting on the whole matter and delays sending the paperwork through to Kevin. He realises that this may be the end of Tony's education and that there will be pressure placed on his whole family as he is likely to lose his jobs if word gets around that he has been expelled from school for drugs. As Peter is contemplating this dilemma, he receives a mobile phone call from Kevin demanding that he get the paperwork to him immediately and asking why there has been a delay. Kevin tells Peter that one of the parents has already contacted him to ask if the school has gone soft on drugs as she has just heard that a mature aged student has been caught with drugs. Peter realises Kevin is angry about this, but feels very uneasy about a simple knee-jerk reaction in what he sees as a complex case. On the way to his office on Monday morning, he stops off at Mary's office (one of the other Assistant Principals) to see what she thinks.

Reference

Cranston, N., Ehrich, L.C. and Kimber, M. (2006). Ethical dilemmas: The "bread and butter" of educational leaders' lives. *Journal of Educational Administration*, 44(2). pp. 106-121.

Discussion

1. Where do people get their sense of ethics? Can you learn to be ethical?

2. Peter must decide if it would be more ethical to support the policies of the school in which he is an Assistant Principle or take up the cause of Tony who's life will likely be changed if he is expelled from school. Which position would you take and why?

3. Are there other options that Peter could pursue in resolving his ethical dilemma and what are the likely outcome of each?

4. Should leaders consult others when they are confronted with ethical issues that are not clear to them?

5. Is it possible for Peter to seek a win/win solution in this situation for his school and for Tony?

Key Leadership Lessons

1. Leaders set the standard for others to follow. Therefore, it is very important for leaders to have a clear sense of ethics and to be consistent in their ethical practices.

2. Leaders often have to make difficult ethical decisions. In this case Peter has to consider school discipline policies, compassion and care for students, and parental and community expectations of the school. However, in the end result they wil do what they think is right no matter what the cost.

3. Cranston, Ehrich, and Kimber (2006) undertook some research with school leaders in Australia to identify the nature of and extent to which ethical dilemmas were part of their daily lives. The authors found that ethical dilemmas were widespread, and the two most frequently cited dilemmas both related to people issues: (1) student issues; and (2) staff issues (such as under-performing staff). Especially difficult were decisions that created a struggle between justice and mercy.

4. With the right mind set and sense of ethics, leaders can sometimes turn difficult situations into win/win situations by doing what is right and helping those that may be adversely affected find suitable alternatives.

BIOGRAPHY

Neil Cranston is Professor in Educational Leadership and Curriculum in the Faculty of Education, University of Tasmania. He teaches, researches and supervises postgraduate students in leadership and has recently co-authored/edited two books with Lisa Ehrich, *What is this thing called leadership: Prominent Australians tell their stories* (2007) and *Australian School Leadership Today* (2009).

Professor Neil Cranston
Educational Leadership & Curriculum
Faculty of Education
University of Tasmania
Private Bag 66, Hobart, Tasmania 7001, Australia
Tel. +61 03 6226 7404 · Email: Neil.Cranston@utas.edu.au

Lisa C. Ehrich is an Associate Professor in the School of Learning and Professional Studies at Queensland University of Technology. She has taught and researched in the field of leadership for over 15 years. In 2009, she co-edited a book with Neil Cranston entitled, *Australian School Leadership Today*, published by Australian Academic Press.

Lisa Catherine Ehrich Associate Professor
School of Learning & Professional Studies
Queensland University of Technology
Victoria Park Road, Kelvin Grove, Queensland 4059, Australia
Tel. +61 07 3138 3038 · Email: l.ehrich@qut.edu.au

Megan Kimber is a Senior Researcher in the School of Learning and Professional Studies at the Queensland University of Technology. Her research traverses Australian politics, administration, and ethics, and she has taught Australian politics and education policy.

Dr Megan Kimber
Research Officer
School of Learning & Professional Studies
Queensland University of Technology
Victoria Park Road, Kelvin Grove, Queensland 4059, Australia
Tel. +61 07 3138 5922 · Email: m.kimber@qut.edu.au

CHAPTER THREE

1

How Leaders And Companies Treat People Matters: Voices Of Women Garment Assembly Workers In Nicaragua

Virginia E. Schein

Major Focus of the Case

What do garment assembly factory workers, street vendors and crop pickers have to do with management and leadership? If management education is to be a matter of world affairs, then it requires an understanding of workforce participants outside of traditional organizations. Management students need to expand their perspective to encompass a more global community of workers. This community includes the working poor in developing countries who sew garments in the assembly factories, run small businesses on the street or pick coffee on the mountain sides. While such workers are far removed from those working in the carpeted offices of large corporations, they, too, are participants in the economic development of their countries.

To date the working poor in developing countries have received scant attention from management scholars. Creative ways for business leaders to engage in socially responsible endeavors, such as poverty reduction, will emerge only if the voices of disadvantaged workers are included in the management and leadership learning process. The purpose of this case is to make leaders aware that the way they treat people matters and to especially call attention to the need for leaders to help and not ignore or mistreat the disadvantaged.

Introduction

In Nicaragua, the second poorest country in the Western hemisphere, I met with 12 women, mostly union members, who were employed in the garment assembly factories in the Free Zone in Managua. Using a translator, I interviewed the women in groups of six, with each session lasting about two to three hours. The meetings were held on a Sunday and arranged secretly, as the women would have been fired had any factory owner or supervisor been informed of the meetings. What follows is a portrayal of the working lives of these women in their own words.

The Work

In assembly line fashion, most of the women sew pieces of garments produced mostly for the United States market. They are paid by the piece, and sew around 1000 to 1500 pieces a day. The women work long hours, often between 60 to 70 hours a week.

– *I wake up at 4am to make food for my children. I leave at 6am to get to work and arrive at quarter to 7am. I leave the job around 8pm or 9pm; they give us half an hour for lunch.*

– *I sew the outside of pants pieces. First I work from 7am to 5pm and I give back my pieces. Then I start again from 5:15pm to 10pm and do about 350 more pieces. I work from Monday to Friday and sometimes on Saturday.*

– *When they have a lot of production they don't let anyone go home because we have to work even if we are sick. Some days we start at 7am in the morning one day and work until 10am the next day, more than 24 hours.*

– *Sometimes we have to come to work on Saturday and Sunday at 6 in the morning. When there is a lot of production we spend all Saturday night working and continue until Sunday morning.*

The Money

They work these long hours for very little money. What they can earn doesn't go very far and is not enough to take care of themselves and their families.

– *We do not make enough for everything that we need to buy. I have to borrow some money to cover all my expenses.*

– *Right now there are no gains of the job. We can't bring a lot of things to our houses. All that we can buy is five pounds of rice and eat it all the time.*

– *The money that we get is not enough for anything. All the money goes into paying water and electricity and food.*

– *The saddest thing for me, and I think that is the same for everyone, is the payment day. We work till we die and when we get the money, outside of our work are the "tabanos" (bloodsuckers). Because of the low salary, it's impossible to buy everything with cash so we buy some things by credit, which is expensive. They wait for us outside the factories to pay them. Sometimes when we arrive home there's no money left.*

The Working Conditions

The working conditions are poor and the supervisors are described as abusive.

– *The work is continuous, one next to another with a hundred machines in a line and everyone working very fast, without looking at anyone. You cannot talk.*

– *From 7am to 5pm, maybe we go one time to the bathroom. You have water by your chair so you don't get up.*

– *When we began there was not much ventilation and it was very hot. The noise of the machines hasn't changed a lot. Now there's some fan system ventilation.*

– *The supervisor screams a lot when the work is not perfect, but when the work is fine she is pretty calm.*

– *The supervisors scream. They insult you. There are line supervisors from Nicaragua that in order to maintain their positions they mistreat workers.*

– *When they don't like our work, they send us a memo. You can be fired after three memos.*

– *I'd love to do another job. Here the work is very continuous and tiring. The supervisors are not nice at all.*

– *Now we have just only ten minutes to eat. We have to go to the market, eat like chickens and then come back to work. I don't have enough time to eat.*

– *If we don't agree to work on Sunday, or maybe you get sick, they just take the money away from your salary.*

– *Sometimes we take pills. It makes you work faster, you don't feel hungry, you don't feel tired.*

– *People have problems with the lungs, tonsillitis, cough, fever, problems with the eyes, tuberculosis, gastric, skin infections, and allergies.*

The Women's Perspective

These are the only jobs the women can get. They are well aware of the low wages and poor conditions – they know the score.

– *We are not against the foreign investments, but I am against the fact that they don't respect my rights as a worker. We need the job and they need our work. This is a country where we are not getting what we should for the work we do. We are the 2nd or 3rd country around the world where the labor is cheap.*

– *The investors should realize that they are stepping on our land, not in their land. They have to respect us. I think this is a bad policy because the government opens our country's doors to them, that's fine, but helps them (investors) instead of helping the people. That's wrong. They are in my country and they should have to respect me.*

– *We have to change this government. Why do you think the investors come here? They know our government has no shame. It allows them to violate our rights. What we earn in a week is not enough to afford the necessities for our children.*

– *Please tell consumers in your country to demand better conditions for us. We make nice clothes and the quality is good.*

– *People pay a lot for the clothes, but what we get is almost nothing. Someone must be getting good profits, don't you think?*

A woman who had been invited to the United States shared her experiences with the other women.

– *I saw the clothes in the stores. Everything looked so nice. I saw the prices. Everything there was so calm and here everything is so tense, noisy. I thought: They don't know how much it costs us to make them and how much we get as a salary. We earn just cents. I wanted to say to the people in the store: "We make them, we work really hard for that and we can't even buy corn. I can't buy anything."*

The Union

Most of the women were members of a union, some in leadership positions. They spoke of the benefits of having a union, the firings and sanctions against them for being members and the fears of some to join a union.

– *They tried to take some money out of my salary for a defect but as I am a union organizer I know my rights. I told them I was not going to permit that, and they said, OK, we will not take even five cents.*

– *They wanted to fire me (for speaking up) but they can't do that because I am in a union.*

– *When we didn't have a union they (bosses) got mad about everything. They didn't agree with us. Now that we have a union they treat us better.*

– *I think there is a lot of difference in my company from before when there was no union to today when we have a union. They are respectful of the law, there's more respect of the worker and the worker knows his rights.*

– *I've changed. Now I have more force, more courage now. I feel more protected by the union.*

– *I've never been afraid. I am a leader in the union. There's a lot of mistreatment and injustice for the workers but I don't demonstrate any fear.*

– *Once they fired me because we started to form a union. We were 25 people fired. We came together for that injustice and after a while we got our positions back, because we pressured and fought.*

– *I was fired because I asked for my rights. We tried to start a union, but the company fired us. I can't find a job. I am on a black list.*

– *Some women are afraid to join a union. When I began to go to organizing meetings, my husband said I was sleeping with another man.*

– *Some women are afraid of joining a union because they see us, you work hard (for the union), your husband leaves you, and you don't get financial support from the union.*

– *Not all women are organized because they are afraid of being fired.*

The Future

The women spoke of their dreams for the future.

– *My dream as a single mother is to learn something, to be a hair dresser, to be a really good dress maker, so I can work at home and be with my children more.*

– *My dream is to give my children education. I'd like them to know more things so they can do more than me – mostly for going up. We are down and we are going to be here forever, but they can go up.*

– *It would be good to have a program where our children could go and learn things and people take care of them. A school for single mothers would be helpful.*

One woman, in a union leadership role, concluded the session with these thoughts.

– *The important thing is that there are women that form and organize unions. There are women who have been thrown out of their jobs for being in the union. But because of their experiences, they are more able to help and understand other people's experiences. They continue working to organize the rest of the women. We want to have a shop where we can sell our products. We are going to have workshops, first in beauty classes, like hair cutting. We have other plans for the future, such as computer classes, technical and administrative workshops, workshops in labor rights. Everything is part of a master plan that is looking for a better future. That's our characteristic as Nicaraguans. We were born struggling and we die struggling too.*

Discussion

1. What style of leadership (and underlying assumptions) are the factory owners using? What style of leadership (and underlying assumptions) are the women seeking?

2. How could the factory owners and leaders lead, treat, and motivate their workers differently? Consider the working conditions, how workers are treated, things that could be done to make employees feel valued and improve their skills and their life, etc.

3. It takes courage and determination to be an effective leader. What can be learned about leadership from the women union organizers and their sacrifices and the risks they are taking?

4. If you were the leader of the factory where the women work, what would be the first five things you would do?

Key Leadership Lessons

1. That workers want to make a quality product and are willing to work hard are leadership lessons that still require attention. The women are treated as if they are unmotivated, needing to be pressured, monitored and yelled at in order to work at an efficient pace. In reality, the women are highly motivated to do a good job. They seek only to work under more humane conditions and to be paid a living wage.

2. Caring and concerned leaders can make an enormous difference in the lives of disadvantaged workers. Attending to the interests of the worker can bring about improvements in such basics as health, housing, and food supply. Leaders that care about their workers have the opportunity to enhance the well being of the workers and provide their families with hope for a better future.

3. Committed leaders can be found in surprising situations and places. The women union members lead with courage under conditions of poverty and exploitation. They work tirelessly to bring about changes for the garment workers, despite the potential for firings and loss of income.

4. The issues of the working poor in developing countries are often dismissed or ignored. These workers are neither naïve nor passive victims. They are aware of the injustices and seek to improve their situation. If businesses want to engage in socially responsible leadership, they need to listen to and learn from the voices of the marginalized members of the global community of workers.

BIOGRAPHY

Dr. Virginia E. Schein is an International Consultant and Lecturer in the area of Gender and Leadership and Professor Emerita of Management and Psychology, Gettysburg College. She has also been a professor at the Wharton School of the University of Pennsylvania, Baruch College of the City University of New York, Yale University and Case Western Reserve University. Dr. Schein is a past president of the Work and Organizational Psychology Division of the International Association of Applied Psychology (IAAP) and served as a United Nations/NGO representative for IAAP. She is a member of the Global Task Force for Humanitarian Work Psychology. Dr. Schein is internationally recognized for her ground breaking research on gender stereotyping and requisite management characteristics and she lectures worldwide on gender and leadership. Her widely cited research spans three decades and five continents. She is the author of *Working From the Margins: Voices of Mothers in Poverty* (Cornell University Press) and co-author of *Power and Organization Development* (Addison-Wesley series). She received her undergraduate degree from Cornell University and her Ph.D. in Industrial-Organizational Psychology from New York University. She is a Fellow of the International Association of Applied Psychology.

September 27, 2010

Virginia E. Schein Ph.D.
Organizational Psychologist
Professor Emerita of Management and Psychology, Gettysburg College
Email: vschein@gettysburg.edu

2

The Importance Of Leadership Style On Morale, Performance And Culture

D. D. Warrick

Major Focus Of The Case

It is well documented that a leader's style can have a significant impact on employee morale and the performance and culture of a team or organization. There are leaders, for example, that that use a style that results in high morale and performance and creates a culture that raises aspirations, encourages excellence, motivates people to excel, values open and candid communication, relies on involvement, teamwork, and innovative thinking, and that achieves enviable results and high morale. However, there are also leaders that use a style that results in low morale and performance and creates an ineffective or dysfunctional culture that discourages open communications, rarely relies on teamwork and collaboration, discourages innovative thinking or making needed changes, and that creates barriers to relationships, morale, and performance. This case focuses on the leadership style of two CEOs in the same company and the impact of their leadership style on the company.

Introduction

Leadership style refers to the manner in which a leader operates and interacts with others. Everyone has a style of doing things and dealing with others and our style with all of its strengths and weaknesses has consequences and works for us or against us. Most people have a dominant style that is used most of the time and one or more back up styles. The more consistent and helpful one's style is, the more likely it is to bring out the best in others and facilitate getting things done and the more inconsistent and harmful one's style is, the more likely it is to create barriers to relating to people and getting things done.

The leadership styles theories can be traced all the way back to the 1940s when studies led by Ralph Stogdill at Ohio State (Stogdill, 1957) discovered that a leader's style is based on two independent variables, the emphasis a leader places on consideration (people-oriented behaviors) and initiating structure (**performance-oriented behaviors**). When considered together these two variables lead to four basic leadership styles. Additional studies by the Robert Kahn of the University of Michigan (Kahn, 1968), Blake and Mouton (Blake and Mouton, 1964), Hershey and Blanchard (Hershey and Blanchard, 1988) and others led to similar conclusions and models, all based on two independent variables that basically translate to a leader's emphasis on people and performance. *Figure 1* shows a model of the four basic leadership styles and their predicted consequences based on leadership styles research on the impact of style on employee satisfaction and morale, performance, and the culture of teams and organizations. This model will be helpful in understanding the leadership styles of the two CEOs in the case and why they experienced the results that they did.

Background Of Company A

Company A (not the real name of the company) is a geographical survey company that employees about 200 employees of which about 40% are highly trained professionals with Masters and Ph.D. degrees. The founder was a respected scientist with a Ph.D degree. He served as CEO for about ten years and built the company from a start up to one of the leaders in the geographical survey field. He was a people oriented leader who was genuinely concerned about the welfare of employees. Employees loved working for the company and for the leader who enjoyed being involved with the professionals in sharing ideas. They had considerable freedom in doing their jobs, often collaborated in coming up with new ideas, were paid well, and enjoyed being part of a

Figure 1:

THE FOUR BASIC LEADERSHIP STYLES

HIGH

HUMAN RELATIONS STYLE
Places a low emphasis on performance and a high emphasis on people. Very warm, caring, and attentive to people needs but reluctant to hold people accountable and push for results. Tends to create a permissive environment that relies on involvement, teamwork, inputs form people, and being a people pleaser. Avoids making people responsible for their behavior or results, or for confronting problems and conflicts. Maintaining harmony and good relations is a higher priority than getting results.

HIGH PERFORMANCE STYLE
Places a high emphasis on both performance and people. Very results oriented but also excels at valuing, motivating, developing, and fully utilizing people. Strives to create a well-organized and challenging work environment with clear goals and responsibilities and a culture that values openness, innovation, involvement, teamwork, continuous improvement, and a commitment to excellence. Treats people as equals and creates a sense of ownership by all for achieving the desired results.

LAISSEZ FAIRE STYLE
Places a low emphasis on performance and people.. Provides minimal direction, attention to people needs, and accountability. Abdicates responsibility for leading, developing, and caring for his or her people, and leaves people on their own to make their own choices with inadequate information and guidance. Tends to be noncommittal and avoids making tough decisions or addressing problems or conflicts.

AUTOCRATIC STYLE
Places a high emphasis on performance and a low emphasis on people. Very task oriented but not very people oriented. Tends to dominate most situations and relies on power, control, manipulation, and hard work to achieve the desired results with minimal apparent concern for the needs or ideas of others. Has difficulty giving up control and involving or empowering others. Rarely gives compliments but is quick to point out weaknesses. While well intended, gives the impression of "my way or the highway".

(Left vertical axis: EMPHASIS ON PEOPLE)

LOW   E M P H A S I S   O N   P E R F O R M A N C E   **HIGH**

successful company. The company continued to grow and to be profitable until the last two years when competition for business increased, costs became an issue, revenues and profits were steadily declining, and the board had growing concerns about the future of the company.

The board eventually decided that the founder was more of a leader than a manager and that a strong turn around manager with manufacturing experience was needed to shape up the organization, get costs under control, and grow the business. The founder was made Director of Research and Development and the new CEO in his first year proceeded to cut costs, tighten controls, reorganize departments, down-size the organization, push for greater and greater productivity, and try to manage the organization back to success.

LEADERSHIP STYLE CONSEQUENCES

AUTOCRATIC LEADER

Although the emphasis is on high performance, it often breeds counterforces of antagonism and restriction of output. Frequently results in hostile attitudes, a suppression of conflict distorted and guarded communications, high turnover and absenteeism, low productivity and work quality, and a preoccupation with rules, procedures, red tape, working conditions, status symbols, and trying to cater to the whims of the boss. Develops dependent and uncreative employees who avoid responsibility and openness.

LAISSEZ FAIRE LEADER

Employees become apathetic, disinterested, and resentful of the organization and their leader. Results In the lowest employee productivity and satisfaction of all the leadership styles.

HUMAN RELATIONS LEADER

While this style may keep employees happy, there is little evidence to support the notion that keeping employees happy and treating them well results in high productivity. The preoccupation with keeping people happy and involved often interferes with high achievement, causes employees to lose respect for their leader, results in the emergence of informal leaders, and causes problems to be smoothed over. Such an atmosphere can be frustrating to goal-oriented people.

HIGH PERFORMANCE LEADER

Results in high employee productivity, satisfaction, cooperation, and commitment. Reduces the need for controls and formal rules and procedures. Results in low employee absenteeism and turnover. Develops competent people who are willing to give their best, think for themselves, communicate openly, and seek responsibility

Temporarily, as costs were cut, profits improved. However, they eventually began to suffer again as multiple problems began to emerge in the organization. The board authorized bringing in a consultant to interview a cross section of employees, survey all employees, and help the leaders turn around the organization.

The assessment confirmed the growing concerns of the board, the leaders, and the employees. The culture had changed from a people oriented culture that valued employees for their expertise and ideas to a manufacturing culture based on strict controls and the constant pressure to get better results and cut costs. The culture was characterized as a high pressure, fast paced, fire-fighting, political, chaotic, production line type of environment filled with tension, stress, and the fear of making mistakes or being part of the next cuts. Managers and employees felt that they were rarely recognized for doing a good job or encouraged to share ideas but were "hammered" when anything went wrong. These factors led to low morale (3.0 on a 7 point scale with 7 being the highest possible rating), leaders and employees looking out for their own interests rather than the interests of the organization, a breakdown in communications from the top and throughout the organization and a reluctance to communicate openly, share ideas, or make improvements for fear of retribution, minimal teamwork and collaboration within and between departments, sacrificing quality for quantity, a number of employees complaining of burn out, and no time to think, solve problems, learn, grow, share ideas, or build relationships or teamwork.

Evaluating The Leadership Style Of The Founder

The founder was very passionate about the company, the quality of services the company provided, and building a company the employees were proud to work for and work in. He was respected for his knowledge and skills related to the field the business was in and his openness, approachability, and involvement in sharing ideas. He was a visionary leader who let the members of his top management team have considerable autonomy. They only met a few times a month as a team and did not have any common goals they were pursuing as a team. He left running the business primarily in the hands of the Chief Financial Officer. He enjoyed being a leader but was not particularly skilled at management skills such as strategic planning, organizing the company for success, setting up controls and tracking and managing key metrics, and dealing with person-nel issues. The lack of attention to management issues and performance is what led the board to replace him with a CEO with strong management skills. Keeping the founder around in a lesser position was awkward for the founder, the new CEO, and the employees.

Evaluating The Leadership Style Of The New CEO

The new CEO had high hopes of being able to turn the company around and make it a growing, profitable company again. He had been involved in a number of manufacturing turnarounds and took pride in being honest and straightforward and willing to make the tough decisions to cut costs, reorganize, downsize, and remove ineffective leaders. After taking over as CEO he spent a few weeks getting to know the business and then developed a plan with goals and milestones for getting the business back on track. He could be personable, engaging, and even encouraging at times but was basically known as a no nonsense, get to the point, results oriented manager who wasn't great on people skills. He didn't relate well to the professionals as he wasn't trained in their discipline and was primarily interested in the business aspects of the company. The new CEO mostly used the top management team to carry out his plans and orders although he did occasionally ask them for input. He had little patience for mistakes or a lack of results and those who did not meet his expectations were quick to know about it. He assumed that the resistance and lack of desired results he was experiencing was primarily due to working with leaders and professionals who were not experienced at running a business right and being held accountable.

Efforts To Rebuild A Successful Company

The consultant reviewed the results of the assessment with the CEO and then the top management team and worked with the top management team to become a more united, focused, effective top leadership team (a team with a greater leadership focus) with a vision and strategy for the future and plan for making the company successful as a business and a place to work. The team agreed on the type of culture it would take to make the company successful and what the leaders would need to do to rebuild the culture. After about a month of working with the leaders, the consultant also started working with the leaders and their departments to share the results of the assessment for the organization and their department and involve the departments in targeting improvements for the organization, their departments, and efforts to build teamwork and collaboration between departments.

A follow-up assessment six months from the initial assessment showed significant improvements in the company culture, teamwork within and between teams, morale, and productivity. Business and profits began to slowly improve as well. All appeared to be going well until the next month when the CEO who had now been with the company a little over a year and a half resigned. He was reasonably coachable during the efforts to rebuild the company and cooperated in the changes that needed to be made. However, it became increasingly clear to him that he was not a good fit for the company and the efforts to rebuild the company. Now the anxiety level in the company was high once again as the leaders and employees had many discussions about the type of leader the board would appoint next and if their considerable efforts to rebuild the company would be wasted.

References

Blake, Robert and Mouton, Jane S. (1964). *The Managerial Grid.* Houston: Gulf Publishing Co.

Hersey, Paul and Blanchard, K.H. (1988). *Management of organizational behavior: utilizing human resources,* 5th edition. New Jersey: Prentice Hall.

Kahn, Robert L. (1968). *Productivity and job satisfaction.* In Maneck S. Wadia, Ed. Management and the behavioral sciences: Text and readings. Boston: Allyn and Bacon, pp. 134-143.

Stogdill, R.M. and Coons, A.E., Eds. (1957). *Leader Behavior: Its description and measurement.* Columbus, Ohio: Bureau of Business Research, Ohio State University.

Discussion

1. Evaluate the board's decision to bring in a CEO with strong management skills to turn the company around.

2. Boards may not be that knowledgeable about the type of leader it takes to build a healthy, high performance organization or they may not be that aware of the internal dynamics of the organization they are selecting a leader to lead. What should boards look for in selecting top level leaders? Also, what are some things boards could do to increase the probability of making good choices and decrease the anxiety of people in the organization during the selection process?

3. Using Figure 1 discuss the dominant leadership style of the founder and the likely impact of the style on morale, performance, and the company culture. What would you consider to be the founder's major strengths and opportunities for improvement as a leader?

4. Using Figure 1 discuss the dominant leadership style of the new CEO and the likely impact of the style on morale, performance, and the company culture. What would you consider to be the new CEO's major strengths and opportunities for improvement as a leader?

5. If the board hired you as a consultant to advise them on selecting a new CEO, what would you tell them about the importance of leadership style and what to look for in a new leader?

6. What is your dominant leadership style, how consistent and predictable are you as a leader, and what are the major strengths and opportunities for improvement of your style?

Key Leadership Lessons

1. Leaders are the number one key to building successful organizations. It is very important that those who are selecting leaders are well informed about the importance of leadership style and the skills it takes to build healthy, high performance organizations.

2. Few leaders understand the far reaching implications of the emphasis leaders place on people and performance. It determines leadership styles, parenting styles, personal styles, the culture of teams and organizations, and even the success of organizations.

3. It is very important for leaders to be aware of their leadership style and the impact of their style on morale, performance, and culture. If you know reality you can almost always do something about it. Awareness makes it possible for leaders to continuously learn and grow and improve their style.

4. There is a controversy in the leadership literature about whether leaders should change their leadership style with different situations. The suggestion is that leaders should use an autocratic style in some situations, a laissez faire style in others, a human relations style in yet others, and a high performance style in most. This would make it difficult to know and relate to leaders. The leaders, people in general, and parents that are easiest to work with and relate to are those who are consistent in their style and that use a style that emphasizes both people and performance. Style should remain consistent. It is a leader's skills that should change with different people and situations. Discuss as a group if you agree or disagree with this position.

BIOGRAPHY

Dr. Warrick is an award winning educator, consultant, and author who specializes in coaching and developing leaders and in organization development, change, and transformation. He is a Professor of Management and Organization Change at the University of Colorado at Colorado Springs where he holds the life time title of President's Teaching Scholar and has received the University's highest award, the Chancellor's Award. He has received awards for being the Outstanding Organization Development Practitioner of the Year, the Outstanding Human Resources Professional of the Year, the Outstanding Educator of the Year, and was recently named the Best Professor in Organisational Development.

D. D. Warrick
Professor of Management and Organization Change And
President's Teaching Scholar
Graduate School of Business
University of Colorado at Colorado Springs
1420 Austin Bluffs Parkway, Colorado Springs, Colorado 80918
Tel. 719-488-2240 · Email: ddwarrick@aol.com

3

Leadership Styles Of Incident Commanders Responding To A Simulated Terrorist Attack

Dr. David Brown

Major Focus Of Case

This Case Study addresses different leadership styles used in responding to terrorist-evoked critical incidents and the consequences of each style. Critical incidents necessitating multi-agency actions are now seen by terrorists as being the most effective approach to create maximum crises due to the demands placed upon a unified inter-agency leadership response (Alexander, 2002; Borodzicz, 2005). For example, the London July 2005 suicide bombings targeted members of the community and infrastructure (train and road transport) necessitating a coordinated emergency response from police, fire and ambulance/medical services.

A unified inter-agency response is characterised by incident commanders being able to coordinate the specific actions of their emergency service with the responses of other emergency agencies. Such co-ordination requires incident commanders to demonstrate both **vertical leadership capability** (leadership within their specific emergency service) and **horizontal leadership capability** (leadership integrating their responses with those of the other emergency agencies). **Vertical processes** describe the flow from strategic through tactical to operational decision making within each specific emergency agency. Decision making processes across the emergency agencies necessary to develop a unified inter-agency response are described as **horizontal processes**.

The prevalent emergency management models of leadership based upon a vertical command and control structure place severe limitations on horizontal leadership capability. Within the command and control structure the hierarchical role of rank clearly designates the vertical leadership decision structures. However, these same vertical structures may be counterproductive in the development of horizontal decision making processes by restricting the leaders of a response to a critical incident to strictly controlled and prescribed sets of rules and procedures (Perrow, 1984). The central question related to this Case is, do these sets of rules and procedures designed to control risk and optimize safety requirements encourage a leadership style that severely limits the scope and flexibility of the leadership response? The case also has implications for organizations and the leadership styles they use and the likely consequences.

Introduction

The scenario depicted in the desk–top simulation involves multiple explosive devices placed in an airport check-in area and transport access tunnel near the airport. The incident response teams include an incident commander and at least three members from each of the emergency agencies (police, fire, ambulance/medical) usually involved in the response to such a critical incident. The simulation utilizes a multi-media approach and data concerning the critical incident were presented to the response teams via video tele-casts, phone, and fax. The majority of this information was made available to all team members; however, some was only relayed to the incident commander. The nature of the incoming reports concerning the characteristics of the critical incident reflects the often chaotic and fragmentary manner in which information is received following a suspected terrorist attack. It is the incident commander's task to act as the leader of the team's response and assimilate all of the incoming data and coordinate the response planning of the various agencies (police, fire, ambulance/medical) involved. The leadership styles of two of the designated incident commanders and the responses of their multi-agency teams are reported in this Case Study.

Incident Commander 1

The incident commander was a senior police officer trained in emergency management. On receiving notice of the emergency, the incident commander immediately formed the police officers in the team into a group. The incident commander assumed command and control of this group and instigated and directed their planning response to the suspected terrorist attack. At this point in the simulation, the incident commander left the other members of the team to plan their independent responses. The senior fire officer in the team assembled the other fire officers into a small group, some distance apart from the "police group", and commenced to direct their response planning process. Both the "police" and the "fire" groups proceeded to develop comprehensive responses to the complex demands associated with a terrorist attack involving multiple bombings.

The comprehensive plans were developed independently from, and without any collaboration with, the other group. During the police and fire groups' deliberations, the senior ambulance/medical officer in the team also formed his members into a group and commenced their planned response, again this was done independently from the police and fire groups. Thus, three independently conceived, comprehensive response plans (police, fire, ambulance/medical) were developed in response to the demands of the terrorist attack.

During this process the incident commander was solely concerned with the police response and did not attempt to coordinate that response with those of the other groups (fire, ambulance/medical). It can be seen that the incident commander focused on vertical leadership processes from tactical through to operational decision making within that specific emergency agency (policing). Throughout the planning response to the simulation there appeared to be vertical leadership structures within each group (police, fire, ambulance/medical) with a senior officer assuming leadership for the development of the planned response for their specific group. However, the incident commander did not assume a horizontal leadership approach and consequently a unified inter-agency response between the groups was not developed.

Of significance, was that the planned responses of the fire and ambulance/medical groups were severely limited by the incident commander's lack of a horizontal leadership style. Important information received from the various sources (video tele-casts, phone, and fax) concerning the nature of the terrorist attack was not conveyed by the incident commander to the fire and ambulance/medical groups. Similarly, the fire and ambulance/medical groups did not source information directly from the incident commander, or communicate to the incident commander their response plans. The incident commander's failure to implement a horizontal leadership style severely limited the unified strategic planning approach necessary to develop a fully integrated response between the emergency agencies (police, fire, ambulance/medical).

Incident Commander 2

The incident commander was a senior police officer with emergency management training. At notification of the simulated terrorist attack the incident commander appointed one of the team members to act as a recorder so that a written record would be available of all decisions and planned actions. The incident commander then ascertained who were the different members of the team and their areas and levels of expertise. This was followed by the incident commander giving a summary briefing to the team of what was known of the incident at that point of the emergency. The members of the response team then formed groups relevant to their area of expertise (police, fire, ambulance/medical) and began to develop specific response plans.

During this process the incident commander systematically moved around the groups updating their information regarding the critical incident, and sourcing their opinions regarding the most appropriate actions. While specific response plans were formulated within the groups (police, fire, ambulance/medical), at set times during the critical incident the incident commander reformed these groups into one "round-table" gathering. During these round-table gatherings the incident commander ascertained the priority actions and needed resources of the specific groups. Most importantly, during these round-table gatherings, the incident commander identified areas where the planned responses of the different groups intersected and liaised with them to bring about a multi-agency coordinated response.

The incident commander provided space during the round-table discussions for members from the different groups (police, fire, ambulance/medical) to familiarize themselves with the challenges being faced by members of other groups. The team dynamic created by the incident commander promoted information sharing, joint decision making and planning between all team members. A specific group was now able to vocalize just what they needed from another group, and how the planned actions of one group could facilitate/impede the actions of another group. There was agreement amongst members of the team that this approach was the most efficient way to develop a strategic response to the demands of the emergency.

During these round-table discussions the planned responses to the terrorist attack developed a defined uniform structure. The incident commander sought the opinions of the experts in each emergency management area (police, fire, ambulance/medical) and organized a collective action plan. The incident commander coordinated the tactical and operational plans within the specific groups with broader strategic planning needed to develop a unified response across the groups (police, fire, ambulance/medical). During the response to the critical incident the incident commander displayed a leadership style that was at times directive, consultative and participative.

Discussion

1. Discuss the differences between vertical and horizontal leadership styles and the implications for today's organizations.

2. Evaluate the leadership style of Incident Commander 1 and the consequences and do the same for the Incident 2 Commander.

3. Drawing from this case discuss how organization requirements and practices can influence leadership style.

4. In regards to this case discuss why leaders responsible for responding to terrorist attacks should be well informed about the factors that influence leadership style and the importance of understanding leadership styles and their consequences.

Key Leadership Lessons

1. Leaders need to understand the importance of leadership styles and there consequences.

2. A Command and Control leadership style has limited use in today's fast moving times when collaboration is important to the success of an organization.

3. Leaders who are not well informed about the importance of leadership style may not be aware of organizational requirements and practices and cultural norms that are encouraging an inappropriate leadership style.

4. To be effective leaders need to rely on others and don't need to make all of the decisions.

References

Alexander, D.E. 2002. *Principles of Emergency Planning and Management,* New York: Terra Publishing, Harpenden & Oxford University Press.

Borodzicz, E.P. 2005. Risk, Crisis and Security Management, Hoboken NJ., John Wiley&Sons.

Perrow, C. 1984. *Normal Accidents: Living with High-Risk Technologies.* New York: Basic Books.

BIOGRAPHY

Dr. David Brown has held professorial appointments at
La Trobe and Griffith Universities, and served terms as Head of
School / Head of Department and as Associate Dean. Dr. Brown
has conducted research with major private and public sector
organizations including the Victorian Auditor General's Department,
Queensland Police Service, Queensland Premiers Department, the
Meat Research Corporation, BHP-Billiton, Sydney Water, and Victoria
Police. Dr. Brown has been a member of professional organizations
including the Australian Human Resource Institute, the American
Academy of Management, the National College of Organisational
Psychologists, and the International Commission on Occupational
Health. Dr. Brown's current research involves conducting simulations
of emergency and crisis situations and evaluating the leadership
capabilities and performance of incident commanders.

Dr. David Brown
Honorary Visitor, School of Management,
La Trobe University, Victoria, Australia.
Email: d.brown@latrobe.edu.au

4

The Far Reaching Consequences Of Leadership Style And Leaders Jumping From Symptoms To Solutions

Glenn H. Varney

Major Focus of the Case

This is a true story that focuses on the importance of leadership style and the consequences of jumping from symptoms of a problem directly to solutions. The latter practice is often referred to as "shooting from the hip" and most often leads to missing the target. Frank Leader is a real leader of a large organization, including several thousand people. It took a major fall in his career for Frank to learn that leadership involves engagement of employees which leads to ownership of the problem, commitment to solutions, and investment in making change work.

Introduction

When you read this story place yourself in Frank Leader's shoes. Try to understand why he imposed his solution on the organization. How do you think Frank acquired his leadership principles? How did he get a top leadership position in his organization without running into the problems he encountered in this case? As you go through the case put yourself in the position of one of his employees and ask yourself how you feel about Frank's behavior and what message you would like to convey to him about his leadership style.

The Story

My name is A. Frank Leader, and this is my story about how I became an effective leader as the result of a life changing career crisis. I am the youngest of four boys. My father was a machinist in a small company, and my mother worked in the local school cafeteria. My parents were strict and had high expectations for "their boys". I graduated from high school about the time of Dessert Storm, and with all of the patriotic intensity of an 18 year old, I joined the Marine Corps for a three year hitch. I did a tour overseas and rose to the rank of Sergeant.

After my discharge, I attended college and graduated with a degree in Industrial Engineering. I felt that my training in I.E. positioned me to work in a manufacturing firm where I could put my skills to good use organizing and designing work systems that would produce high performance. I was employed as a System Engineer for company that produced molded plastic parts, and within ten years I was a supervisor on my way up the management ladder.

By this time I had formed a set of leadership principles that I firmly believed were applicable to improving efficiency and performance results in any organization. For example, I believed:

1. A disciplined and direct leadership style was the best way to manage and control output.

2. System efficiency was the best way to keep costs down.

3. The work force had to be well trained in operations and specifically their immediate jobs.

4. Strong and tight supervision is required to immediately correct work force and operational problems.

5. The customer is always first, especially in producing high quality products which are always delivered on time.

6. Reward/punishment is the best way to motivate people.

7. Keeping up to date requires continuous benchmarking and utilizing the latest tools and practices such as "zero defects", "lean manufacturing", "supply chain concepts", etc.

These principles worked well for me as I advanced in the organization, and I was ultimately promoted to Vice President of Distribution, responsible for four large product warehouse operations. Everything seemed to go well for the first two or three years. We had an acceptable number of returns and complaints from customers (missed delivery dates, incorrect product mix, items missing from orders, etc). Turnover was a little higher than I would have liked. But all in all I thought everything was under control until one day I received a call from the Vice President of Human Resources. She advised me that we had a union organizing attempt underway in our largest Distribution Center, located in South Carolina. She said we needed to get on this problem now in order to "head off the union". So I took her advice and we attacked the situation head on and put a number of measures in place:

1. We initiated a union avoidance program involving the entire workforce of 110 associates.

2. We began supervisory training in how to communicate with and control the workforce.

3. We introduced a series of work-group roundtable meetings with associates to solicit their concerns, complaints, and ideas.

4. We installed a gain-sharing plan designed to reward associate member contributions.

5. We began training in the use of "lean" tools and practices for the workforce.

6. We increased inventories to ensure that we met our customers' needs.

I was certain that another part of the problem was that my Distribution Center Manager was weak and needed to be more forceful in his relationships with the workforce. He insisted that he was "on top of it" and that he "knew his associates". I disagreed and told him that he had 30 days to get it right or find another employer.

Things went from bad to worse. It was reported that the union organizing drive was moving forward and picking up steam; customer complaints were up; we were not meeting budget. Worst of all, from my point of view, our biggest customer called the President and complained about quality, missed delivery times, product errors, etc. etc. The gain sharing plan that we had designed with the help of two outside consultants to get the workforce to line up with management looked like it was going to give away the shop. With all of these problems threatening I decided that it was time for me to move into the distribution center and take personal charge of the situation. Here are the actions that I took:

1. I fired the consultants who set up the union-avoidance program and the gain sharing plan. Over the strong objections of the task force that had designed it, I also changed the gain sharing formulae to reduce the economic impact on the distribution center.

2. I reorganized the associates' shift patterns, rotating associates on shifts so that they did not form "buddy" groups.

3. I put in "checkers" to control all shipments to customers.

4. I removed one of the supervisors who seemed to be sympathetic to the union.

5. I froze all salary increases.

6. And I made it known that if productivity didn't increase and costs go down, plus fewer customer complaints then heads would roll.

Things did not improve. Performance continued to deteriorate. We began to get threats from the customers that they would take their business elsewhere if things didn't improve fast.

The union showed no signs of backing off their organizing attempt. Finally I got a call from the President saying that he was coming to the distribution center to look into the "mess" himself. He arrived with the Vice President of Human Resources and spent one day out on the floor talking to associates and supervisors. At the end of the day I was given my walking papers! All he could say to me was "if only you had stayed out of it". I asked what he meant by that statement. His reply was: " things had started to work out and people were settling down until you decided to take over. You screwed everything up, so I told the associates we are going back to the original plan".

What a blow to my ego. I just couldn't believe that all the experience I had gained and all that I had learned in my career had failed. I was out of work for six months during which time I met with a career counselor who told me, "Maybe you should be looking at yourself as the source of the problem. Times have changed and perhaps I haven't kept up to date." The idea shocked me. I couldn't be to blame or could I? But I had time on my hands so I decided to do a self evaluation. I asked a friend of mine to help me figure out what went wrong and she agreed to look into my leadership approach and how it got me in trouble.

References

A leader is best when people barely know he (she) exists, not so good when people obey and acclaim him (her), worse when they despise him (her). But of a good leader, who talks little, when his (her) work is done, his (her) aim fulfilled, they will say: We did it ourselves!

Lao-Tzu, 6th Century, B.C., Chinese Philosopher

Discussion Questions

1. Evaluate the strengths and weaknesses of Frank's leadership principles and leadership style.

2. Evaluate the strengths and weaknesses of Frank's approach to dealing with the union organizing attempt.

3. Evaluate the strengths and weaknesses of Frank's action plan for taking charge of the Distribution Center.

4. Discuss the potential consequences of leaders jumping to conclusions and solutions and treating symptoms before taking the time to know reality and share examples you have experienced, read about, or heard about.

5. How can leaders guard against jumping to conclusions and solutions and possibly treating symptoms?

Lessons Learned

1. It is important to for leaders to be aware of their leadership philosophies and style and the the likely consequences.

2. Leaders need to check out reality before treating what they assume to be reality.

3. Some simple principles for making changes are:

   (1) Engaging stakeholders in identifying the issues increases the likelihood of discovering reality.

   (2) Involving stakeholders in developing solutions increases the quality of the solutions and ownership and commitment to solutions.

   (3) Changes need to be monitored to evaluate what is working and not working so needed adjustments can be made.

BIOGRAPHY

Glenn H. Varney of this case is a recognized scholar/practitioner who has written extensively in the field of Organization Development and Change. He is active in the Academy of Management, OD&C Division and received the OD Network Life time Achievement award in 2009. Glenn has devoted his career to teaching leaders how to apply the scientific process to changing organizations.

Glenn H. Varney
Professor Emeritus of Management
College of Business Administration
Bowling Green State University

Tel. 419.352.7782 · Cell 419.261.7023
Email: gvarney@bgsu.edu

5

Leadership Style And Development In A Growth-Oriented Chinese-Australian Family Firm

Jin Ye, Dr Melissa A. Parris & Dr Dianne Waddell

Major Focus of The Case

It has become evident that the founders of family firms have many fundamental choices to make regarding the extent and mode of family involvement in a business and the governance structure they might adopt. A family business benefits from the sources drawn on family involvement, but it also suffers from the problems generated by the delicate nature of the relationships involved, which leads to a threat against the growth and survival of family business. This case focuses on the leadership style of a dynamic Chinese leader who built several successful family businesses.

Introduction

Family business is acknowledged as a vital and significant sector of the Australian economy, with the vast majority of private sector businesses in Australia being family businesses. In 2002, it was estimated that approximately 67% of Australian businesses were family owned and/or controlled by families with an estimated wealth of $3.6 trillion (Smyrinios and Walker 2003). Although there are no firm statistics to map the presence of Chinese family businesses in Australia, the majority of Chinese immigrant[1] entrepreneurs prefer to run family firms that provide them with flexibility, independence, and a more settled life (Collins 2002). These families provide critical resources and support to emerging enterprises in terms of finance, labour and social capital. In turn, these businesses have been established as a means of providing support for the entrepreneurs and their families (Aldrich and Cliff 2003).

Leadership in a family firm is a tense process that is always embedded within a family context where there are high levels of emotions. To reduce the interference of emotional links, the founder pays more attention to managing a clear distinction of responsibilities and acknowledged differences in the way each individual approaches the business. The trust among family members fosters a working relationship where they are able to talk about their own ideas and expectations openly. At the same time, the founder needs to establish the mechanics and managerial ways to work with non-family employees in the business. The following case illustrates that under the founder's leadership; the business has experienced consistent growth and provided more opportunities for the employees and family members in the future.

---

1 Chinese immigrants are a heterogeneous group; the term primarily refers to people with Chinese heritage emigrating from China, Malaysia or other parts of Asia. When we use the term Chinese immigrants, we mean any ethnic Chinese who has immigrated to the Australia (first generation).

Building The First Successful Business

This business is a child care service company with centres located across suburban Melbourne, Australia. This is a medium-sized family firm jointly owned and managed by a husband and a wife. Tim[2], who is in his early 50s, came to Australia from Malaysia to study engineering. His early professional career was shaped in some of the world's most recognisable multinational corporations. His intention to enter into private business in child care was fuelled by his wife's interest. With a Master of Business Administration, he was responsible for the overall business strategy decisions as Chief Executive Officer, while his wife was charged with managing daily operations as Chief Operating Officer. They created a working partnership that enabled them to complement each other with their different skill sets.

Tim and his wife have over 16 years' experience in the child care business. They started up their first centre in 1994, with a capacity of 60 children. With increasing demands, they gradually expanded their service by building and buying more centres. By 2002, they had 6 profitably run centres. In 2005, they had received offers to sell the company which they had accepted.

Building The Second Successful Business And The Leadership Style And Principles That Made The Two Businesses Successful

After a one and half year retirement, they went back into business in 2007. With the support of an external partner, they were able to grow the business considerably in a short period of time.

The childcare service now has ten centres in operation, providing much needed childcare and family services to multicultural Australian families. The company employs more than 100 non-family employees, 10 of whom are centre managers. The daily operation is delegated to each centre manager that enables Tim to think more strategically about the long-term development of the business over the next five to ten years. The aim is to run the firm as a professional management business. He places highest priority on firm growth through expansion and new service development. He also emphasizes building high performance teams to achieve further growth. The business needs to undergo management restructuring to ensure more non-family managers could be appointed to cover all aspects of the business.

In order to acquire the necessary knowledge to understand the company's situation as fully as possible, Tim and his wife visit each centre once a week to listen to employees' reports and solve any apparent problems. They know most staff members' names and maintain the direct contacts among their clients and employees in order to receive necessary feedback and listen to their concerns for improvements. Tim adopted an approach to encourage greater openness both in his management style and opportunities for the business. He invested in training and education workshops for employees' professional development and communicated his long-term plans for the business growth. He believed the high quality of human resources was a significant factor to ensure business survival, stability and growth.

In terms of business succession, Tim feels that time is some years away. He has considered a move towards a state of separate ownership and management for the business.

He wants to establish a governance structure that requires decisions to be delegated to professional managers in line with business expansion, in which a board of directors, supervisory committee and management teams could participate in business decisions. He is keen to recruit and train high-level management team members (i.e. centre managers) that groom them for

---

2 Pseudonyms have been used to protect participants' confidentiality. Age and other profile details are based at the time of the interviews were conducted with participant.

their areas of responsibility and increase their level of control. He prepares these experienced professional managers for the eventual handover of the managerial control, so he can dedicate more of his time to charity and voluntary interests. However, Tim still maintains a dominant position in the business with final decision-making authority.

Tim is not sure about the intergenerational involvement for the business, but feels he has to be fair and try new ideas that seem appropriate. He has not expected his children to join the business at the expense of their interests. The family expectation is that the children have an opportunity to pursue whatever they are passionate about, which influences their university and career choices. He acknowledges he chooses to give them their freedom to try out new thinking in the business and potential diversification, rather than dominate in deciding the level of their involvement and forcing them to comply with his wishes. He is also aware he needs to keep building up the business and ensure it has the potential to grow and becomes a viable career opportunity in order to attract them to the business in the future. Considering the possibility that his children might join the business, he described how he would develop a monitoring structure that established their credibility in the business and assert their responsibility over their areas, because he felt there was still a long way for them to go in terms of development and awareness in the business environment. He also described when the business had experienced significant growth and diversification, he could allow his children to choose to either maintain the business as it is, or even separate sections and run them independently. He seems to be far more objective when discussing future career options for the future of business and the family.

References

Aldrich, H. E. and Cliff, J. E. (2003) 'The pervasive effects of family on entrepreneurship: Toward a family embeddedness perspective', *Journal of Business Venturing*, Vol. 18, No. 5, pp.573-596.

Collins, J. (2002) 'Chinese entrepreneurs: the Chinese Diaspora in Australia', *International Journal of Entrepreneurial Behaviour & Research*, Vol. 8, No. 1/2, pp.113-133.

Smyrinios, K. X. and Walker, R. H. (2003) *Australian family and private business survey*, The Boyd Partners and RMIT, Australia.

Discussion

1. How would you describe the leadership style of Tim and his wife?

2. What are the leadership principles that Tim used to build a successful business?

3. What are some things Tim could do to retain the high quality of employees and continue to build a healthy, high performance organization?

4. If the founder employed a professional leader and manager to replace him as the CEO, what are the major strengths he should look for?

5. If the next generation decided to join the business, what could the founder do to integrate them into the firm, increase the probability of acceptance of their credibility and decrease anxiety over their roles, and insure the future motivation of non-family members?

6. Are sound leadership principles not culture bound?

Key Leadership Lessons

1. Being a successful leader requires character, an effective leadership style, a clear leadership philosophy, and a vision for the future.

2. Successful leaders continue to transform their companies and make needed changes.

3. Skilled leaders create organisations that attract and retain talented employees.

4. Leaders of family firms must find ways to balance the growth and motivation of both family employees and non-family employees.

BIOGRAPHY

Ms Jing Ye is a PhD candidate in the School of Management and Marketing at Deakin University, Melbourne, Australia. Her thesis focuses on the cultural influence on succession in Chinese-Australian family businesses.

Jing Ye
School of Management and Marketing
Faculty of Business and Law
Deakin University
221 Burwood Hwy, Burwood VIC 3125, Australia
Tel. +61 3 9246 8033

Email: jingye@deakin.edu.au

Dr Melissa Parris is a Senior Lecturer in Management at Deakin University, Melbourne, Australia. Her research focuses on individuals' workplace experiences and the personal effects of these, and has resulted in several international journal articles. Melissa's research activities have spanned the areas of middle management, workplace teams, experiences of downsizing, and the concept of authenticity in the workplace. She is currently investigating the relationship between cultural background and managers' career aspirations.

Dr Melissa A. Parris
School of Management and Marketing, Faculty of Business and Law
Deakin University, 221 Burwood Hwy, Burwood VIC 3125, Australia
Tel. +61 3 9244 6276, Email: melissa.parris@deakin.edu.au

Associate Professor Dianne Waddell is an Associate Professor of Management and an Associate Dean in Teaching and Learning at Deakin University, Melbourne, Australia. She has published and presented many book chapters, refereed journal articles and refereed conference papers on change, leadership, e-business, and program management. Her current research interests include family business and quality management.

Dianne Waddell Associate Professor
School of Management and Marketing, Faculty of Business and Law
Deakin University, 221 Burwood Hwy, Burwood VIC 3125, Australia
Tel. +61 3 9244 6265, Email: dianne.waddell@deakin.edu.au

CHAPTER FOUR

1

Experiencing Whitewater:
Navigating The Challenges Of The New Workplace

- -

Angela N. Spranger & William M. "Bill" Daniels

Major Focus Of The Case
- -

In today's corporate arena, leaders face a mass of priorities that are all treated as equally critical by key stakeholders, leaving the leaders wondering how to get it all done. They focus on treating employees and associates as valued partners, meeting customer needs, staying up to date, and being involved in the latest company changes and initiatives. To be successful, leaders need management skills, people skills, change skills, and a whole host of other skills.

Introduction – A Day In The Rapids
- -

"Completely unacceptable." Those were the words swimming in Ed's mind as he left his one-on-one session in the vice president's office, only to head down the hall to the same VP's conference room for a late afternoon meeting. He'd been called to the office to discuss a sudden change in the production schedule for his division's major product. The due date had shifted to the left far more than was comfortable. The VP made it clear that Ed's division was not meeting weekly production goals sufficiently to hit the new deadline, and he had stated explicitly that failure to achieve the shipping date would lead to the organization losing this key contract – which would be "completely unacceptable."

What the VP didn't realize was that these particular components are made to precise tolerances that require special inspections, adding time to the production schedule. Meeting the deadline wasn't an option, though, so Ed knew that although he traditionally ran a one-shift operation, in order to meet production requirements the Division would have to consider adding a second shift. Beyond the problem of convincing people to volunteer for second shift work, Ed only had a set amount of overhead funds for a shift differential to reward those who do go to evening work.

His mind racing, Ed walked into the meeting with his portfolio, a late-day cup of coffee, and a frown. He was the director of a program division with 700 salaried employees in a manufacturing company with over 10,000 hourly and salaried workers. As a seasoned manager (he had 28 years in the company, 19 of those in management), Ed had seen a lot of organizational changes come and go. Many of them were viewed as "flavor of the month," or "fly by night" – the current hot topic on the VP's agenda, until something pushed it out of the way. Nothing really stuck, and no one committed to any of the organizational development initiatives, because there was just too much else to do. "We're always putting out fires" was one of Ed's trademark complaints.

Remembering the Old Days
- -

Ed could remember when issues were clear around here. "This organization built its reputation for world class products on the strength of a do-or-die work ethic," Ed thought, "because workers and managers alike recognized our product was not just multimillion-dollar projects. We built safe, intimidating, effective weapons that could either prevent or deliver destruction, and we built the best! We did it on time, on budget, and our sons and daughters in the military could depend on our products. We were national defense, and proud of it! So what's changed?"

In the wake of OSHA reviews and new legislation, the company earned and maintained the highest safety ratings. But that drove up costs, and caused schedule delays on a few major contracts – which damaged customer satisfaction. The customer didn't seem to understand that to do what we do really is a do-or-die commitment, and employees' safety requires new policies, equipment, and procedures. Not too long ago, a union rep leaked a story to the local paper about a quality issue that could have led to fatal disaster – and not only did it go national, it went viral. Talk about a customer relationship disaster!

They used to say in Ed's MBA classes (which he took while he worked full-time and supported his family, thank you very much, and what's with these young folks who want accolades just for coming to work every day?), that of the three-legged stool made of cost, schedule, and quality, you could have two of the three. The old joke was, "two out of three ain't bad." But now, Ed thought, "we're expected to achieve in all three areas and then some!" He just didn't know if he could keep up.

The Priorities Keep Piling Up

As he entered the VP's meeting the stress on Ed's face was evident. Along with cost, scheduling, and quality concerns in his program area, one of his hotshot young associates with more education than experience had gotten Ed's secretary to commit Ed to meet with him about "risk and opportunity management for customer satisfaction," all the latest buzzwords. And Ed had just received an email that the program had gotten 112 new scope of work changes from the customer.

On top of that, because it was 4:30 on Monday afternoon, it just had to get even better: this meeting. The VP's email said it was a "critical, mandatory management meeting" to discuss the division's organizational engagement survey results. Ed had his unopened results packet in his portfolio and didn't look forward to opening it; with recent hires from outside the division and frustrating HR policy changes, Ed just knew the numbers weren't going to be good. He looked down the table for friendly faces and saw Stacey, his Learning and Organizational Development consultant, who smiled at him as if everything would be ok. Stacey always had a people focus and an idea for how to get associates more involved in solving the division's problems; she even managed to get the Quality Coordinator and Finance guy to agree with her sometimes. She had been promoting Gallup Q12 principles and the four I's of transformational leadership, but who had time for all that navel gazing? Ed knew he needed to spend more time with her to solidify his succession plan and get her help on supervisory leadership development in his division. But right now, Ed just didn't want to think about it. He'd get his supervisors together to start working out all these problems tomorrow morning.

As he settled in to wait for the meeting to start, Ed thought, "in the old days the focus might have been on the cost and schedule issues, and I could juggle those. But the negative publicity from the quality issues, and the time and money it's going to take to recover from that... I just don't know. And just in time for our OSHA safety audit, why are we suddenly having a rash of onsite accidents? It's all too much. Maybe I do need some risk and opportunity management, especially now that I have to break the news about this schedule change causing a second shift. I just don't see any opportunities here. How can I satisfy my one major customer who wants ideal cost, schedule, quality, safety – all while manipulating the work scope - everything? And what about the people, my resource for getting it all done – how can I get them on board to sort out this mess when they feel like they're losing benefits and being overlooked? I feel like a Vegas act, juggling flaming chainsaws!" Just then, the VP walked in, his mouth set in a grim line.

Discussion

1. Would you say that the pressures Ed faces are typical or not typical of leaders at his level in today's new organizational world?

2. List and discuss some of the critical skills today's leaders need to develop to be successful.

3. From a leadership perspective what could Ed do to be more effective?

4. From a management perspective (planning, organizing, controlling, delegating etc.) what could Ed do to be more effective?

5. What are other things Ed could do to get control of his situation and increase his effectiveness and reduce his stress?

6. Who could Ed go to for possible help in his situation?

Key Leadership Lessons

1. Skills in leadership such as providing vision, direction, inspiration, and clear goals, priorities, and values will become increasingly important in a fast moving, high pressure, high demand organization world where leaders can't do everything and must free others up to become increasingly self-directing.

2. Effective leaders will also have to be skilled managers to effectively manage themselves, their people, and their responsibilities.

3. Surrounding yourself with the right people and learning to delegate is a leadership essential.

4. Knowing what not to do and what not to change is as important as knowing what to do and what to change.

5. Manage upward as well as downward and be willing to negotiate what is most important.

BIOGRAPHY

Angela Spranger is a doctoral student in Organizational Leadership at Regent University. She holds an MBA in Marketing and a Master's Degree in Human and Organizational Learning. Angela has worked in recruiting and staffing, labor-management relations, and instructional design. She is the training and organizational development specialist in a Program Division at Newport News Shipbuilding, a Division of Huntington-Ingalls Industries, taking a "theory-into-practice" approach to organizational leadership and development. Angela has facilitated workshops on career development, effective facilitation, career blind spots, and decision making and conflict resolution.

Angela Spranger, MBA, MA Ed., SPHR
14 Omera Place, Hampton, VA 23666
Tel. 757-880-8972 · Email: angesp1@regent.edu

William M. "Bill" Daniels is a colleague and manager at Huntington-Ingalls Industries who has accumulated over 25 years of progressive management experience in the Planning and Production Control functions for multiple Division-level programs in the 18,000-plus member organization. Specifically, Bill has led departments in the Aircraft Carrier Construction, Submarine Construction and Overhaul, and Aircraft Carrier Refueling and Complex Overhaul programs. He is a graduate of the esteemed Apprentice School at Newport News Shipbuilding, and has earned a Bachelor's Degree in Business Administration from Averett University. Bill's experience and observations led to a series of conversations from which this case emerged; he encourages managers and students alike to consider the changing demographics of the workplace relative to the cost-schedule-budget-quality dilemma and seek ways to balance organizational and employee demands.

2

Developing Leaders:
A High Potential, Unique Approach

William J. Rothwell, Ph.D., SPHR

Major Focus Of The Case

A large insurance company was facing a problem: weak management bench strength resulting from a combination of early retirement offers, downsizing, and expected Baby Boomer retirements. To address this business problem, two change champions helped the company launch an accelerated high potential leadership development program at the entry management level. The program made use of a systematic approach to recruiting, selecting, and developing workers for operating (line) management positions. The program combined real-world experience with classroom training and weekly briefings.

Introduction

This case study focuses on how to champion change and how to develop a high-potential leadership development intended to prepare new hires at entry level for line (operating) management positions. The case is organized into the following sections: (1) case background; (2) forecasting supervisory needs; (3) the recruiting and selection process; (4) the components of the leadership development program; (5) the first six weeks; (5) the first year (after the first six weeks); and (6) program results.

Case Background

The Superco Insurance Company – a fictitious name for a real, well-known company – faced a crisis. As a result of a generous early retirement offer and several waves of downsizing, top executives perceived that the company had grown "weak in bench strength" at all management levels. To make matters worse, an examination of the company's management workforce revealed that high percentages of managers at all levels on the company's organization chart would be eligible to retire within just a few years. Top executives therefore resolved to take immediate corrective action. But, at first, they were unsure about what to do.

One company executive decided that the creation of an accelerated high potential leadership development program might be the appropriate solution to the problem. She was aware that numerous companies, particularly banks and other insurance companies, had previously experienced great success with such programs. Accordingly, she discussed the idea with top managers, conducted research to identify the exact parameters of the "talent shortage" potentially facing the company, benchmarked accelerated leadership development programs at other insurance companies and banks, and (working on a committee with others) prepared a detailed proposal to establish and implement an accelerated high potential leadership development program.

The company's CEO took the proposal to the Board of Directors, which approved the program and identified management and leadership development as a strategic goal. In addition, a position was approved for a Management Development Director to oversee and coordinate a full range of leadership development programs – including those for existing executives, middle managers and front-line supervisors as well as the accelerated high potential leadership development program. (The accelerated high potential leadership development program is hereafter abbreviated as the HiPo trainee program.) The Management Development Director was also put in charge of all company recruiting efforts, employee relations, and internal training.

Forecasting Supervisory Needs

The first step of the HiPo trainee program was to clarify existing needs, particularly at the critically-important supervisory level which served as a "feeder" for middle management and top management ranks. The Management Development Director conducted an annual survey of line (operating) managers to use for forecasting anticipated needs for supervisory talent in their respective areas of responsibility. Based on the forecast results, the company would "go outside" to recruit potential entry-level talent. The budget for the positions available each year would match the perceived needs when the HiPo trainees finished their program. The idea was to have HiPos ready to assume front-line supervisory positions after their training. In this organization, a front-line supervisor oversees the work of hourly workers. It should also be mentioned that a high potential (HiPo) is a worker who is perceived to be successful in his or her current job but is also perceived to be capable of promotion.

The Recruiting and Selection Process

It was decided that, as part of the goals of the accelerated high potential leadership development program, the company would seek a widely diverse, multicultural group of recruits to reflect (among other distinctions) different ages, sexes, races, and ethnic heritages. In other words, the "trainee program" was not restricted to recent college graduates only. Since the company had a history of problems with job posting – the company suspended job posting during downsizings because employees were thought to apply for every position, whether qualified or not, to seek very small pay raises – internal applicants were not considered for the HiPo program.

The Management Development Director took trips to colleges to seek HiPos for the program. Faced with competing against more famous firms, the MD Director gradually learned some special "tricks of the trade" in recruiting. One "trick" was to incent college faculty with meals at nice restaurants if they forwarded resumes from promising third-year undergraduate students. A second "trick" was to study the backgrounds of the company's existing HiPos at all levels to find patterns that they shared in common. He discovered that many had attended the same college, a local school whose graduates had heard of the company and were familiar with its sterling reputation as an employer.

Of course, recruiting was not limited to colleges alone. The Management Development Director also took proactive steps to place ads in newspapers, opening announcements on the company's website, and also targeted special mailings to every minority and protected-class employee organization in many States.

The selection methods used to pick trainees was especially rigorous. Applicants completed a lengthy application form designed especially for the program and were screened through a 1-hour structured interview. Successful applicants were then subjected to 3 independent interviews with HiPo executives in the organization. Only applicants who received 3 "hire" recommendations independently from the HiPo executives were given job offers.

Program Components

The chosen few hired into the HiPo program – it was anticipated that there would be only a small number of positions for the program each year – would participate in a combination of classroom training, job rotation, and short work assignments. Each recruit would spend at least 14 months in the program with no possibility of promotion out of the program during that time. This policy prevented managers from "cherry picking" the best recruits from the program early, thereby short-circuiting their exposure to different parts of the company and leaving behind only those trainees with less perceived potential.

The First Six Weeks

Before their first day, HiPo trainees received an overnight package with the company's employee handbook. They were told they would have a quiz over it on the first day. Additionally, they were given a list of frequently-asked questions (FAQs) to anticipate many questions – such as "where to park?", "what to wear?", and "when to expect the first pay check?"

All HiPo trainees would receive a first-day orientation, conducted by the Human Resources Department, which would introduce them to their benefits and company work rules. About a month after the date they were hired, trainees would receive an in-depth classroom orientation to the organization, its strategic plan, its products, its competitors, and its customers.

Following orientation but during their first 6 weeks of employment, they were expected to participate in a "tour" in which they conducted informational interviews with 80-100 of the company's 300 management-level employees. While on a tour, trainees would meet individually with company management representatives to ask questions about their divisions, departments, and work units. All tours began with a one-on-one discussion with the company's Chairman, and that meeting gave trainees the proper impression that they were very important people in the organization. At the end of the tour, trainees were expected to have completed the preparation of a "tour guide" that described the names, organization charts, work processes (as depicted on flowcharts), key forms, and other information about each area they visited. That "tour guide" became their source of information about "who does what in the company" – and "how they do it." (Copies of earlier guides, prepared by their predecessors, were available to serve as models.)

The First Year (After the First Six Weeks)

Although trainees would remain on the payroll of the Human Resource Department until they were finished with their program, they would rotate through at least 3 different major operating divisions after their tour. During a 4-month rotation, trainees would be guided by a Learning Contract that described the responsibilities during the rotation, the expected outcomes, and timeframes for completion of assignments. At the end of each rotation, trainees would receive a formal Training Progress Report to describe their performance and enumerate future training needs. While on rotation, trainees would report on a daily basis directly to a line (operating) manager.

The company's executives believed that all trainees should perform "useful work" – and not just participate in training. This view was in keeping with the company's philosophy that the HiPo program represented a form of "boot camp" in which trainees would be "put through the paces" – and challenged at every turn – so as "to build the right work ethic early in the individual's development."

Each trainee was destined to receive different "kinds" of rotations to build the competencies essential to success in the organization. An analytical rotation was designed to give trainees responsibility for meeting the requirements of a troubleshooting assignment, tapping the expertise of experienced workers in the process. A customer service rotation was designed to expose trainees directly to the company's customers (insurance policy owners and sales representatives). A presupervisory rotation was designed to give trainees exposure to the actual work duties of a front-line supervisor by making them an understudy or "assistant to" a HiPo supervisor. Most trainees, it was decided, would begin with an analytical rotation because that helped to acquaint them with the organization. All trainees would eventually participate in a presupervisory rotation, which was deemed the most important, because they were destined if successful to enter a supervisory position upon program completion.

While on rotation, trainees received planned, individualized coaching from company supervisors, managers, and executives. Often they were paired with experienced hourly employees – or assigned to an experienced, exemplary supervisor. They were expected to perform while learning but also to learn while performing. However, because they were given coaching or classroom training about what to do before they needed to do it, many managers liked to joke that trainees did not face a "sink or swim" experience because the company had "thrown them a life preserver." Their Learning Contract provided written documentation of the training they were to receive – and the results they were expected to achieve. In other respects, their rotations were based on "best practices" in company management rotation programs.

One afternoon each week they attended classroom training. The topics varied. Typically, they would hear about a topical issue from someone within the company, an industry representative, a customer, or a vendor. On occasion, they would participate in hands-on exercises in which they were asked to work through "critical incidents about supervision" that had actually occurred in the organization and were gathered from experienced workers or their own successful predecessors in the HiPo program.

While HiPo trainees were on rotation, the Management Development Director would periodically meet with the managers in the areas into which trainees had been rotated. The managers offered confidential information about how the individual trainees – and all the trainees – could improve faster and better. The MD Director used that information for continuous program improvement.

After completing the structured training program, each trainee would become eligible for promotion to supervision. Company managers were not required to select them. Trainees thus competed for promotions with promising hourly employees and experienced supervisors from the industry recruited from outside. Trainees were thus under some pressure to "prove themselves" at every turn throughout the management training program. They understood, at time of hire, that they could be terminated for poor performance in training. But, of course, company policy required progressive discipline to be applied even with trainees to ensure that they were given ample opportunities to improve prior to termination.

Program Results

After three years the accelerated high potential leadership development program was hailed as a resounding success by the company's supervisors, managers and executives. Turnover in the program remained extraordinarily low, and most turnover occurred because individuals discovered they were "not cut out to be supervisors." Morale among trainees remained exceptionally high. As a final tribute to the program's success, some managers started discussing the possibility of requiring all future supervisors – even those promoted from within or hired from outside with experience – to go through the program. There was even discussion about establishing similar, but parallel, programs for other job categories – including technical workers, salespersons, and hourly employees.

Discussion Questions

1. The first change champion in the case was the company executive who saw a need and got the company interested in a high impact leadership development program. What did she do to champion the new program and what lessons can you learn from her about championing change?

2. The second change champion was the newly appointed Management Development Director. What did he do to champion building a unique program and what can you learn from him about championing change?

3. Typical leadership development programs do little to actually prepare leaders to lead. What were some of the unique aspects of the program in the case?

4. Are there things you would change or improve in the leadership development program?

5. What are some other innovative ideas that could be added to a unique leadership development program like the one described in the case?

Key Leadership Lessons

1. Effective leaders are always looking for new and better ways to do things and are willing to champion needed changes.

2. Effective leadership development programs must be based on a strongly-felt business need. Company leaders must preserve their commitment to the program over time and be willing to take an active role in it rather than delegating everything to others.

3. Recruiting and selecting are critically important. Individuals participating in selection should themselves be high potentials, since people tend to choose people like themselves.

4. The company's on boarding process required the HiPos to meet as many supervisors, managers and executives as possible. That helped the HiPos to achieve social integration faster. It also allowed the HiPos to learn all facets of the business in a short time span.

5. There can be a synergistic relationship between hands-on experience and planned training sessions. The two, when combined, seem to have more impact than either one by itself.

6. Rotations are most effective when there is a learning plan to guide what people are expected to learn from the rotation and when they receive a formal performance review after the rotation.

BIOGRAPHY

William J. Rothwell, Ph.D., SPHR is a Professor on the University Park campus of Penn State. He leads a graduate emphasis in Training/Organization Development. Before arriving at Penn State in 1993, he was an HR professional for nearly 20 years and headed up HR efforts in a State government agency and then led a comprehensive Management Development program at a large insurance company. In addition to serving as a professor, he is also President of Rothwell & Associates, Inc., a consulting firm. He has authored, coauthored, edited or co edited over 300 books, book chapters and articles – including 68 books. His most recent books are *Invaluable Knowledge* (Amacom, 2011), *Effective Succession Planning,* 4th ed. (Amacom, 2010) and *Practicing Organization Development,* 3rd ed (Pfeiffer, 2010). In 1999 he published a book entitled *Developing In-House Leadership and Management Development Programs: Their Creation, Management, and Continuous Improvement* (Greenwood Press).

William J. Rothwell,
Ph.D., SPHR Professor
Department of Learning & Performance Systems
310B Keller Building, University Park, PA 16802
Tel. 814-863-2581 · Fax: 814-863-7532 · Email: wjr9@psu.edu

3

Working With People Problems

L. J. Cumbo, Jr.

Major Focus of the Case

The manager of a general accounting department with 14 employees could clearly see that morale was low and getting worse. He commissioned a consultant to find out what was going on and learned that one of the reasons for the low morale was that his best performing employee was spreading rumors about him. How should he handle this situation?

Background

Steve Hall (not his real name) was Manager of the General Accounting Department at one of the largest privately held trucking companies in the United States with 60 terminal locations nationwide. Although drivers and some other operations employees were organized as Teamsters, few office employees were unionized. The General Accounting Department was responsible for general ledger accounting, accounts payable, bank reconciliations from multiple banks, cost accounting, and state fuel tax compliance. Separate departments handled revenue accounting and payroll accounting.

Low Morale

Hall had been the manager of General Accounting for sixteen years and had served in other positions within the company prior to his current appointment. The department was comprised of fourteen accounting clerk positions and four administrative assistants. Hall felt that morale had declined within the most recent year, and that departmental members seemed less interested in their work and in the camaraderie that had always been typical of the group. After numerous discussions with key employees, Hall requested that a consultant be commissioned to evaluate departmental morale. The consultant conducted a survey of all employees, followed by interviews with about half of the group members. Using a benchmark morale study of all company office employees from six years earlier, the consultant concluded that morale was significantly lower than in the earlier study. He also indicated that a number of employees reflected in interviews that "it's not as much fun to work here as before" and "it was a lot better before all the rumors started."

Who's Spreading Rumors?

Hall had suspected some rumor-mongering, but wasn't sure how many and which people might be involved. In subsequent scheduled performance review meetings, he brought up the subject of rumors with seven subordinates. To his surprise, each of them pointed to the same co-worker as the only person who was spreading rumors. That employee was Mary Brown (not her real name), the most senior member of the group and, in terms of virtually all measures of employee performance, the best of the clerks. Mrs. Brown's tenure in the department predated that of Hall. Hall and his colleagues were rightfully impressed with Mary Brown and her speed, accuracy, work output, and knowledge. She also had a nearly perfect attendance record and was never late to work. In Hall' view, she clearly was the most valuable employee under his direction. In fact, during her recent performance review, he had noted that she "outperforms any two other clerks in the office" and that she "has an excellent work attitude and pride in performance." She had, however, been known to sometimes enjoy creating and spreading rumors and gossip.

From individual interviews with all employees in the department, Hall concluded that she was the sole source of a number of untrue and malicious rumors about him, a co-worker, the company, and the department. For example, she was traced as the source of rumors that Hall was fired from a previous job for "running around with the office girls," that he company was about to fold, and that pay in the department was much lower than in other similar departments in the company. Hall was therefore virtually certain that he was facing an unfortunate dilemma.... the false rumors were causing the loss of morale, and Mrs. Brown, his most valuable group member, was the source and chief spreader of the malicious rumors.

Discussion

1. Should Mr. Hall fire Mrs. Brown or explore other alternatives?
2. What would be several negative and positive ways to handle this situation and what would be the likely consequences of each?
3. What would be a few important principles leaders should follow in handling people problems?
4. If you were Mr. Hall, how would you handle this situation?
5. What could Mr. Hall do to stay on top of what is going on in his organization and avoid future problems?
6. What are some alternatives Mr. Hall could consider for re-building his department and improving morale?

Key Leadership Lessons

1. Leaders need to be in close touch with the people and teams they lead.
2. It is important for leaders to do occasional informal or formal evaluations of their teams to assure they know what is going on.
3. Leaders need to be active in building healthy, high performance teams.

Suggested Reading For Additional Insights

Baker, J. S., and Jones, M. A. (1996). The poison grapevine: how destructive are gossip and rumor in the workplace? *Human Resource Development Quarterly, 7*(1), 75-86.

French, J. P. R. Jr., and Raven, B. (1960). The bases of social power. In D. Cartwright and A. Zander (Eds.), *Group dynamics* (pp. 607-623). New York: Harper and Row.

Guerin, B., and Miyazaki, Y. (2006). Analyzing rumors, gossip, and urban legends through their conversational properties. *The Psychological Record, 56*, 23-34.

Hallett, T., Harger, B., and Eder, D. (2009) Gossip at work: unsanctioned evaluative talk in formal school meetings. *Journal of Contemporary Ethnography, 38*(5), 584-618.

Kurland, N., and Pelled, L. H. (2000). Passing the word: toward a model of gossip and power in the workplace. *Academy of Management Review, 25*, 428-438.

Newstrom, J. W., Monczka, R. E., and Reif, W. E. (1974). Perceptions of the grapevine: Its value and influence. *The Journal of Business Communication,* 11(3), 12-20.

Smith, B. (1996). Care and feeding of the office grapevine. *Management Review,* 85(2), 6.

BIOGRAPHY

Dr. Cumbo is an educator, consultant, and author. He is Hull Professor of Business and Economics at Emory & Henry College in Emory, Virginia where he has won the Excellence in Teaching Award and has served many years as a department chairman and as chairman of the Division of Social Sciences. Dr. Cumbo also serves as President of Cumbo & Associates, Inc., a Virginia systems and strategy consulting corporation with a specialty in small and mid-sized client organizations. Dr. Cumbo received his BS degree in Accounting from East Tennessee State University, his MBA from the College of William and Mary, and the PhD in Business from Virginia Tech.

L. J. Cumbo, Jr.
Hull Professor of Business and Economics
Department of Business Administration
Emory & Henry College, PO Box 947, Emory, VA 24327
Email: ljcumbo@ehc.edu

4

Reigniting Demotivated Employees: Reversing Career Entrenchment

Angela Spranger

Major Focus of the Case

Effective leaders are skilled at motivating people, especially those who are not highly motivated or have become disenchanted. This is a case about a leader who took a strong interest in re-motivating a former star employee who was suffering from career entrenchment. The phenomenon of career entrenchment happens when employees see little opportunity for growth or advancement, and feel stuck in their current roles.

A Leader Who Cares About Her People

Liz was proud to have been promoted to her new position: Director of a major operating division, at a company location with thousands of employees. An African American woman in a very masculine, old-school organization, she had every reason to be proud. It didn't take long, though, to find out she had a serious problem on her hands. A long-service, highly-skilled professional, Dan, had become convinced that with Liz's promotion, his career path had hit a dead-end. With no growth prospects, Dan's motivation plummeted. He came in each day, kept to himself, rejected meetings and did just enough to stay afloat; he was practicing for retirement and getting his financial house in order so he could walk out comfortably.

The Problem of Employee Entrenchment

Several researchers have addressed the topic of career entrenchment (Blau & Holladay, 2006; Carson & Carson, 1997), in which employees remain in a position that offers minimal opportunity for engagement or growth. Some call this phenomenon "on-the-job retirement," but the experience of entrenchment is much more than a catchphrase or a joke. In terms of organizational engagement or psychological attachment, more recently termed psychological capital (PsyCap) (Luthans, Avey, Avolio, & Peterson, 2010), entrenchment involves a loss of hope and optimism, and a reduction in resilience, with only an employee's sense of efficacy providing the PsyCap required to keep coming in each day. Those capacities of hope, optimism and resilience are proximal outcomes resulting from leader intervention, but when leaders fail to intervene, PsyCap decays. Hope, realistic optimism, self-efficacy and confidence, and resilience waste away (Luthans, et al., 2010). It's as if work becomes a psychic prison and the employee is just waiting to get out (Morgan, 1998).

Dan's area of expertise was established and he'd progressed through his job family until he had earned its top rank. He had the respect of his peers as well as his leadership. When Liz was promoted to Director, it closed off the only opportunity that Dan could see – even though he hadn't really wanted the Director job anyway. Liz saw Dan's many strengths, and she wanted him on her team. She resolved that she couldn't just allow this high potential, high value human capital resource to waste away and then walk away. Liz needed to get Dan re-engaged.

Alternatives For Motivating Entrenched Employees

Carson & Carson (1997) offer four responses to the realization of career entrenchment. The individual may choose to exit immediately (retire, or leave the workforce altogether), voice his or her concerns and ideas to improve the situation (an option used only if exit is impossible), demonstrate loyalty by finding ways to expand the job and demonstrate organizational citizenship behaviors (OCBs) such as training and mentoring others, or by simply waiting for something to change. Psychological capital can absolutely decay in such a situation, as only the person's ability to perform (efficacy) is activated on a daily basis.

But leadership initiative can alter this trajectory. Of the four responses to career entrenchment, only one requires full engagement and a "reboot" of hope, optimism, and resilience: loyalty. A leader activates the loyalty response by identifying and accessing the subordinate's strengths and finding ways to deploy those strengths for the benefit of the group and the organization. Many organizational leaders make the mistake of ignoring the high performer, expecting the individual to maintain the status quo. Instead, an effective leader might focus on helping that valued employee deploy and develop his or her strengths in new and unique ways. Luthans, Avey, Avolio & Peterson (2010) studied the effects of specific psychological capital interventions in which developmental dimensions designed to affect each of the four proximal outcomes (hope, realistic optimism, efficacy/confidence, and resilience) were manipulated to produce a sustainable performance impact. Defining goals and pathways and implementing obstacle planning were two dimensions that increase hope and build efficacy and confidence. Developing positive expectancy strengthens the employee's realistic optimism. The employee's experiences of success provide a basis for mentoring and modeling effective behaviors for others. One responsibility of senior leadership is to be attuned to the needs of junior leaders and colleagues, and to find ways to enhance their psychological capital. Investing in colleagues in this way builds assets and reduces organizational risks.

What Liz Did To Motivate Dan

"I began to meet with Dan regularly and talk with him about how I make decisions, how I do course corrections when things don't turn out just right – because that's a big part of it, being able to help people recover from an error. And I made sure he knew, as all my team knows, that I want the facts, the honest and complete facts. And soon I started hearing him use the same language and methodology I was using, and even to tell people that that's what he was doing."

Corporate leaders choosing to personally mentor specific individuals, teaching them their decision making processes and analytical methods, is a form of transformational leadership that can increase and even multiply the associate's PsyCap and organizational commitment. An effective leader deliberately works with a star employee who has shown signs of fading. She can do this by defining new goals and pathways and implementing obstacle planning, to restore the employee's hope, and re-engage him in the organization. Allowing that person to demonstrate his or her skills, and finding new and relevant ways to recognize and reward successes, strengthens the employee's realistic optimism.

"When I moved on," Liz says, "he was there, already prepared to take over the organization. I was so proud! Dan had stopped putting all his energy into retirement and started thinking about who else he could mentor and bring along, as I had done with him."

Discussion

1. Effective leaders are close to their employees and quick to spot issues such as a lack of motivation. What should leaders look for in general to spot a lack of motivation and specifically to spot career entrenchment?

2. What are some of the costs of having employees who have lost motivation?

3. What are some ways leaders can motivate employees to utilize more of their potential? Draw from what Liz did and create other ideas as well.

4. What are some of the consequences of having leaders who do not address employee motivation?

Leadership Lessons

1. Effective leaders recognize the contributions of star colleagues, and those leaders take the time and energy to motivate them, to bring out the best in them.

2. The best leaders are approachable, good listeners, who create an environment where employees feel safe sharing their needs.

3. It is important for a leader to let people know that you personally value them and that the organization values them.

4. Good leaders make a point of asking employees for their input on the most effective rewards and opportunities for empowerment. Giving people incentives that matter can completely change their outlook and re-engage them in the organization's goals.

5. Good leaders will try to motivate employees and utilize their potential. However, they also know when enough is enough and they need to take corrective action.

References

Blau, G., & Holladay, E. B. (2006). Testing the discriminant validity of a four-dimensional occupational commitment measure. *Journal of Occupational and Organisational Psychology* , 79, 691-704.

Carson, K. D., & Carson, P. P. (1997). Career entrenchment: A quiet march toward occupational death? *Academy of Management Executive*, 11 (1), 62-75.

Luthans, F., Avey, J. B., Avolio, B. J., & Peterson, S. J. (2010). The development and resulting performance impact of positive psychological capital. *Human Resource Development Quarterly*, 41-67.

Morgan, G. (1998). *Images of Organization: The Executive Edition*. San Francisco: Berrett-Koehler.

O'Reilly, I. C., & Chatman, J. (1986). Organizational commitment and psychological attachment: The effects of compliance, identification, and internalization on prosocial behavior. *Journal of Applied Psychology*, 71 (3), 492-499.

BIOGRAPHY

Angela Spranger is a doctoral student in Organizational Leadership at Regent University. She holds an MBA in Marketing and a Master's Degree in Human and Organizational Learning. Angela has worked in recruiting and staffing, labor-management relations, and instructional design. She is the training and organizational development specialist in a Program Division at Newport News Shipbuilding, a Division of Huntington-Ingalls Industries, taking a "theory-into-practice" approach to organizational leadership and development. Angela has facilitated workshops on career development, effective facilitation, career blind spots, and decision making and conflict resolution.

Angela Spranger, MBA, MA Ed., SPHR
14 Omera Place, Hampton, VA 23666
Tel. 757-880-8972 · Email: angespl@regent.edu

CHAPTER FIVE

1

The Synergistic Robin Hood:
Building Upon Strengths To Make Productive Teams

Mark L. McConkie

Major Focus of The Case

Because so much that we do in organizations we do in and with groups, leadership involves the processes of selecting, managing, and influencing effective teams. The first step in team formation is the ideal in the leader's mind as to who should be a part of the team. It is tempting for leaders to choose friends, people like themselves, people they know they do or can get along with, or people with similar backgrounds. A far more productive strategy, however, is that of choosing excellence – men and women who have talents, skills and abilities which the leader himself lacks. Choosing high talent associates sets the stage for synergistic interactions which accelerate production rates, allows for and encourages both individual and group growth, and inevitably focuses group attentions on achieving higher levels of performance – as these fictional accounts from the life of Robin Hood illustrate.

Introduction

Synergy is the process of building upon strengths in such a way as to create an end result that is stronger, more productive, and more complete than would be the case by simply combining the constituent subparts. In other words, "the whole is greater than the sum of the parts." The interaction of high-performance players dramatically increases the likelihood of producing synergistic interactions, which suggests that effective leadership surrounds itself with talents and skills which it in itself lacks. An effective organization leader, therefore, surrounds himself/herself with men and women who can do all kinds of things which he/she cannot, and even with people who do many of the same things the leader does – only does them better. Leadership, then, is not being more technically proficient that others, rather it is the process of discovering, directing and unleashing the creative genius and talent of others. Great leadership, therefore, surrounds itself with great talent – as this case study from the life of Robin Hood illustrates.

Robin Hood:

Well do you know the story of the famous shooting match at Nottingham, staged by the evil Sheriff in order to capture the errant Knight, Robin of Locksley. Robin, legend records, came disguised and won the shooting contest by splitting the arrow of Gilbert 'O the Red Cap, who has launched his arrow to the very center of the target. Robin's greatness, however, lay not in his archery, but in his skill as a leader and manager.

EPISODE ONE: **Robin Meets John Little**[1]

On a given morn in merry England, Robin went seeking adventure. Shortly he came upon a stream over which a single log was stretched, forming a bridge wide enough for but one man to cross over at the time. Approaching the log Robin spied a giant of a man with a large, cast iron frame, standing at the other end of the log, preparing to cross to Robin's side. An impetuous and eager youth, Robin called to him and commanded that he step aside, so that he himself might pass unobstructed. The deep voice at the other end of the stream refused. Warning and counter warnings were issued from either side, but neither was willing to accept the claim of the other. A challenge was issued – honest accounts differ as to who offered it – and Robin set out to find a staff. Having secured one, he met the stranger half way, where the quarterstaff cudgeling began in good earnest. The two exchanged bruises and blows for an hour, neither gaining the advantage. Even the birds and animals hid their eyes for fright. Finally, with one Herculean sweep, the tall stranger hit Robin with a thrust to the side, which sent him flying into the water beneath.

The stranger laughed as Robin fumbled for his horn, which he finally found, and blew. Within moments Will Stutely appeared, and immediately asked Robin why he stood waist-deep in the flowing font. "Why merry," quoth Robin, "yon stout fellow hath tumbled me in neck and crop into the water, and hath given me a drubbing besides."

"Then he shall not go without a ducking and eke a drubbing himself!" cried Will Stutely. "Have at him, lads!"

"Nay, forebear!" cried Robin; "he is a right good man and true, and no harm shall befall him. He has bested me at something, and is good enough therefore to join our Band."

Then, turning to the tall stranger, Robin said: "Sir, you have bested me, and fight more ably with a cudgel than do I. You are therefore good enough to be a part of my Band. Will you join with us, and become one of our team?"

Stretching forth his hand, the stranger said he would be honored. Introductions were exchanged, and the stranger said his name was John Little. Robin changed his name to Little John, and he was formally inducted into the Sherwood Forest Gang, and appointed Number Two Man under Robin.

EPISODE TWO: The Tanner of Blyth Bests Little John and Joins the Band

Walking through the woods one day, Robin overheard two men shouting, as if in anger. Approaching the noise they created, he peered through the shrubbery, and saw the quarrel in the making: "As you may have seen two dogs that think to fight, walking slowly round and round each other, neither cur wishing to begin the combat, so those two stout yeoman moved slowly around, each watching for a chance to take the other unawares, and so get in the first blow. At last Little John struck like a flash, and "...the contest began in good earnest, each exchanging blows for nigh on thirty minutes, until the ground was all plowed up with the digging of their heels, and their breathing grew labored like the ox in the furrow."

But Little John suffered the most, while Robin, laying beside a bush rejoiced at such a comely bout of quarterstaff, averring all the while that he had never seen Little John so evenly matched. At last, Little John threw his mightiest blow at his opponent, who took the blow only to return it upon Little John, who, losing his balance, fell to the dust. Then, raising his staff, stout Arthur, for thus was he named, dealt him another blow to the ribs.

"Hold!" roared Little John. "Wouldst thou strike a man when he is down?"

"Aye, merry, would I," quoth the Tanner, giving him another thwack with his staff.

"Stop!" roared Little John, "Help! Hold, I say! I yield me! I yield me, I say, good fellow!"

"And so thought I," cried Robin, bursting forth from the thicket and shouting with laughter, stretching forth his hand to the Tanner, and crying, "Thou hast bested the man who bested me and art better than the both of us. Thou art, therefore, good enough to be a part of our Band. Wilt thou join with us?"

The Tanner agreed, his name was changed, and he became a stalwart of the Sherwood Forest Gang.[2]

EPISODE THREE: **Robin Signs Will Scarlett to the Team**

Walking the byways of Sherwood Forest on a given day, Robin encountered a graceful stranger, walking with a curtsy and smelling roses as he walked. In the conversation which ensued, Robin challenged him to a duel. The stranger, dressed in red, reluctantly agreed, as he had no alternative. As the stranger had no sword, he walked to the side of the road, leaned over, and uprooted a tree. Little John and the Tanner, watching at a distance, cringed. The stranger acted as if he had done naught to speak of. The fight then began in solemn playt, and so much dust was thrown into the air that the on-lookers could see nothing, "but only hear the rattle of the staves against each other."

After a long and ferocious battle, the stranger landed a blow on Robin's pate that sent him sprawling in the dust. "Hold!" cried Robin, when he saw the stranger raising his staff once more. "I yield me!"

"Hold!" cried Little John, bursting from his cover, with the Tanner at his heels, "Hold, we say!"

"Nay," answered the stranger, confidently, "if there be two more of you, and each as stout as this good follow, I am like to have my hands full. Nevertheless, come on, and I will strive my best to serve you all."

"Stop!" cried Robin Hood, "we will fight no more. Take my vow, this is an ill day for thee and me, Little John. I do verily believe that my wrist, and eke my arm, are palsied by the jar of the blow that this stranger struck me."

At this point, Robin stood, extending the hand of fellowship to the stranger, saying: "You, good fellow, have bested me at something, and seeing that you are better at the quarterstaff than am I, I judge you worthy to join our Band. Will you not become a part of our team?"

The stranger agreed. Introductions were exchanged, and Robin changed the stranger's name to Will Scarlet, for he was dressed in red.

EPISODE FOUR: **Robin Enrolls Midge the Miller**

Some days later, Robin, Little John and the Tanner were walking the paths of Sherwood when, in the long distance, they espied a miller, walking towards them with a large sack of flour.

He carried the sack with such ease that Robin called him "a credit to all English yeomanry," and proposed to his two companions that they play a trick upon their unsuspecting fellow. They agreed that they would feign a robbery, take the miller and his flour into the forest, feed him a feast, then give him some money and send him on his way, better fed and richer than when they found him.

When the miller approached close enough for conversation, Robin and his companions announced they wanted his gold: "Our good Gaffer Swanthold sayeth that gold is an over-heavy burden for a two-legged mule to carry; so we would e'en lift some of this load from thee."

The miller denied having any gold, but the three from Sherwood insisted it was hidden in the bag. Upon Robin's instructions, they leaned over to search the bag, whereupon the miller seized two large handfuls of flour and thrust it in their faces, blinding and half-choking them. As they struggled to see and breathe, the miller threw more flour into their faces, and struck them repeatedly with his staff.

Finally, a near-blinded Robin cried, "Stop! Give over good fellow, I am Robin Hood."

"Thou liest, knave," cried the miller, giving him a rap on the ribs that sent up a great cloud of flour like a puff of smoke. "Stout Robin never robbed an honest tradesman. Ha! Thou wouldst have my money wouldst thou?" he sputtered, as he gave Robin another blow.

Rolling in pain, Robin finally found his horn, which in short order called forth Will Stutely and some of his companions, who immediately lifted staves to protect the floured three.

"No!" cried Robin, "This good man is clever of mind and quick of hand, and his wit is faster than that of the three snowmen you see before you, and he is therefore worthy of membership in our little Sherwood Kingdom." Then, turning to the miller, he said: "You, Noble Sir, have bested myself and two of my best men, and therefore qualify for membership in our Band. Would you join, and become one with us?"

The miller said that he would. Names were exchanged, and Robin said that rather than calling him "the miller's son," as had heretofore been the practice, he should be called by his proper name, Midge. Thus he became Midge the Miller, a member of Robin's Band.

EPISODE FIVE: **Robin Finds a Chaplain In Friar Tuck**

Seeking an adventure one morning, Robin's musings were interrupted by the sound of two voices conversing. He approached the stream from whence the voices came. Crawling through the foliage, he could spy but one man, who was large, and wearing the dress of a friar. The friar sat eating, drinking, and singing to himself.

"Who is it?" said Robin, "who sits by the wayside and talks with himself?"

Upon hearing Robin's voice, the friar immediately put his steel cap on his head. But when Robin got close, he suggested to the Friar that it would be good Christian service were he to carry Robin across the stream. Looking straight down the helm of Robin's drawn sword, the friar saw good wisdom in the service, and humbly carried Robin across the stream. Robin, during the journey, made the mistake of sheathing his sword.

As the friar was setting Robin safely on the foreign side of the stream, he quickly drew Robin's sword from his unsuspecting sheath, and pointing it to the throat of the King of Sherwood, politely but firmly suggested that His Royal Sherwood Highness return the favor to the church which the church had just rendered to the state.

Robin wisely obliged, splashing through the stream to the nether side, carrying the hefty priest through the flow. As he was wading, however, he slowly loosened the friar's sheath cord, so that when he set the friar on the ground, he could quickly grab the friar's sword as the friar had previously done to him.

The conversation quickly followed the point of the blade, and Robin soon found himself upon the shoulders of the wading monk, who was working himself toward Robin's preferred shore. Midway through the stream, however, the friar, with one mighty heave, threw Robin into the water.

Upon reaching the shore, a fierce sword fight ensued, in which neither man could gain the advantage. Finally, after an hour of contest, the friar forced Robin to drop his sword.

They then exchanged names, and Robin said: "Thou art the fairest swordsman I have fallen in with for many a day. Indeed, thou hast bested me at the crossed swords, and I therefore find you good enough to be a part of my Band. Wilt thou join with us?"

The friar agreed, and Robin said that of all the names by which he was called, he liked "Friar Tuck" best. They agreed that he would be thusly called.

References

[1] Howard Pyle, *Some Merry Adventures of Robin Hood.* New York: Charles Scribner's Sons, 1946.

[2] Pyle, pp. 98-104.

[3] Peter Drucker, *The Effective Executive.* New York: Harper & Row, 1967, p. 73.

Discussion

1. Are fictional accounts, such as these episodes from the life of Robin Hood, legitimate mechanisms to illustrate and teach leadership principles to people who work in real world, non-fictional settings? Why?

2. Robin is hungry to surround himself with people who are more able than he is.

   a) What does that say about Robin?

   b) What effects will it produce?

   c) What does it suggest about those he hires?

   d) How is it likely to impact their ability to perform?

   e) How will it affect Robin's performance?

3. What elements combine to enable a team of highly talented individuals to synergize?

Key Leadership Lessons

1. We live in an age of groups, teams, units, divisions and departments – an age of complex tasks accomplished by teams of experts with diverse skills and competencies. This imposes upon leaders the responsibility of selecting team members whose unique skill sets interact one with another in a way which maximizes their potential. The interaction of highly skilled workers increases the likelihood of such maximization. Often this means leaders will be surrounded by individuals whose abilities exceed those of the leader, whose role it is to facilitate or direct the usage of those skills to maximum benefit. This means leaders provide vision and direction.

2. Effective leadership builds on strengths; ineffective leadership organizes to avoid weakness and therefore builds toward mediocrity. Steel magnate Andrew Carnegie illustrated the concept by having his tombstone inscribed with the words: "Here lies a man who knew how to bring into his service men better than he was himself."[3] To build on strength is to multiply the performance capacity of the whole.

3. Effective leadership seeks to create synergy, that process whereby divergent skill sets "explode" in their interaction one with another to the creative and productive good of the group or organization. One of the first steps in creating such interaction is uniting high talent people in the performance of a shared goal or task –and that is leadership's role.

4. The leader who surrounds himself/herself with high talent people – particularly with people whose talents exceed those of the leader him/herself – pushes him/herself to greater achievement by that very act. To work with excellence is to inspire continued excellence.

BIOGRAPHY

Professor McConkie specializes in organization behavior, management development and ethics. He is a Professor of Public Administration in the School of Public Affairs at the University of Colorado at Colorado Springs. He has consulted, lectured and taught in 49 of the 50 states, and in over 30 nations. He has consulted widely with organizations in the public, private and not-for-profit sectors, and has over 100 scholarly publications or presentations..

Mark L. McConkie
Professor of Public Administration
School of Public Administration
University of Colorado at Colorado Springs
1420 Austin Bluffs Parkway, PO. Box 7150, Colorado Springs, Colorado
Tel. 80933-7150 ·Tel. 719/255-4011 · Email: mmcconki@uccs.edu

2

The Challenges Of Building A Leadership Team: Patience Or Performance In A Turnaround

Erik Hoekstra & Bethany J. Schuttinga

Major Focus of the Case

When change is needed, a turnaround leader taking over a poorly performing department, function, or entire organization needs to calibrate the appropriate speed of change. While the leader will likely have the broad outlines of the new vision and a sense of the new performance metrics in mind before arriving, once in the role the leader must determine whether current staff can catch the vision and reenergize individual performance or whether some degree of "wholesale change" in staff may be needed to get performance and culture change moving.

Further, if personnel changes are needed, the turnaround leader needs to make decisions about how such change should occur, how many significant personnel change decisions the organization can handle, and the timing of needed personnel changes to move the organization ahead productively. In some situations, moving quickly is important – but the leader who moves too quickly may face additional resistance and a breakdown in trust. How can a leader know when to push, how fast to move, and what are the determining factors in such a situation?

Introduction

One of the key responsibilities of a CEO in any organization is selecting and leading the senior team. No matter how capable the Chief Executive is individually, unless the organization is very small, no leader will be successful without a capable and highly motivated senior leadership team (Wageman, Nunes, Burruss, and Hackman, 2008). Building the internal culture of that team is a critical function and as much an art as a science. Individual team members also come to the table with varying degrees of talent and motivation. The Chief Executive must be able to assess both the motivation level and the talent level of each person well and know whether the particular mix of these talents and motivations can come together to make a successful team (Lencioni, 2002). In some cases, motivation can be adjusted upwards through coaching and in some cases training and development may be able to increase talent. Sadly however, there are situations in which the leader simply needs to make changes to the senior team by exiting ineffective team members, replacing them, or restructuring the team for higher performance.

When a senior leader needs to drive for change and push for organizational improvement, a key factor is the optimal speed of change that can be delivered (Kotter, 1996). Change which is too rapid may cause disruption and lack of trust, leading to long-term problems and distractions. Change that is too slow may create frustration (or exit) for high achieving employees and also frustrate customers or key organizational supporters. Having a change plan, and knowing how fast to move, is a critical success factor for leaders, particularly those in new leadership roles (Ciampa and Watkins, 2005).

Background Of The New College President

When Lucy Smith (not her real name) was hired as the President at her alma mater, Alma College (not the real name), the Chairperson of the Board of Trustees had said, "I trust you in this role and I've got your back. The Board has hired you because we know that you'll be the change agent we've been looking for. We look forward to great things".

Smith had graduated from Alma 20 years earlier and had a meteoric rise in higher education. She quickly completed a Ph.D. in medieval history, but was always more of a manager than an academic. In her student days, she was known for being a campus leader and after her hire at Ohio State University she had quickly moved from the classroom into an Associate Provost role. When the Provost position came open at Ohio State University she was quickly appointed as the interim and within a year she was appointed as the Provost. Her ability to read people and situations was her calling card and she loved being at a major research institution in a leadership role.

She had twice spurned, with appreciation, the overture from the Board of Trustees of her alma mater for the post as President. While she knew Alma needed a turnaround, she wasn't looking for another position and knew the history and tradition that had plagued the school since her student days. Alma was dear to her heart, but as a religious school of 2000 undergraduates, it didn't have the prestige of OSU. It also was situated in the college town of Alma Falls, an old-line textile, agricultural, and steel manufacturing town. A great small town yes, but the college employees comprised nearly 25% of the town. It was also a tight-knit community with many familial connections. Anna knew that being a change agent in the town would be challenging both professionally and personally.

However, the Chair of the Board of Trustees had been very convincing and in an informal meeting on campus, she had heard from several high potential young faculty members who expressed their desire for change at the college. The Board of Trustees had a good vision for the college, the college had been relatively successful in raising money to build some new buildings, and there was enough of a cushion in the budget to allow for some flexibility in personnel during the change process.

Three Months Into The Job

She was now three months into the new job and it was clear what the issues were....people. She had inherited a mostly deflated and quite disconnected executive Cabinet leadership team which included a Vice President for Enrollment Management, Vice President for Academic Affairs, Vice President for Student Development, Vice President for Business and Finance and a Vice President for Advancement. Beyond this senior leadership team, it appeared that the college was stuck in mediocrity with deans, department chairs, directors, a registrar, librarian, and an athletic program in disarray. Her immediate predecessor had been a people pleaser and had lasted about 6 years.

Her executive team lacked focus and it was clear through Cabinet meetings and individual meetings with the VP's, that she was in danger of losing an excellent performer if the change did not come soon enough. Although enrollment was steady and on the increase, Dr. Smith felt uneasy about the level of commitment of her Vice President for Business and Finance. With a new baby and three other small children at home, Dr. Smith found her Vice President distracted and unfocused. If Smith was going to move the college to the next level, she needed someone who could lead well and focus intently in the areas of capital planning and debt management. Alumni support and fundraising efforts had been average in the past. Her Vice President for Advancement expressed early on when Smith arrived that the fundraising efforts had high potential but ultimately the efforts suffered because of the lack of long term planning and that donors had nothing to be truly excited about at Alma.

In addition, Smith also saw a need for change in the academic side of the organization. Long standing faculty expressed regret that the academic-focused glory days of the college were long past and blamed the administration for taking the college down a path of mediocrity. It was clear that it would be an uphill battle to both garner the respect of the faculty and to muster the energy to rejuvenate the faculty ranks. The pulse of the student body was generally positive and although Smith was fairly confident in the skill set of her Vice President for Student Development, she was concerned about some of the personality traits and the lack of development she was seeing in this leader.

Deciding What To Do Next

As Smith pondered her first three months on the job, she had more questions than answers. She had certainly turned around under-performing teams and functions in the past, but not at this senior level and not in as 'public' of a venue as she faced now at Alma. This coming Friday, she was meeting with the Board's Executive Committee for their quarterly meeting. While it certainly wasn't a formal performance evaluation, the Board Chair had said to her, "Perhaps outside of our formal agenda, we could have an informal lunch discussion together. Now that you've been through your first 100 days, it might be helpful for the Board to hear your plan for the college and how you anticipate moving that plan ahead through your senior leadership team."

She had always had a knack when it came to reading people, but the team context at Alma was more dynamic and complex than situations she had previously faced. As she assessed her senior team, she thought about each member and tried to assess their individual talents and levels of motivation. Using a simple, yet surprisingly effective tool (see Figure 1) which she had picked up earlier in her career in a professional development seminar, she mentally mapped each of her direct reports and considered how best to manage them. She also planned to use the tool to help her communicate to the board some of her plans to shake the Cabinet up a bit.

Smith had experienced many organizational changes in the past and thus knew the need to balance speed of execution with capacity of an organization to handle rapid change. Internally, she was torn. She couldn't sort out her head, her heart, and her gut. On the one hand, she seemed to want to *"pull the band-aid off quickly and get it over with, clean house fast, get it behind you, and be bold to drive the change bus......if some people don't want to ride, they can catch a different bus"*. On the other, she knew that too much change too fast might be the organizational equivalent of *vertigo*, making everyone nervous, anxious, and wondering *'who might be next'*. She also knew, both directly from the Board of Trustees and from a 'sense' she had picked up from many donors and some faculty members, that she was expected to shake things up and move Alma forward... and time was ticking.

As she fell asleep on Wednesday night, she weighed her options carefully and tried to place her senior management team (see Appendix A for Leadership Team Biographies) in the various sectors of the Talent Motivation Performance Matrix in her mind's eye. Her schedule was open on Thursday and she intended to pull the grid out formally to assess her people. She also intended to do more thinking about the pace of change she could reasonably expect to chart for Alma before her Friday meeting with the Board. Review the model in Figure 1 and the profiles of the Leadership Team Members in Figure 2 before answering the discussion questions.

Figure 1:

TALENT MOTIVATION PERFORMANCE MATRIX

	BEDROCKS > High motivation Low talent Give recognition for good work Use to coach others Can training & development improve their talent potential?	**ROCK STARS** High motivation High talent Give challenging work to stretch Coach and mentor Take interest in career development Caution, may alienate other team members.
HIGH ↑ M O T I V A T I O N	**GLACIERS ∧** Low motivation Low talent potential Could become rock stars/bedrocks Counsel, establish trust Take action to help, including possible outplacement.	**UNKOWNS ∧** Low motivation High talent May need intense counsel/coaching Are they bored? Inspire, motivate, encourage to reach potential.
LOW	**T A L E N T**	**HIGH**

Biographies of Cabinet Leadership team at Alma College

(all names used are not the real names):

Vice President for Enrollment Management, Mr. V

Mr. V joined Alma in 1996 as an Associate Director of Admissions and in 2000 was promoted to the position of Director of Admissions. In 2003, he was appointed Vice President for Enrollment Management and assumed oversight responsibility for the College's financial aid program. Since his appointment in 2003, undergraduate full-time enrollment at the College has increased by 20% and the academic quality of enrolling undergraduates increased significantly. He also serves as an adjunct faculty member in the Business Department where he teaches a popular course in marketing, and he frequently speaks regionally and nationally on trends in the enrollment management field.

Vice President for Academic Affairs, Dr. W, Ph.D.

Dr. W became the Vice President for Academic Affairs in 1996, coming to Alma from Big Falls College in Franklin, Idaho, where he had served as Vice President for Academic Affairs and Dean of the College since 1990. Prior to 1990, as a cultural anthropologist, he conducted fieldwork on the island of Sardinia where, along with his wife (who currently serves as a faculty member in the natural sciences), he investigated the impacts of the state and capitalist market penetration on the lives of shepherds and their families in the mountainous villages of the Barbagia region.

Since coming to Alma, Merson contributed early in his tenure to the rebuilding of the core program. However, after the completion of the core program, he has been relatively inactive in program growth, scholarship and development of faculty. He has instead spent his time maintaining the status quo and routinely travels with his wife on behalf of the college to Sardinia to conduct research in their interest areas. He holds a Ph.D. and Master's Degrees from Columbia University and a Bachelor's Degree from the University of Chicago. He also has earned a certificate from the Institute for Educational Management (IEM) at Harvard University.

Vice President for Student Development, Dr X, Ph.D

Dr. X completed her masters and doctorate in higher education administration at the University of Florida in 2001. She received her Bachelor of Arts degree at Walla College in Nebraska. Her dissertation research for her doctorate focused on 'Discrimination in higher education against women from rural backgrounds'. While completing her doctorate on a part-time basis in higher education administration at the University of Florida, she also served as the Campus Activities Director and provided oversight for a $500,000 budget and 120 student clubs and organizations. Immediately after finishing her degree in 2001, she joined the executive leadership team at Alma. She was eager to get back to a rural area and has enjoyed all of the friends she has been able to make at Alma. She prides herself on building deep relationships with students and is often a person who is sought out by those who want to talk about the latest controversy in Alma.

Vice President for Business and Finance, Ms.Y

Ms. Y accepted the position of vice president for business and finance in 2007. She has an MBA from Indiana State University and a Bachelor of Arts degree from Alma College. Prior to returning to her alma mater, she served as the university treasurer at California Methodist University in Oak Park, California. Nesbitt also worked for 13 years at Grandview Hospital in Hunt, Indiana, in the position of executive director of business services and facility operations. She and her husband have enjoyed being back in Alma after living all over the country due to all the family they have in the Alma area. Her father-in-law serves on the Board of Trustees and is the President of First National Bank in Alma.

Vice President for Advancement, Dr. Z

Dr. Z joined Alma in 2005 and has a Bachelor of Arts in Journalism from Bethesda College, a Master of Science in Business Education from Washington State University, and an EdD in Higher Education Administration from Montana State University. He has held faculty and administrative positions at Minnesota State University and Bethesda College. Between 1994 and 2005, he served as Vice President of Advancement at Bethesda College. During his service at Bethesda, he was recognized by a national association for "Excellence in Fund Raising" in the area of development program performance. He was also recognized for building a strong advancement team and leading them by example with the highest integrity and care for donors. For the past five years, he has been a successful advancement consultant.

References

Ciampa, D. and Watkins, M. (2005). *Right From The Start: Taking Charge in a New Leadership Role.* Cambridge, MA: Harvard Business School Press.

Kotter, J. (1996). *Leading Change.* Cambridge, MA: Harvard Business School Press.

Lencioni, P. (2002). *The Five Dysfunctions of a Team.* San Francisco: Jossey-Bass.

Wageman, R., Nunes, D.A., Burruss, J.A., and Hackman, J.R. (2008). *Senior Leadership Teams: What It Takes To Make Them Great.* Cambridge, MA: Harvard Business School Press.

Discussion

1. What are the major strengths that Dr. Smith brings to her new job as President of a college and what are the major challenges she faces?

2. Using Figure 1 and the profiles of the Cabinet members in Figure 2, place yourself in Dr. Smith's position and evaluate the strengths and weaknesses of the leadership team and each team member.

3. If you were the president in this situation would you pursue change quickly or more slowly?
What are the advantages and disadvantages of each?

4. Try to be as innovative and imaginative as possible and discuss and list at least five alternatives the President could take and the potential implications of each.

5. What are steps the President could take in building the leadership team into a highly effective team?

6. Discuss possible options or actions leaders with aggressive change agendas should consider in making successful and sustainable changes.

Key Leadership Lessons

1. Building a highly effective top leadership team is a major key to the success of organizations.

2. Few teams have all of the ingredients needed for team success. Leaders need to be able to assess t he strengths and weaknesses of teams and team members. There are many alternatives for improving the effectiveness of teams and team members before wholesale changes need to be made. Still every leader has to assess how much time and resources to invest before making the tough decisions.

3. Senior leaders have a responsibility to create momentum for change and improvement in organizations. The climate and culture of any organization sets the tone for expectations throughout the organization and gives followers clear signals of appropriate action. Senior leaders are not universally responsible for the culture and climate of the organization, but how they work with their senior leadership team does have a large impact on culture and climate.

4. It is important for senior leaders to effectively manage their board of directors and the expectations of the board. It the new leader doesn't clarify expectations, the results can be disastrous.

5. The appropriate pace of change is an important and challenging factor for leaders to consider, particularly when entering an organization from the outside. Push too fast or too far and you risk alienating important organizational groups or creating organizational stress or burnout. Move too slowly or be too timid and you risk missing key opportunities to move the organization forward in meaningful ways.

6. Leaders set the performance standard for individuals in various ways. Allowing poor performance, particularly within the senior leadership team, signals to others in the organization a 'low bar' for performance that will permeate the culture and hurt the organization. Ensuring that the senior leadership team members are held to clear expectations for high performance will similarly signal a 'high bar' for performance that will yield many benefits to the organization.

BIOGRAPHY

Dr. Hoekstra serves as the Provost at Dordt College. His previous professional background includes roles in leadership development, executive coaching, organizational consulting, industrial construction, wholesale distribution, retail management, and serving as a business faculty member. Desiring to see workplaces become places of realized potential, he focuses directly on corporate culture and leadership development as keys to organizational effectiveness. Hoekstra has led seminars for internal and external audiences in the areas of negotiation, constructive confrontation, performance coaching, delegation, team-building, and change process leadership. Dr. Hoekstra holds a Bachelor's Degree in History and Philosophy from Trinity Christian College, a Master's Degree in International Management from The Rotterdam School of Management of Erasmus University in the Netherlands, and a Ph.D. in Organizational Learning and Human Resource Development from Iowa State University. His research interests include corporate culture, servant leadership, and organizational effectiveness. He has co-authored several publications on coaching, delegation, servant leadership, and change management, including The Manager as Change Agent, (Perseus 2000)

Dr. Erik Hoekstra Provost · Dordt College
498 4th Ave NE, Sioux Center, IA 51250
Tel. 712-722-6333 · Email: ehoekstra@dordt.edu

BIOGRAPHY

Bethany J. Schuttinga currently serves as the Vice President for Student Services and Associate Provost for Co-curricular Programs at Dordt College. As Vice President for Student Services and Associate Provost for Co-curricular Programs, she is responsible for promoting partnerships with academic departments, serves as the chief judicial affairs officer, and oversees professional staff in housing, academic support services, career services, health programs, security, campus ministries, and counseling services. Ms. Schuttinga has served at Iowa State University in Student Affairs administration. As Assistant Dean of Students and Director of Judicial Affairs, her primary responsibilities included providing leadership as the chief judicial administrator for adjudicating cases of academic dishonesty, plagiarism, fraud in research, and complex, violent and/or serious behavioral violations for graduate and undergraduate students. Schuttinga earned a Bachelor's Degree in Psychology from Dordt College and a Master's Degree in Counseling and Student Personnel from Minnesota State University. She is currently a doctoral candidate in Educational Leadership and Policy Studies at Iowa State University.

Bethany J. Schuttinga
Associate Provost for Co-Curricular Programs
Vice President for Student Services
Dordt College, 498 4th Ave NE, Sioux Center, IA 51250
Tel. 712-722-6076 · Email: bschutti@dordt.edu

3

Collaborative Leadership: Using Large Group Meetings To Cause Rapid Change And Breakthrough Performance

Steve Cady, John Hine, Jonathan Meenach & John Spalding

Major Focus of This Case

By 2010, new challenges faced global businesses as the economy slowed, consumer confidence took a dive, and cost pressures continued to mount. Experts predicted many years of slow growth with the potential for another recession in the U.S. In this chapter, we describe ConAgra Foods June 2010 leadership meeting through the lens of a collaborative transformation model: DxVxFxS > R. We tell the story from the perspective of the top leader, senior leadership team, and top level of 150+ leaders. Our goal is that you gain understanding and ideas for engaging your organization and clients for collaborative innovation on a large-scale.

Introduction: Anticipation Through Collaboration

Questions facing any large organization are how to prepare for a seemingly unpredictable future? What role do leaders and their teams play in these times? How do organizations create a culture of forward thinking innovators - anticipating and, as Wayne Gretzky replied to a question about his innate ability to score (Gretzky, 1989),

"...skate to where the puck is going to be."

In sports as well as business, the capability to innovate with anticipation is the "holy grail" of leadership. It seems that collaboration is the answer. The Center for Creative Leadership analyzed its requests for service from clients in 2009 and found that two-thirds of those requests were from organizations asking for help to improve some aspect of the collaborative environment. Leaders continue to realize that collaboration and interdependence are key components to change and organizational function in the 21st century (McGuire, Palus, Pasmore, & Rhodes, 2009).

What follows is the story of how one company decided to systemically change the manner in which it behaves, by changing the way leaders collaborate and lead in order to thrive and grow the business. ConAgra Foods Inc. is a Fortune 500 (ranked 178) company and one of North America's largest packaged food companies (Fortune, 2010). In 2005, Gary Rodkin joined the company and as chief executive officer has led the change from a holding company for dozens of brands and businesses to a more unified operating company. The company's current mission is: **"One company. One goal. Making the food you love."**

Gary Rodkin's first task at ConAgra Foods was to streamline and stabilize the business by rallying employees around the "One company" mission - setting the stage for collaborative leadership which would make its debut at the 2010 Annual Leadership Meeting. Rodkin started by asking the senior leadership team to rethink the "How" for the future. Accomplishing this goal would entail shifting from a culture of tactical operations (focused on managing the business) to strategically leading the business to new heights of innovation and growth.

Rodkin's notion of corporations resonates with thinkers from around the world such as the classic notion of "creative destruction" (Schumpeter, 1975), where the likes of Lehmen, NW Airlines, Google, and Facebook come and go overnight. While some people suggest businesses are too big to fail, others disagree. They see a disappearing corporate hierarchy as companies move to a model of mass collaboration in order to meet the demands of customers and differentiate their business in an ever increasingly competitive global landscape (i.e., Tapscott, 2006).

In response - rather - in anticipation, Rodkin decided to tackle the opportunity head-on. He charged his planning team to come up with a more radical design for the upcoming leadership meeting; one that would make a clear statement. The leadership event would be a change from past meetings that inherently resulted in a parade of reporting on the status of the business, to an approach that would build upon his vision for "how" collaborative leaders will operate in the future.

A Formula for Collaborative Change

Breakthrough performance requires breaking through resistance, but in a different way. Leaders must come up with their own individual and then collective sense of what matters. Getting to "what matters" is captured in the formula DxVxFxS.

D x V x F x S > R

D = Share a common ***data-base*** of information to create a ***desire*** for change.

V = Craft an inspiring ***vision*** *(strategic plan, priorities, goals, etc.)* that is positive, compelling, and possible.

F = Determine a set of ***first-steps*** in the direction of the vision (action plan, steps, commitments, etc.) that are concrete and measurable.

S = Ensure there are ***supporting mechanisms*** to promote follow-through by establishing clear communication, education, advocacy, structure and processes, policies and procedures, and resource allocations.

R = ***Resistance*** to change. The collection of people and groups whose "world view" is one of maintaining the status quo and unwilling to support change. Resistance is a positive piece of data telling us what is needed for success.

Begin with a common understanding of critical **Data** that surfaces collective **Dissatisfaction** with what people are experiencing today and a **Desire** for something better (i.e., readiness for change). Then, create a joint **Vision** of "what we yearn to be," and follow that with a clear set of short-term **First Steps**. It is important to include measures of success and specific **Supporting Mechanisms** to ensure accountability and continuous improvement so the change process will stay on track. Once the collective agreement, as a critical mass, is greater than the collective **Resistance**, individual and group paradigms shift. Change begins immediately. In fact, it already has. The momentum accelerates away from present state in a "wise" direction and **Transformation** is realized (Beckard & Harris, 1987, Cady & Dannemiller, 2005, Dannemiller Tyson Associates, 2000).

Clarifying Purpose & Outcomes

Tammy Williams, Director of Communication and External Relations, was in charge of managing the event. Knowing that Rodkin was looking for a different type of meeting, she pulled together a team of subject matter experts focused on change and collaboration in the workplace. Given that Williams' is known throughout ConAgra Foods for well designed and professionally produced events - that deliver results, she approached the design and planning of the meeting with Rodkin's objectives in mind,

> *"I expect to see a group of people really come together and get engaged over this initiative to really start thinking about how we achieve breakthrough results."*

The team identified the purpose of the leadership meeting as: ***"to step up our commitment to growth and momentum."*** The outcomes were to leave the meeting with alignment and engagement on three things:

1. What it means to be a leader at ConAgra Foods: Defining the next phase of SAC (Simplicity, Accountability and Collaboration) and our distinct leadership qualities of Vulnerability, Authenticity and Courage, as it relates to our responsibility for creating a culture of growth and higher levels of performance.

2. The key bets we are placing across all of our businesses to win in fiscal year 2011 and how that fits into the fiscal year 2011 Must Do's (the "what" of the organization).

3. A short list of externally focused break-through ideas for changing "how" we work to greater advantage: these will drive the "how" – specifically, our leadership behaviors. Note, this is not a redesign of any fiscal year 2011 plans, but a way to be progressive and use break through thinking for how we work to achieve greater growth, improve customer/consumer satisfaction and engage our employees at all levels of the business for fiscal year 2011 and beyond.

The Leadership Meeting Through the Lens of DVFS

Prior to the meeting, leadership was asked to provide innovative ideas, that when implemented, would affect "how" the enterprise operates. The planning team communicated to the attendees that this meeting would be different with regard to their role as leaders. ConAgra Foods' leadership competency model has one element entitled Leadership Qualities - Authenticity, Courage, and Vulnerability. These qualities proved to be essential for holding very frank discussions that ensued, dialogue and deliberation essential to innovation.

Max-Mix tables maximize systems thinking & organizational learning

Arrival – Shifting the Culture "Right Up Front"

As the 150 + leaders arrived to the meeting place, they walked into a room environment that was immediately different (Photo 1.). Participants began to informally connect, discussing the pre-work, the meeting itself, and other topics that emerged. The room was set up in round tables with eight people each **assigned to sit** in groups that maximized the **mix of perspectives**. People were sitting with people they had never met, at best they may have heard of or spoke with over the phone. The senior leadership was spread throughout the room and was expected to participate as well. This "max-mix" seating communicated an important message tied to collaboration and the need to connect across the enterprise. In essence, each table became a **microcosm** of the whole leadership body for the organization, setting the stage for the creative tension necessary to generate the breakthrough ideas.

Database (Desire for Change)

Creating a common database is a core principle of systems thinking and a learning organization. (Von Bertalanffy, 1972) In many organizations, facts are not shared in a way that ensures everyone (or a critical mass) is on the same page often resulting in rumors and dysfunctional decisions. Leaders can prevent this downward spiral of secrecy, blame and turf protection by promoting and instilling dialogue, respect, initiative and collaboration (Kanter, 2003).

In order to connect the whole room of leaders around a common data-base, Rodkin and the Senior Leadership Team (SLT) presented the current state and seven fiscal year 2011 Must Do's. For example, Must Do No. 2 adds a food safety and quality component, as well as an improved nutrition challenge. While the Must Do's included similar elements from previous years, there were important new objectives and points of emphasis developed for the current fiscal year.

A feature of collaborative events is to design the meeting so that information is shared in short presentations, allowing the participants at their tables to translate, interpret and check for alignment. By switching the flow of conversation to the tables everyone gets involved, stays engaged and experiences what collaboration really means as they formulate better questions and internalize the information.

Vision

The next phase in the meeting was to move toward creating a vision for what is possible. The 20 + tables in the room crafted over 40 breakthrough ideas for consideration. The ideas were posted on flip charts and shared with the whole room. Each table then selected a representative to meet collectively that evening with the SLT to whittle down the 40 ideas to a critical few. In order to make it to the final round for Day 2, it was necessary for the SLT to agree that they could support this idea.

How this discussion unfolded in the room had a dramatic impact on those present. There was open debate among the SLT. The other leaders witnessing this discussion were energized and inspired by the debate and the willingness of the SLT to be authentic, courageous and vulnerable. They were encouraged to get into the discussion and identify ideas they felt passionate about. The discussion began to change the thinking in the room from tactical to strategic. It was no longer a presentation of ideas developed and vetted in advance and presented as a done deal. Rather, Rodkin challenged the leaders in the room in "real time" to go deeper to look for innovation in the ideas generated that day. They were challenged to make connections, think collaboratively, and create provocative propositions for the "HOW." These discussions led to agreement on eight breakthrough ideas to be the core for the Open Space discussion on the second day.

On Day 2, the room set-up communicated another form of discussion - **Open Space Technology** (Photo 2). Participants walked into a room set-up in one big layered circle.

In the center of the room was a circular elevated stage in the form of the ConAgra Foods logo. Rodkin opened the morning with some operational business and meeting participants provided a review of the feedback from day one. Cady introduced the open space format by describing what occurred the previous evening that led to the eight Breakthrough "HOW" Ideas.

Each of the ideas had two or more of the table representatives serving as conveners. Their charge was to passionately present the idea in the center of the Open Space.

(Photo 2) *The Open Space Technology room and an authentic conversation with the Senior Leadership Team.*

As each idea was presented in the center of the open space, it was placed on a wall entitled, "Market Place." The ideas were not complete. Also, the table representatives were convening ideas, not necessarily leading the idea. Each person in the room was to sign up for one idea that they would be willing to put their time and energy toward seeing succeed.

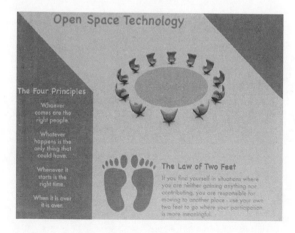

Before leaders went to work on an idea, the Four Principles and the Law of Two Feet were shared with the group. This again reinforced a shift toward collaborative leadership. The idea that a person could sign up for one idea and then choose to move to another idea is critical to ensuring "the feet do the voting." The process is powerful as the ownership and accountability shift to the participants in the room. When someone publicly selects a Breakthrough Idea team and pronounces an idea, others step forward to commit to working on that idea, it is now in their hands to see it through.

One inspiring moment occurred for a group working on a breakthrough HOW idea. Mid way through Day 2, all the work groups reconvened as a whole around the open space to give updates on their progress. They were also invited to present a breakthrough request or question "real time" of the SLT. The intention is that breakthrough results require breakthrough "asks." By this time, the SLT had modeled collaboration and built trust necessary for bold action. The convener asked a hot topic question. He asked the SLT if they agreed on a specific definition on a key concept from an operations perspective (Photo 2.). Rodkin looked at the other SLT members and together responded "no." With that, the room broke out in applause in direct acknowledgement of the leadership's connection with the Leadership Quality of Authenticity. One participant's reaction to the call for authenticity and vulnerability while leading at ConAgra Foods was,

"Just because we have been doing something for 20 years doesn't mean we have been doing it right. At ConAgra Foods we do not do a very good job of change management. We need to be vulnerable, and open to change in order to really look at new ideas and thoughts, to be more effective."

After the updates, the teams went back to their small group work and continued developing concise action plans for the next six months to significantly move their ideas forward. They focused on the key steps, measures, roles, and a timeline for actions. The teams then came back at the end of the day to give their progress report with commitments to action.

Supporting Mechanisms

While each of the elements in DVFS can occur in sequence, they are addressed throughout the process as well. This is particularly applicable with the "S" in that supporting mechanisms were emphasized throughout the two-day meeting. Prior to the event, during the design process, the templates for strategic planning and implementation were incorporated into the process. It was important to connect the Annual Operating Plans (AOPs) with the Must Dos and overall strategic plan.

In setting things up for the work back home after the event, it was essential that there were public pronouncements outlining concrete commitments to action. It ensured everyone got involved and stays focused over time. The difference for a collaborative meeting is purposeful action. Each of the Breakthrough Idea teams reported out on their action plan tied to a clear statement of purpose and outcomes.

Ending on a Good Note

Wrapping up an event is much more than a simple "thank you and good bye." As the meeting drew to a close, Rodkin discussed the importance of follow-through on the ideas being implemented. He gave a date for Breakthrough Idea teams to provide written progress reports (within one month) and then a second date for team leaders to provide an in-person update to the SLT (within two months). Following the meeting, he also identified key SLT members who would serve as champions of each Breakthrough Idea team.

The phrase "thank you" is one of the most powerful acts of leadership. Giving credit is essential to effective delegation. While speaking, Rodkin was handed a slip of paper. One of the divisions in ConAgra Foods was chosen as a supplier of choice for the company's largest customer. The room broke out into applause as Rodkin motioned for the leader to stand. As he stood, the room responded with a standing ovation.

After weeks of design work, advance work, and two days of intense collaborative discussion and action planning, the group left energized and upbeat. They experienced a different kind of meeting, a collaborative meeting, where they witnessed leadership competencies in action, where they co-created a set of ideas they felt passionate about and committed to seeing ConAgra Foods achieve breakthrough performance. When asked about the future of ConAgra after the collaborative event, Rodkin's response was,

"I feel really good that we are going to raise our confidence level,
meaning our ability to actually achieve our objectives and hopefully beat them
because we are going to be thinking and acting differently."

Discussion

1. How would you describe the leader's leadership style? Would you want to work for this style of leader?

2. What was the leader trying to accomplish with this type of meeting?

3. Discuss your understanding of collaborative leadership and how it differs from traditional leadership.

4. Discuss your understanding of the formula for collaborative change. Is there anything you would change about the formula?

5. In large group meetings, what are the benefits of having people sit in mixed groups versus allowing people to sit where they want with people they like?

6. Discuss the four principles of Open Space Technology and explore examples of how you could use this approach in organizations.

7. Evaluate what you liked best and would possibly change about the strategy that was used.

8. What changes in the organization occurred because of this intervention and do you think they will last?

Key Leadership Lessons

1. It takes collaborative leadership to create a collaborative culture. Collaboration cannot be delegated. It starts at the top.

2. Leaders need to explore innovative, effective, and efficient ways to make strategic planning an important and collaborative process.

3. Large group meetings are high payoff/high risk endeavors that require professionals to run.

4. When designing collaborative meetings ask three questions: (1) What is the purpose? (2) Who needs to be involved? (3) What conversations (agenda) need to take place?

5. In large group meetings include those who will be implementing the decisions in the decision-making process. Remember that people support and defend what they help create.

6. Speak honestly and authentically. Transparency shifts the culture and builds trust.

7. Sometimes it is necessary to mandate collaboration. Don't make participation optional.

References

Beckhard, R. & Harris R. (1987) *Organizational Transitions: Managing Complex Change.* Addison-Wesley Publishers.

Cady, S. H. & Dannemiller, K. D. (2005). "Whole System Transformation: The five truths of change." *Practicing Organization Development: A Guide for Consultants, 2005 ed.* (Rothwell, W. J. et al). San Francisco, CA: Jossey-Bass. p. 440-455.

Dannemiller Tyson Associates (2000) *Whole Scale Change: Unleashing The Magic in Organizations.* Berrett Kohler Publishers.

Fortune 500 Annual Rankings of Corporations. Retrieved from: http://money.cnn.com/magazines/fortune/fortune500/2010/snapshots/299.html

Gretzky Quote from Hockey Experience. Retrieved from: http://www.colorpilot.com/typep_famous-quotes.html

Kanter R.M. (2003) *Leadership and The Psychology of Turnarounds.* Harvard Business Review.

McGuire J. B., Palus C. J., Pasmore W. & Rhodes G. B. (2009) *Transforming Your Organization: Global · Organizational Development White Paper Series.* Center For Creative Leadership.

Schumpeter J. (1975) *From Capitalism, Socialism and Democracy.* Harper Publishers.

Tapscott D., Williams A. D. (2006) Wikinomics: How Mass Collaboration Changes Everything. Portfolio Publishers.

Von Bertalanffy L. (1972) *The History and Status of General Systems Theory.* The Academy of Management Journal. The Academy of Management. December 1972, p. 407-426

BIOGRAPHY

Dr. Steve Cady is Graduate Faculty member at Bowling Green State University where he serves as Director of the Institute for Organizational Effectiveness. He has also served as Director of the Master of Organization Development Program and the Chief Editor for the Organization Development Journal. He is author of The Change Handbook, Stepping Stones to Success, and the Life Inspired DVD with WBGU-PBS. Some of his clients include Chrysler, Tavistock Group, Dana Corp., Toledo Diocese Schools, Area Office on Aging, Mercy College, Alcoa, BP, City of Toledo, and Lake Nona. Prior to receiving his Ph.D. in OB with a support area in Research Methods and Psychology from FSU, he studied at the UCF where he obtained an MBA and a BSBA in Finance.

Steven H. Cady
Bowling Green State University
The Cady Group
580 Craig Drive 8-234, Perrysburg, OH 43551
Tel. 419.255.6800 · Email: steve@stevecady.com · www.SteveCady.com

John Hine is the Sr. Director of Organization Development and Learning for ConAgra Foods. His experience as both an internal and external consultant to Fortune 100 firms serves him well in his current role of designing and installing ConAgra Foods learning infrastructure, as well as consulting on change initiatives, and implementing learning. Prior to joining ConAgra, John held positions with Ford Motor Company, Provant and AchieveGlobal providing learning solutions, implementation support and organization design and process consulting. John holds a business degree from Michigan State University and a master's degree in Organization Development from Bowling Green State University.

John Hine
Senior Director of Organization Development & Learning
ConAgra Foods
One ConAgra Drive, M/S 1-120, Omaha, NE 68102
Tel. 402.240.5696 · Email: john.hine@conagrafoods.com

BIOGRAPHY

Jonathan Meenach is a graduate of the Bowling Green State University Master of Organization Development program and has his Bachelor of Science Degree in Exercise Science from Miami University. His has coached on all levels within an organization, from C level executives all the way to individual contributors for clients such as Kroger, Medtronic, Nationwide Insurance, and Chevron. His areas of expertise include leadership development, career development, stress management, and personal health, wellness, and productivity. Clients he has engaged with include ConAgra Foods, Mercy College, Patrick Henry Local School District, as well as the City of Toledo Department of Public Service.

Jonathan Meenach
Director of Business Development & Services
The Cady Group
580 Craig Drive 8-234, Perrysburg, OH 43551

Tel. 419.255.6800 · Email: Jonathan@thecadygroup.com

John Spalding has a master's degree in Organization Development from Bowling Green State University and participated in the Dannemiller - Whole Systems Practicum in 2003. Some of the organizations John has worked with include University Christian Fellowship, The City of Detroit Health Department, Clarcor/TFS, The Sisters of Notre Dame Schools, Dana Corporation, and G1NBC.com. John has management experience in the field of MR/DD and Youth Development. John as teaches Industrial Organizational Psychology at Owens Community College. In addition, he has conducted various service research initiatives for retail organizations and in education as a learning and literacy consultant.

John Spalding
Organization Development Consultant
S&G Endeavors
670 Islington Street,Toledo, OH 43610
Tel. 614-519-5867 · Email: g1ntol@gmail.com

CHAPTER SIX

1

Leadership In A Turnaround Situation And A Multicultural Environment

----

Dr. Lloyd Gibson and Dr. Regina Gibson

Major Focus Of The Case

Leadership style in a turnaround situation, especially in a multi-cultural environment, is very important to the success of the organization. As the organization is transformed to a successful one, the leader may have to adapt his or her style. This case focuses on the leadership of a new CEO recruited to overcome a crisis situation in a small community bank. The CEO also faced the additional challenges of being from a different culture than the most of his employees and of interacting with the founder and previous CEO who had quite a different leadership style. In the process of turning around the bank and implementing a new strategy for the bank, the new CEO also transformed his leadership style in order to reduce anxiety and gain the respect and confidence of the employees, the board of directors, and the community.

Introduction

In a business turnaround situation, a multicultural environment can affect the way leaders address the responsibilities of leadership. The tried and tested leadership approaches might not be effective, especially when a leader has been recruited for a business turnaround and transplanted into a culture with values different than his or her own.

New practices may need to be adopted by business leaders in order to deal with the challenges of managing and leading employees with a different culture, and various models, such as Hofstede's four cultural dimensions model (1991), have been suggested as a basis in the study of culture and leadership. In situations of cultural diversity, however, the leadership model which has been recently used as a framework for new leaders (Robinson and Harvey, 2008) is the "Personal and Corporate Values Journey Chart" (Robinson, 2002) derived from the early work of Don Beck and Christopher Cowan (1996) of the National Values Center, Texas, USA.

This model charts the changes in leadership style of a new leader in a multicultural environment. According to this model, the accumulated experience and knowledge of the new leader results in progress along the values journey, and movement along the chart results in a type of "creative tension" (Senge, 1990, p. 9). As shown in a simplified version of the Values Journey Chart in **Figure 1**, creative tensions result in six leadership styles or stages which may be plotted at specific points on the Values Journey Chart. These leadership stages, as described in **Table 1**, are: (1) Paternal, (2) Tough, (3) Authoritarian, (4) Entrepreneurial, (5) Facilitative, and (6) Synergistic. This model will be helpful in analyzing the leadership style of a new CEO in the case of a struggling Chinese American community bank.

Figure 1:

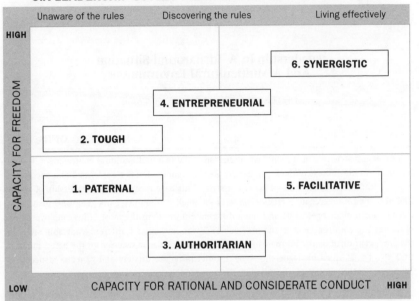

SIX LEADERSHIP STYLES FROM THE VALUES JOURNEY CHART

Table 1:

SUMMARY OF LEADERSHIP STAGES

LEADERSHIP STAGES	APPROACH	REINFORCEMENT	CULTURE	MOTIVATING NEED
1. PATERNAL	Provide safety	Survival	Submissive	Security
2. TOUGH	Force	Self-reliance	Egocentric	Independence
3. AUTHORITARIAN	Instruct	Conformity	Duty-compliant	Stability
4. ENTREPRENEURIAL	Delegate	Affluence	Success-striving	Achievement
5. FACILITATIVE	Facilitate	Peace	Harmony-seeking	Sustainability
6. SYNERGISTIC	Integrate	Flexibility	Synergy-seeking	Sustainability

Background

The situation addressed in this case involves a community bank in a large Midwestern city. The owners, employees, and customers of this bank were primarily Chinese American. The bank was founded and led by a Chinese American with no previous banking background. At the time of this case, the bank was operating under a written agreement with the state and federal regulators, and the directors were facing monetary penalties as a result of non-compliance with the written agreement. Approximately 90% of the employees, more than 90% of the customers, and two-thirds of the board of directors were Chinese American. English was the third or fourth language for most of the Chinese American employees. The Chinese American employees were accustomed to an autocratic approach by the previous CEO and almost none of them had any experience in banking outside of their experience at this bank.

The bank was unprofitable and suffering losses of more than $100 thousand per month. The Chinese American individual who was the founder, Chairman, President, and CEO since the bank was formed more than 15 years before, had been recently required by the regulators to step down as the President and CEO and a search firm was hired to find a new President/CEO. The Board's preference was for the new leader to be a local Chinese American and an experienced banker who was familiar with the type of regulatory issues the bank faced. There were no candidates who met all of these requirements and the board used a search firm to identify potential candidates. Finally, the three members of the search committee recommended a candidate who was Caucasian and non-local, but had significant banking experience, particularly as it related to this bank's situation. The new CEO was then hired as the result of a split vote by the board members.

First Stages of New CEO Leadership

The new President and CEO could not officially start work until the Board obtained approval from the regulatory agencies, both state and federal. The regulators included the state banking agency, the Federal Reserve, and the FDIC. Upon receiving a contingent job offer from the Board, the new leader came in from out-of-town by plane and went from the airport to a taxi cab to the board room and straight into a meeting with the regulators about the bank's situation. In this meeting the regulators listed the problems they thought should be addressed and they threatened possible monetary fines and penalties for the board members.

After hearing the issues raised, the new leader, who was not yet officially in the position of President and CEO, immediately began to negotiate with the regulators and asked for up to 90 days to make initial changes and address selected issues. The regulators agreed and told him that they would fast-track the process by which the bank would receive their approval for him to start work, given the precarious position of the bank. However, it took two weeks to obtain all necessary approvals. The new President came in as an observer during these two weeks without pay. During this time the new leader identified and prioritized the problems that had to be addressed. Four of these problems had already been identified by the regulators and were included in the written agreement between the bank and regulatory agencies: (1) lack of appropriate governance by the board of directors, (2) non-compliance with regulations, (3) poor asset quality, and (4) poor asset/liability management. Clearly the losses being experienced by the bank were a critical issue, but it was necessary to look at the underlying causes. The losses were the result of bad loans requiring additional expense to increase the loan loss reserve, operating expenses far in excess of what was appropriate for a community bank of that size, and general mismanagement coupled with an inability to address regulatory issues.

Beyond the above mechanical problems, there were issues around communication and trust both within the bank and between the bank and the outside world, including its customers, the regulators, and the local community. This made it extremely important that the new leader quickly establish both credibility and a rapport with all of the relevant constituencies: employees, directors, regulators, customers, and community groups. In order to accomplish this, the new leader had to overcome language and cultural differences between him and his constituents. During this process the new leader also had to create a team where one had not existed in order to address all of the problems identified.

Acknowledging The Leadership Style Of The Founder

The founder had started the bank with an entrepreneurial approach working with certain board and community members by filling a niche, Chinese Americans, who were underserved. His leadership style then changed to one that was authoritarian and remained so at the time of the case. The developments over the previous year leading to the written agreement with the regulators had created a very stressful environment for all of the employees and the directors. Even after the founder was removed from his position, many employees still looked at him as being in charge. The employees were used to him being an autocratic leader who would often embarrass them in public and change his mind as to what he wanted them to do. However, there were a few knowledgeable employees who ran the bank on a day-to-day basis in spite of this lack of leadership.

The Changing Leadership Style Of The New CEO

The new CEO entered the situation that was previously described with the goal of turning the company around as he had done with another community bank several years earlier. He had also been involved in other turnarounds within larger organizations. He took pride in being able to complete these successful turnarounds while working primarily with the existing staff in an honest and straightforward manner and maintaining a high level of integrity. However, he was also willing to make the tough decisions to cut costs, reorganize, and make appropriate changes to address the particular situation while building a successful team. He exhibited a tough leadership style the first day he walked into the bank by negotiating an agreement with the regulators to allow the bank at least 90 days to address existing problems by gaining their initial trust and confidence and quickly laying out a plan as to how these problems would be addressed. However, in order to put together such a plan, he spent his first two weeks before officially starting as CEO to get to know the employees and the bank better. He then developed a plan with goals and milestones for addressing the most pressing problems facing the bank. The new leader quickly developed a reputation as being highly intelligent and knowledgeable in banking and gained respect within the bank. At this point he used a combination of tough and authoritarian leadership styles as he established himself in what was a crisis situation. As part of this approach, he had to negotiate with outside consultants, businesses with problem loans, and the banking regulators. He also had to create a new management team in order to successfully implement the turnaround plan. This included a change in the board, the hiring of a new CFO from the outside, and some internal changes in management. All of this had to be accomplished while restoring the community's confidence in the bank.

The new CEO realized that the new management team, which included the new CFO and other internal officers, had to be confident and willing to carry out the turnaround plan. In order to develop his new team, the new CEO began having weekly meetings with senior management and held meetings with all employees by traveling to their offices. In this way, he maintained a much higher level of visibility and interaction with the employees than his predecessor. The initial plan was successful and the regulators upgraded the bank after 90 days. In the next 90 days the bank was able to reduce operating costs by renegotiating contracts, selling off one of their buildings, and reducing staff by 20%. This was an extremely difficult time, but the bank was returned to operating profitability within six months and regained the confidence of community members while producing organic growth in the bank's retail business for the first time in more than a year.

During his first several months, the new CEO also began to teach himself both Mandarin and Cantonese phrases and attended many Chinese New Year celebrations. Later, he and his wife, and sometimes daughters, attended Chinese dinners, dragon boat races, and charity events, including a Miss Chinatown contest, with his employees and the founder and his wife. The new CEO and his wife even walked in a Chinese Community Day parade with other VIP's in the Chinese American community. Employees, the board members, and the many of the bank's customers were encouraged to attend these events. Although, his Chinese was limited to a few words and phrases, the new CEO attempted to speak Chinese to his employees whenever possible, and also began to preface his reports to the shareholders with a short introduction in Chinese. As a result, the employees, some members of the Board, and the Chinese American community grew to know and become comfortable with the new CEO.

At times, in order to accomplish the turnaround goals, it was necessary for the new leader to adopt a more paternalistic style toward his employees. At many stages in the turnaround process, it was important that the employees and directors felt safe and secure, particularly after the reduction in staff and the sale of the building. It was also important to the new CEO that everyone bond together for survival to create a team going forward.

Eventually, the CEO's leadership style became entrepreneurial as a longer range plan was developed with the board of directors and senior management. The focus at the later stages of the turnaround was to develop and implement a successful business plan designed to grow the bank. Once this plan was developed, the CEO made additional efforts to communicate more with the employees in order to facilitate discussions about the implementation of the plan throughout the bank. Suggestions from the employees for the new business plan were beginning to be considered as the bank continued to be profitable. However, at this point it was announced that the bank was being sold.

References

Beck, Don E. and Cowan, Christopher C. (1996). *Spiral dynamics: Mastering values, leadership, and change.* Oxford: Blackwell Publishers.

Hofstede, Geert H. (1991). *Cultures and organizations: Software of the mind.* London: McGraw Hill.

Robinson, David A. (2002). *A phenomenological study of how entrepreneurs experience and deal with ethical dilemmas,* PhD thesis, Rhodes University, Grahamstown.

Robinson, David A. and Harvey, Michael (2008). Global leadership in a culturally diverse world. *Management Decision,* 46(3), 466-480.

Senge, Peter M. (1990). The leaders' new work: Building learning organizations. *Sloan Management Review,* 32 (1), 7-23.

Discussion

1. Evaluate the board's decision to bring in a CEO from outside the company, outside the area, and from a different culture. When is it appropriate for boards to hire CEOs from outside and what should they look for considering that making a wrong choice can have far reaching consequences.

2. Using Figure 1 and Table 1 as a reference, describe the leadership styles of the founder and the new CEO.

3. If a board of directors hired you to turn a company with a culture different than yours around, what would be the first three things you would do to address the situation?

4. What valuable lessons can you learn from the new CEO and how he helped change the bank, manage the change process, and make the bank successful?

5. In a technical sense, style describes a person's approach to relating to others. Some experts would say that the new CEO had a consistent leadership style but was changing his leadership skills with different situations. Was the new CEO actually changing his style or his skills and how would you respond to a leader who changes styles with different situations?

Key Leadership Lessons

1. It is very important for leaders to understand their leadership style and its consequences as the implications can be far reaching.

2. In a multicultural environment, and especially in a turnaround situation, leaders are key to improving communication and confidence in the organization. It is very important for leaders to take the time to study and learn to effectively work with cultures that may be different from their own.

3. A turnaround situation can result in high stress levels for everyone involved. The wrong leadership style can result in even more anxiety which may affect morale and performance. The leader must always be aware of the impact of his/her leadership style and be willing to adapt to new situations.

BIOGRAPHY

Dr. Lloyd Gibson has 28 years of banking experience, including 14 years as the president and CEO of three different community banks. Included in this experience were two successful turnarounds of problem banks. He has also worked as a senior credit officer, chief lending officer, and head of commercial lending. Dr. Gibson obtained both his Bachelor of Science and Master of Arts degrees in mathematics from the University of Pittsburgh. He earned his Master of Business Administration degree with a major in finance and public management from The Wharton School of Business. He received his Doctor of Science in Information Systems and Communications from Robert Morris University. Dr. Gibson has taught courses in management and strategic management. In addition to his current position at Stratford University, Dr. Gibson serves as a trustee on the board of Pittsburgh History and Landmarks Foundation. Dr. Gibson and his wife, Dr. Regina Gibson, have written several papers together including one entitled "Chinese American Online Banking: Multicultural Acceptance of Information Technology," which received the Best Paper Award in the research category at the 49th Annual Conference of the International Association for Computer Information Systems in October of 2009.

Lloyd G. Gibson, D.Sc.
Dean, School of Business
Stratford University
7777 Leesburg Pike, Falls Church, VA 22043

Tel. 703 821 8570 · Email: lgibson@stratford.edu

Dr. Regina Gibson is the President of Gibson Research and Consulting and also serves as an adjunct professor in the Business School at Stratford University in Falls Church, Virginia. As a professional engineer, her experience has included engineering and economic analyses for the oil and petrochemical industry. Dr. Gibson obtained her Bachelor of Science degree in chemical engineering and chemistry from Carnegie Mellon University, her Master of Business Administration degree with a concentration in management and entrepreneurship from The Wharton School of Business, and a Doctor of Science degree in Information Systems and Communications from Robert Morris University. Her research has included studies of entrepreneurial attitudes, technology acceptance, and online mentoring.

Regina Ann Gibson, D.Sc.
President, Gibson Research and Consulting
Adjunct Professor, Stratford University
Email: gibsonresearch@gmail.com

2

Award Winning Leadership: A Case Study Of Saudi Chamber Of Commerce - Eastern Province

Vijayalaxmi Moovala

Major Focus Of The Case

This case study focuses on the leadership style of the Secretary General of Saudi Chamber of Commerce: Eastern Province, Adnan Abdullah Al Nueim, who brought about significant changes in the Chamber, and transformed the bureaucratic, traditional work environment into a customer friendly, proactive, and service oriented one. Under the dynamic leadership of Adnan, the Chamber received awards for the best work environment (2008 & 2009) in Saudi Arabia among all non-profit organizations. It also won the award for best customer care (2008) in the government sector. Adnan, himself was given the award of Corporate Management CEO of the Year (2009) in the semi- government sector of the Middle East. The case highlights the strategic management and human resources mechanisms of the Chamber. A profile of the leader, style, qualities, values and, people orientation is outlined. The factors that contributed to the Chamber winning the prestigious awards in the Middle East region form a part of the case.

Saudi Chamber of Commerce: Eastern Province

The Saudi Chamber of Commerce[1]: Eastern Province, a semi-government service organization in the Kingdom of Saudi Arabia, was established in 1952. The Chamber's vision was to lead the development of Eastern Province[2], the largest province in Saudi Arabia, through effective mobilization of resources and diversification of economy. Under the dynamic leadership of the Secretary General, Adnan Abdullah Al Nueim, the Chamber which had an employee strength of 215 including 11 women [in July 2010], was poised to scale great heights in the professional corporate world through its leadership effectiveness and management practices.

Best CEO of the Year

Adnan, a 38-year old, dynamic, and well-educated Saudi national, joined the Chamber in 2003 in a supervisory position, and within a short span of four years was promoted to the position of a Secretary General. He was adjudged as the **"Corporate Management CEO of the Year" – 2009**[3], by the *Middle East Excellence Awards Institute* which was the platform to recognize achievements of professionals and organizations from the region. This award honored the distinct achievements of Adnan, who as a leader brought about significant changes in the Chamber, by establishing strategic direction and building professional management teams. The tipping point in favor of Adnan was the successful implementation of an executive/management

1 www.chamber.org.sa
2 Eastern Province covers more than 36% of Saudi Arabia's total area. Its coastline, over the centuries, has served as a vital link in East-West trade.
3 http://www.meawards.com/criteria.asp?awardid=574

development program, which resulted in a noticeable improvement in attracting and retaining executive talent, and enhancing employee productivity/ performance at the Chamber. In addition, the coaching/ mentoring processes, employee incentive programs, and a fair performance management system that were implemented in the Chamber played a role in Adnan getting the award.

Strategic leadership and core values

On assuming the leadership position in 2007, Adnan set about with the most important task of formulating the vision, mission and core values of the Chamber. The strategic focus of the Chamber was on five key areas:

1. Membership [subscription]
2. Products/ services provision
3. Business development and investment
4. Internal business environment
5. Financial resources

Objectives were determined in the five strategic areas and quarterly reviews were conducted. In these reviews: (i) the content and context of the achievement of objectives were analyzed, (ii) accountability of assistant secretary generals/ managers was highlighted, and (iii) future action plans were agreed upon. Adnan fostered a positive, flexible and progressive work environment in the Chamber. He created a team culture and highlighted the slogan: **Working Together for a Better Future**. The core values espoused by the Chamber were:

• Trust and Integrity
• Customer Service
• Commitment
• Professional Excellence
• Accepting Responsibility
• Group Work
• Gratitude & Appreciation

Employees of the Chamber believed that core values depict the behavior of the organization and hence, should be implemented and exhibited.

Management Philosophy

A personal interview conducted [by the author] with Adnan provided valuable insights into his leadership thoughts and philosophy. His vision was for the Chamber to be ranked among the top five in the world. Adnan's passion for institutional building was evidenced through the shared vision, shared values, shared decision-making, and human capital development at the Chamber.

Adnan's motto:
'Leaders should have the vision and create the right culture."

The coaching process initiated in the Chamber was a reflection of this philosophy. On one end of this spectrum, was the encouragement given to employees to be ambitious, positive-minded, and enhance their professionalism. On the other end, was the responsibility assigned to managers to develop their successors and empower their subordinates. Adnan encouraged employees to have the drive, initiative, ambition, and demonstrate competencies to compete in the global/ complex environment. He acknowledged and welcomed anyone who aspired and aimed to occupy his position, which indicated a mature, positive, and confident leadership style.

Adnan followed the maxim:
'A good leader develops other leaders and not followers'

An interesting dual approach leadership model practiced by Adnan was that the organization must provide opportunities and create the right environment, to enhance employees' professionalism and objective achievement. The successful formula that was being implemented in the Chamber was:

Figure 1:

ADNAN'S DUAL APPROACH LEADERSHIP MODEL

Organizational approach ⇓	**Leads to** ⇢	**Employee approach** ⇓
[Provide Opportunities + Create Right Environment]		*[Enhanced Professionalism + Objective Achievement]*

Adnan emphasized that his role:

'......is to transfer the vision and guide employees. Employees are highly capable key players in organizational objective achievement. The effective way to gain support for corporate strategy is through employees' involvement and participation. I cannot do anything alone; I am here to support the staff. My time in the Chamber is for employees and subscribers. I can always check emails and catch up with other work after office ours.' [4]

Employee Participation In Decision Making

Adnan had established a strategic committee of thirteen members, including the five assistant secretary generals as permanent members. To ensure employees' participation in strategic decision making/ management, three members of the committee were selected from the non-managerial employees. To encourage women participation in management, one lady employee was selected as a member of the strategic committee. The role of this committee was to formulate and monitor the implementation of the Chamber's strategic framework.

Adnan conducted weekly meetings with the five *assistant secretary generals*. He also conducted joint monthly meetings with *assistant secretary generals* and *department heads*. The minutes of both these meetings, and the monthly activity reports submitted by all departments were posted on the Chamber's intranet which could be accessed by all employees. This was a good management practice endorsing the leadership commitment towards shared vision and values, where the top management believed that employees, irrespective of their hierarchical level, were entitled to know the strategic decision making, and happenings at top management meetings.

This was keeping in line with the management dictum:
'Strategy must descend from the boardroom to the shop floor/customer counters.''

---

4 Excerpt from an interview [conducted by the author] with Adnan on 18th July 2010 at the Chamber in the Kingdom of Saudi Arabia.

Transparency And Open Communication

The Chamber conducted 'employee opinion' surveys annually. A specially instituted committee monitored the surveys, analyzed the findings and prepared the results/ feedback report. The feedback report included a summary sheet in which the suggestions/ complaints/ comments of employees, **even those related to Adnan,** were copied verbatim. The feedback report was circulated to all employees in the Chamber, thereby demonstrating a transparent and open communication style [the original feedback sheets submitted by employees were handed over to the Chairman of the Board]. Adnan addressed issues/ concerns raised in the survey by writing a comment/ solution, and sending it to every employee.

Adnan responded to emails sent to him directly by employees, by personally looking into the issue and/ or assigning the responsibility to the concerned person. Adnan sent short messages of appreciation and personal thanks to employees on their mobiles about their achievements. These messages were forwarded to all other employees, as well. Any good work done by employees was acknowledged by Adnan through appreciation letters and personal emails. Trends such as these endeared Adnan to his employees who contributed to his nomination for the **best corporate management CEO award - 2009.**

Human Capital Development

A noteworthy human capital development initiative undertaken by Adnan was the establishment of a *career development section* in August 2009. The main function of this section which reported directly to him, was to focus on and review key human resources mechanisms; particularly job descriptions, job placement, career and succession planning in the Chamber. A strong believer in 'continuing learning' as a tool for professional success, Adnan encouraged lifelong learning through the *continuing learning program.* This program aimed at raising the level of education and skills of employees. Financial support and moral encouragement were provided to employees interested in developing themselves and furthering their career prospects.

The main challenge that the Chamber faced was with unplanned and unexpected requests/ demands from subscribers. These challenges were overcome through out-of-the-box thinking and empowerment. An 'Excellence and Innovation' program was formulated which was aimed at encouraging employees to be innovative and creative. As a result of this, a healthy competition and open environment existed in the Chamber where employees were empowered to think independently, and those who contributed to this program were also rewarded. The value addition process in the Chamber was mutual; in which the Chamber added value to the employees by enhancing their professionalism and the employees in turn, added value to the Chamber, through their work efficacy and excellent customer care.

In the Chamber, employee development costs were viewed
as human capital investment.

Customer Care Orientation And Excellence

In a major revamp, the Chamber was rebranded, publicized, and projected as a unique, high quality, user friendly, service provider. Adnan was instrumental in the Chamber reaching high standards of customer service through a two pronged approach. On one hand, it focused on customer care and service dimensions which involved offering high-quality customized programs, and services addressing specific issues and individual needs through various outlets.

On the other hand, the Chamber focused on the vital link in the customer service chain, the service personnel/ providers. Employees of the Chamber were well-trained to serve customers and work with partners. The customers of the Chamber traditionally called members were renamed as *subscribers*, which contributed to a major positive change in the mindset among employees about customer care. Subscribers were treated according to their specific needs and, their complaints were viewed as feedback.

The testimony of the customer care orientation exhibited by the Chamber was the customer care award received by it. The Chamber received the **"Best Government Customer Care Award"** [5] for 2008 in the Middle East, for its exemplary performance in serving the public. This award was given by *The Middle East Excellence Awards Institute* on the consideration of not only the customer care services, but also the over-all influence of customer care of the Chamber in the nominated government organization.

Best Work Environment

The leadership style and management practices that prevailed in the Chamber contributed to it being adjudged [among all non-profit organizations] as the **'Best Saudi company to work for'** [6], for two consecutive years, i.e. 2008 & 2009. The award was given by *TeamOne Consulting and the Saudi Research and Publishing Group,* which conducted a survey related to management/leadership style, key human resources mechanisms, and the level of employee satisfaction with the Chamber.

The Chamber focused on good human resources practices to create the best work environment. It instituted 'employee of the month' awards for rewarding employees with outstanding performance, and the 'perfect manager' award to develop managerial competence and ensure that managers followed the best practices in terms of goal achievement and people management.

Award Winning Characteristics

A learned and enlightened leader, Adnan wrote a weekly column in the economic section of the local daily newspaper *ALYAUM* [Today][7] about business related topics. A visionary and a strategist with a focused approach and goal orientation, Adnan exhibited maturity, intellectual development and understanding of people management. He had an open door policy and believed in working in close proximity with every employee. He established personal rapport with employees and learnt from their expertise. Adnan was a role model and led by example. Some personal characteristics that came across strongly were his generosity, warmth, tolerance, and patience. He was unpretentious, had a pleasant disposition, and was accessible to employees.

Adnan had the judicious blend of objective achievement and people orientation.'

Embodiment Of Core Values

Adnan through his leadership had created an organizational culture conducive to employees' exhibiting professional behavior and living by the core values. The trust of employees in the leadership and integrity of Adnan was reflected in the award received by him as the *corporate management CEO of the year-2009.* Winning the *best customer care award - 2008,* indicated that the leaders and employees of the Chamber, walked the talk, by providing excellent **customer service.** **Commitment, responsibility, group work** and **professional excellence** prevalent in the Chamber contributed to it being the best Saudi company to work for. **Gratitude** and **appreciation** that the Chamber showed towards its internal customers, in the form of a healthy work-life balance and professional environment, helped in the provision of excellent customer service to its external customers. Succession planning, coaching, and other progressive measures highlighted in

5 http://www.meawards.com/criteria.asp?awardid=464
6 http://www.bestsaudicompany.com/en/home_en.aspx
7 A daily newspaper published in Arabic from the Kingdom of Saudi Arabia.

this case, were an indication of professional excellence and people orientation that the top management of the Chamber valued.

Discussion

1. Describe the characteristics of Adnan's leadership style that created such a successful organization.

2. As a leader what are specifics that Adnan did to build an award winning organization.

3. Discuss what you like and then anything you would change about the vision, mission, and core values Adnan established.

4. Discuss your understanding of **Adnan's dual approach leadership model.**

5. Assess Adnan's people orientation with special reference to employees' participation in management and his open and transparent communication style.

6. What would be the major lessons you would want to learn from Adnan's approach to leadership and to building a highly successful organization?

Key Leadership Lessons

1. The style in which you lead is just as important as the things you do as a leader.

2. Top leadership direction that includes and encourages employees' participation in the strategic framework of the organization, leads to success. Organizations need to translate strategic plans and decisions into understandable terms and disseminate them to all employees in the organization. The practices in the *Saudi Chamber of Commerce: Eastern Province* of employee participation in decision making and open communication were noteworthy, and indicated top management commitment towards employees' involvement in strategic decision-making and implementation.

3. Implementation of the strategic framework and goal achievement are possible through employees' contribution and individual achievements. An effective leadership strikes the right balance between task achievement and people orientation. Adnan's leadership style exhibited a judicious blend of task orientation and people management, making him an effective leader.

4. Customer care and excellent service is very important for any organization's success. The right formula is to focus on internal customers [employees], who will provide the best service to external customers, who in turn will contribute to the profit margin. Leadership of the Chamber ensured that employees were developed, appreciated and taken care of. This helped in the provision of excellent customer service that the Chamber was recognized for.

5. Human capital development mechanisms pave the way for the survival and growth of organizations. Employees are the best assets of any organization. Implementing career development and succession plans provide the right impetus for the continuity of expertise and effective leadership in organizations. Adnan focused on management development programs and succession planning that ensured the availability of leadership and expertise in the Chamber. This endorsed his effectiveness as a leader, whose focus was on identifying and developing potential leaders.

BIOGRAPHY

Dr. Vijayalaxmi Moovala holds a Master's degree in Business Administration and a
Doctorate in Business Management from India. She has a certificate in psychometric
(occupational) testing: SHL [UK] and is a certified Master trainer of Neuro-Linguistic
Psychology [USA]. Dr. Vijaya has over 20 years of experience in management training
and consulting. She started her career as a Management Consultant and University
faculty member teaching M.B.A. students. Her expertise is in the areas of *human capital
development, applied managerial psychology, strategic and general management.*
She has extensive experience in facilitating management training and development
programs for supervisors and managers of different organizations in India, Kingdom
of Bahrain and other Gulf countries. Dr. Vijaya has provided leadership and guidance
to several human capital development projects. She is research oriented and has
published several management articles in renowned journals. She believes in
self-development and lifelong learning.

Dr. Vijayalaxmi Moovala
Program Manager
Center for Leadership & Management
Bahrain Institute of Banking & Finance
PO Box: 20525, Juffair, Kingdom of Bahrain
Mobile: +973-39263810 · Email: vijaya@bibf.com mvijaya@hotmail.com

3

Monica's Mandate:
Going For Lead Plant Status

Paul Coughlan & David Coghlan

Major Focus of the Case

This case shows the passion for excellence that a visionary leader had as she committed to improvement after improvement in spite of almost overwhelming odds. Monica Moran managed to keep her plant focused, motivated, and involved as she exhibited an excellent understanding of leadership in achieving goals that would have discouraged many leaders. Much can be learned from learning from the leadership skills she exhibited in this case.

Introduction

Monica Moran, Plant Manager at PPM Limited, reflected on the strategic operations improvement initiative which had taken up the past two years. She had exploited methodically opportunities to improve customer value at lower producer cost. In December 2007, Monica began to plan for a post initiative review to evaluate the achievements and to identify opportunities for further improvement. Ultimately, Monica was ambitious to achieve lead plant status for her plant.

In February 2005, PPM had become a subsidiary of a US multinational corporation competing in Europe. The corporation had been under pressure for a number of years from its European distributors to set up a manufacturing plant in Europe. The European distributors were losing out on business opportunities due to long lead times, poor service and the relative strength of the US dollar. The corporation was not interested in starting a new plant, even though some European governments had offered set-up grants. It had explored European companies but, with the exception of PPM, could not find any that would fit with its manufacturing expertise and culture. PPM had been a supplier to the corporation for ten years, manufacturing some of their product for the European market. In addition, Ireland was an English speaking country, with lower manufacturing costs than the USA, and a low corporation tax rate.

Strategic Operations Improvement in PPM

Since 2006, Monica had led an improvement initiative, directed towards a desired future state of the company to become a lead plant within the corporation. During this period, she had designed, developed and implemented an operations improvement program and enacted two *action research cycles* to achieve measurable improvements in manufacturing excellence. Each action research cycle was comprised of a pre-step and four basic steps – *diagnosing, planning action, taking action, and evaluating action.*

> **Cycle 1:** Confirming the role of operations in PPM
> **Cycle 2:** Broadening service to the European market and getting to know the
> European distributors

By the end of cycle 2, PPM had gained an unprecedented level of manufacturing excellence. It was beginning to understand what competing in the industry meant. It had developed a capability to counter the value added migration contributing to the fragile nature of their earlier competitiveness. Now, PPM had to consider how to add value upstream and downstream in order to achieve lead plant status. Monica reflected on her achievements to date.

CYCLE 1: Confirming The Role Of Operations In PPM

Issue/Problem

The vision of PPM was to achieve profitable growth through delivering superior customer value at lower producer cost. This vision was to be achieved by moving from a source-manufacturing site, through contributor to a lead plant within the corporation. By leading the effort to transform the plant, Monica and her senior management team were trying to prepare the company "to set new industry standards, to redefine what is possible, and to forever change the terms of competition". The initial issue was that PPM was too far down the value chain from its customers. It did not know the distributors or end users of the product. Also, the European market viewed PPM as an inferior manufacturing site relative to the corporation's US-based manufacturing facilities.

Pre-Step - Context and Purpose

In 2006, a value chain analysis confirmed that PPM was currently the market leader. The primary activity, operations, was characterised by proprietary manufacturing expertise based on in-house developed process equipment and patented product designs. Underpinning this activity was an infrastructure where quality assurance, cost control, dependability and product line breadth were competitive. Further, the total installed cost of the facility was low and product support to customers was available on a global basis.

An exploration of value-add migration outlined the fragile nature of this market leadership position. It was felt that there would be a decline in the amount of value added in manufacturing as the industry moved manufacturing to lower labor cost countries. Yet, as currently organized, PPM was not in a position to add value upstream - through design and development - or downstream - through customer service and marketing. The purpose of the strategic operations improvement initiative was now clear.

Diagnosing

In January 2007 the division president, the European sales director and Monica met to discuss the emerging perceptions in the European market that PPM's conformance quality and processes were inferior to the corporation's US-based manufacturing facilities. They were concerned that market share in Europe would fall if PPM did not achieve the current ISO quality management system requirements for the design and development, production and, when relevant, installation and service of their products. The European market leaders had devised this technical quality standard and had decreed that, by 2007, this standard would become an order qualifier.

Planning Action

Following the above analysis, Monica outlined the issue and the vision for the improvement initiative to the division president and the PPM management team and, together, they came up with an action plan:

- Gaining accreditation to the new ISO quality standard
- Adding processes similar to the US-based manufacturing facilities
- Hosting at PPM of the divisional European distributors sales meeting planned for June 2007
- Hosting visits from technical sales team at PPM

The action phase of this cycle was planned to take place over three months, between April and June 2007.

Taking action

In April 2007, Monica authorized the purchase of a state-of-the-art heat treatment furnace to allow PPM to become more flexible in response to customer requests for samples and internal test results. Eighty percent of products produced at PPM were heat-treated and, so, having this capability in-house was essential in controlling costs and quality, particularly for automotive industry customers. The furnace would enable PPM to have the same finishing operations as the corporation's US-based manufacturing facilities and, so, to gain the confidence of European customers.

In May 2007, PPM gained ISO accreditation after nine months of planning and changing the current system. Back in September 2006, Monica had set up a project team to achieve this standard. Led by a quality engineer, the team included the engineering manager, the purchasing manager, the operations manager and a number of engineers.

While neither of the achievements had brought PPM closer to the customer or won new business, Monica saw them as stepping-stones to achieving the overall vision. Then, in June 2007, she hosted the European distributors sales meeting. PPM now had its first opportunity to show the distributors the manufacturing facility and the new heat treatment furnace. Further, Monica could announce officially that PPM had gained the ISO accreditation. As importantly, she could get to know the distributors.

Evaluating Action

The facilities improvement and quality accreditation confirmed that PPM could compete. The quality of the underlying manufacturing process approach was key to competitiveness and there had to be a concerted move towards continuous improvement, cost improvement and manufacturing excellence. Having attained the ISO accreditation, PPM was ahead of most European suppliers, ahead of all suppliers at their level in the supply chain and ahead of the corporation's US-based manufacturing facilities. Finally, hosting the European distributors sales meeting gave Monica her first opportunity to meet the distributors and to show them the PPM facility.

CYCLE 2: Broadening Service To The European Market And Getting To Know The European Distributors

Pre-Step - Context and Purpose

The actions in cycle 1, while successful, had taken PPM only as far as meeting with the European distributors on a credible basis of quality in operations. Monica now had to agree with the distributors on how to progress the vision of profitable growth through strategic operations improvement. Cycle 2 developed this action.

Diagnosing

During the European distributors sales meeting, Monica had targeted the German distributor and had described an initiative to achieve customer intimacy in their geographical segment of the market. In the resulting discussion, they had reviewed the European market against their vision, and had identified a new action program.

Planning Action

Monica, with the German distributor, the European sales director and a number of the PPM management team planned and agreed a course of action. The German distributor outlined operational actions for PPM:

- to install a fully equipped test laboratory to carry out tests and reports for the market
- to hire an applications engineer and a quality test engineer to avoid the delay of going back to the USA for all technical questions

- to install a computer-numerically-controlled machine to enable the manufacture and quick turnaround of customer sample requests
- to install automatic camera inspection systems to ensure uniformity of product and zero defects.

PPM was beginning to learn more about its market, the customers and infrastructural priorities for action. The division president supported and approved the emerging action plan. Monica aimed to implement the action phase of this cycle between July and December 2007.

Taking action

Between July and November 2007, PPM built and equipped a new laboratory to carry out product part approval processes - essential tests and reports required with samples for all new orders from customers. This laboratory would carry out a range of other tasks also required by some customers before quoting and in response to later installation problems. The laboratory was built with a mixture of second hand equipment (transferred from the corporation's US-based manufacturing facilities) and new equipment purchased with the President's approval. There was already a state of the art laboratory in the UK warehouse, which had been servicing the European market. However, with the establishment of the PPM laboratory, the European distributors began to use PPM more and, as a result, Monica supported the establishment of broader and deeper contact between PPM quality team and each of the distributors.

This expansion of the role of the PPM quality team created a need to manage the interface with the distributors. In response, Monica promoted one of the members of the PPM engineering team to the role of applications engineer. This engineer would be the main contact with European customers for new enquiries about potential new business and installation queries about the product. Monica sent this engineer to the corporation's US-based manufacturing facilities for three months of intensive training with their applications engineering team.

Between July and November 2007 also, Monica got corporate approval to purchase a new machine for the manufacture of samples. Delivery was scheduled for May 2008. PPM also received a new inspection machine. So, by the mid 2008, they would be equipped to interact on a broad basis with new European customers and to move closer to the European distributors. However, PPM still did not know their customers.

In December 2007, PPM began to quote and to make samples for large volume German customer projects. Monica established daily contact with the sales team at the German distributor. The provision of samples enabled the German distributor to become involved at the design level of targeted customers. Further, Monica saw that PPM supported the distributor's efforts with creative responses to questions and quick turn-around of samples and quotations.

Evaluation Action

By December 2007, PPM had its own fully trained applications engineer. While this position was supported by the corporation's US-based manufacturing facilities for some issues, PPM now had an in-house applications engineering facility to offer directly to customers. This facility promoted new dialogue with the engineering representatives of the German distributor, who appreciated having a fellow applications engineer in the same time zone.

PPM now had many of the building blocks in place necessary to compete successfully for new business. The actions Monica had taken broadened PPM's service to the European market. She awaited still the delivery of the new capital equipment.

Next Steps

In December 2007, Monica reflected on the achievements over the past two years and to identify opportunities for further improvement. She wondered how best to proceed. The ambition of becoming a lead plant was still alive!

Suggested Readings

Coghlan, D. and Brannick, T. (2010). *Doing action research on your own organization*. 3rd ed. London: Sage.

Delany, E. (2000). Strategic development of the multinational subsidiary through subsidiary Initiative-taking. *Long Range Planning*, 33, 220-244.

Ferdows, K. (1997). Making the most of foreign factories, *Harvard Business Review*, March-April, 73-88,

Ferdows, K. and de Meyer, A. (1990). Lasting improvement in manufacturing, *Journal of Operations Management*, 9 (2), 168-183

Kim, C.W. and Mauborgne, R. (2004). Value innovation: The strategic logic of high growth, *Harvard Business Review*, July-August, 172-180

Discussion

1. Monica was a visionary leader with a passion for excellence. What was her vision and what indications did you see of her passion for excellence?

2. Monica used an Action Research approach to change that is commonly used by organization development professionals (diagnosing reality, collaborative action planning, taking action, and evaluating action). Few leaders are familiar with this process. What are the advantages of this approach for leaders and what are the potential consequences when they skip any of the four steps in planning and implementing changes?

3. Identify and discuss some of the steps Monica took as a leader to lead the change process and keep people focused and motivated in Cycle 1 and Cycle 2.

4. What next steps could Monica take as a leader?

Key Leadership Lessons

1. The most effective leaders are visionary leaders who make the vision clear and have a passion for building something special and accomplishing something special.

2. The Action Research approach gives leaders an effective model for planning and implementing changes. Phase one of the Action Research process (diagnosing reality) especially saves leaders from making unin formed decisions and treating symptoms rather than the real issues.

3. It takes leaders with well thought out philosophies and convictions to persevere when faced with one obstacle after another in accomplishing their goals.

    1) The role of a plant manager in the multi-national subsidiary is a complex one. Frequently, the main competition is within the corporation, where subsidiaries effectively compete within one another on cost and efficiencies in order to ensure that corporate management does not close down a subsidiary plant and transfer operations to a lower cost geographical region.

    2) Changing a plant's mandate and achieving lead plant status requires overt and covert change activities by the plant manager and team.

    3) The process of action research, whereby cycles of action and reflection are engaged, strengthens the ability of the leader to take action, to build coalitions and to anticipate the next steps based upon learning from action.

BIOGRAPHY

Paul Coughlan is Associate Professor of Operations Management at the School of Business, Trinity College Dublin, Ireland. His research interests include continuous improvement of manufacturing and product development practices, services innovation, action learning, action research, and commercialization of university research. With David Coghlan, he has co-authored *Collaborative Strategic Improvement through Network Action Learning* (Elgar, 2011).

Paul Coughlan
School of Business & Innovation Academy, Trinity College, Dublin 2, Ireland
Tel. +353 1 8962327 · Fax: +3531 6799503 · Email: coughlnp@tcd.ie

David Coghlan is Associate Professor of Organization Development at the School of Business, Trinity College Dublin, Ireland and is a Fellow of the College. He specializes in organization development and action research and is active in both communities internationally. Recent co-authored books include: *Organization Change and Strategy* (Routledge, 2006), *Doing Action Research in Your Own Organization* (3rd. Sage, 2010) and co-editor of the four volume set, *The Fundamentals of Organization Development* (Sage, 2010).

David Coghlan
School of Business & Innovation Academy, Trinity College, Dublin 2, Ireland
Tel. +353 1 8962323 · Fax: +3531 6799503 · Email: dcoghlan@tcd.ie

CHAPTER SEVEN

1

Growing As A Leader:
The Role Of Leadership Development And Coaching
At The University Of Western Australia

Shelda Debowski

Major Focus

Most stories of change leadership imply that the leader is operating as a charismatic, sole agent in the change process. While this may be the case in some instances, there are many leaders who find it difficult to stimulate and lead change. This is particularly the case in educational communities where academic leaders have limited leadership experience before they move into their senior roles. This case study examines the ways in which organizational developers worked in partnership with higher education leaders to achieve effective change, despite high staff resistance and initial challenges in focusing the community's efforts. The case study illustrates the different roles that can be played by organizational developers through the various stages of change leadership, and the influence and contribution they can make to the change process and to encouraging robust and resilient change leaders.

Drawing on three leaders' experiences from a research-intensive Australian university, the process of complex organizational change is traced. Stemming from a need to better manage resources and/or increase the effectiveness of the organizational unit's strategy, the imperative for change was high for each leader, but staff commitment to the process was sluggish. The profiled leaders faced considerable challenges in harnessing the commitment of the change community. Resistant stakeholders and difficulties in creating an effective leadership presence were two challenges consistently encountered by these leaders.

Organization development professionals worked in partnership with the leaders through various processes of mentorship, consultation, coaching and facilitation. By employing a partnership model, increased staff engagement and ownership of agreed strategies enabled more rapid adoption of the outcomes and encouraged authentic learning by the leaders. The three vignettes demonstrate the complexities of leading change and the desirability of providing professional support to leaders during the long transition processes. The case offers a viable model for leaders who need more than personal charisma to make change work.

Introduction

Pick up any leadership or management magazine and you will see a host of charismatic and/or transformational leaders who have made a profound difference to their organizations – in many cases, so the story goes, as sole agents for change and reform. If you believe the hype, the successful change leader is articulate, strategic and able to draw many people into his/her vision. Self-doubt, opposition, or failed ventures are rarely featured in these accounts of successful change leadership although there are guidelines as to how to gain support from followers to achieve successful systemic change (e.g. Burke, Lake and Paine, 2008; Kotter and Cohen, 2002). These accounts can be quite daunting for a less charismatic leader who suffers setbacks or has little leadership experience. These less than perfect leaders may experience undermining by others, limited employee engagement with the change agenda, and / or considerable anxiety about the best way forward.

Leadership in Higher Education

Faculty leaders in higher education face even more challenges; emerging into leadership roles from a career that has primarily encouraged individual effort, they are then asked to assume responsibility for steering successful collective change across communities that are largely individualistic in nature. The academic leader may have little experience in leading university strategy, groups or business processes. Instead, they are generally skilled in achieving high research performance. Agility of thought, the capacity to interpret and shape strategic directions and the ability to guide disparate community factions may all be foreign concepts to these leaders. In this era of financial crises and government reductions in supporting educational funding, the role of academic leader has become particularly arduous. The leader is expected to build a strong community that is dedicated to achieving effective and sustainable change to improve educational quality. Increasingly, the change process is predicated on the need to address cost overruns and uneconomic systems and practices. Academic communities are not only being asked to change their processes and outcomes, but may also face the challenge of redundancies. Working as a change leader in this context is therefore particularly difficult – and even more so for those who are inexperienced leaders. Faculty leaders are normally appointed for a set period – generally around five years in duration. These inexperienced leaders face large financial challenges, anxious staff members and increasing expectations to achieve global excellence and address skill shortages. Compounded by a lack of leadership contacts, a limited knowledge of the political context, and the need to acquire in-depth understanding of the many management and reporting systems, these university leaders face many challenges in meeting high expectations in their formal leadership roles.

The Dilemma Of Seeking Help

When faced with large scale challenges and difficult contexts, few leaders think about seeking help. Leadership textbooks don't talk about being assisted, and the admission of failure and fear can be seen as a sign of weakness. Further, the acknowledgement by leaders of those who have assisted them in achieving successful outcomes is generally missing from our heroic tales (e.g.Kotter and Cohen, 2002). This case study therefore offers an alternate reality: one where leaders can work in partnership with supportive organization development professionals to address complex change and grow into their roles with confidence. Three leadership vignettes illustrate the different support strategies that can contribute to successful change – and to the development of a leader's assurance and image. First, a brief overview of organization development and its role and its methodologies is provided to set some context.

Organizational Development

The discipline of organization development (OD) is regarded as a transformative agency in many businesses (Swanson and Holten, 2009). Drawing on organizational psychology, business theory, knowledge management and human resource management principles, developers operate as coaches, facilitators, educators and mentors to their leadership communities. They may offer formal educational programmes as well as customised support to leaders. The mix of services will depend on the particular organization and its requirements, as well as the effectiveness of the professionals employed in the area. Effective organizational development professionals operate from high levels of credibility and trust. They need to be fully conversant with the emerging challenges facing their leaders and anticipate the likely issues that will need to be addressed.

Highly expert developers do not provide ready-made solutions, but instead, aim to support the leaders as they build their leadership capabilities and confidence. They work one-on-one with the leader as they clarify their thinking about their leadership challenges, and then work in partnership with the leader in planning and implementing the change process. Their role may extend to facilitation of group consultations, coaching on leadership approaches, integrating the contributions of other professionals as required, and any number of other roles – as the situation emerges. This partnership model ensures leaders are guided into better practices in authentic learning contexts.

Professional Help For Leaders

The University of Western Australia hosts a small but effective OD agency. In the last seven years Organisational and Staff Development Services (OSDS) has shifted from operating as a workshop provider to a highly strategic and influential change agency (Debowski and Blake, 2007). The priority focus for the service is supporting the many academic leaders across the university, particularly those experiencing pressure to reform or change their structures, practices and cultures. These developers work across a number of levels, ranging from providing induction support and leadership programmes for new leaders, brokering leadership networks for leaders to learn from more experienced colleagues, providing opportunities for cross-fertilisation of new ideas across the entire community, facilitating consultation and strategic discussions and coaching and working in partnership with leaders. While the role to be played by the organizational developer will depend on the context, the primary goal is to build a strong connection between the leader and the community; to cultivate cohesive alignment between the change agenda and the prevailing culture that is operating (Latta, 2009).

Klaus – A Dynamic Force for Change

After two years of being a head of school, Klaus had a good idea of what was happening with his small academic community. Despite a great research profile, the school was not profitable, demonstrating an emerging operational deficit that had to be arrested. He could see the potential to push for higher research performance and reduced teaching costs as the main avenues for change. However, within a month of launching his ambitious plan, he was facing two bullying charges from his staff and a massive uprising of many in his community. Klaus approached OSDS for assistance. Over the ensuing six months, a series of workshops were held with his staff. Conducted by a skilled facilitator, these workshops progressively worked through the various issues that needed to be addressed. In the first session the staff were offered a detailed explanation of the performance of the school and shown concerning longitudinal trends. They were aggrieved and angry and sought to find a scapegoat. The presence of the facilitator was critical, as it protected Klaus and kept the group focused on looking forward. By the next session, the group was ready to explore how the deficit might be addressed. Over that six month period they identified and eradicated non-viable classes, redesigned the curriculum, increased the research productivity requirements for all staff and developed higher expectations for quality learning across the entire community. The facilitator worked with Klaus and his school throughout this period, providing a valuable support and sounding board during the discussions. A key role of the facilitator was to maintain the group's focus on positive ways forward. Klaus is now an exemplar and model for the entire university community. His school is financially strong, but even more importantly, ranks as one of the top research performers in the world. He also receives very high ratings from his staff when he undertakes reviews of his leadership. He now mentors many other leaders and readily assists them in their own journey.

Richard – Cleaning Up The Mess

It can be very daunting to move from being a high achieving researcher with a small, active research group, into being the dean of a very troubled and damaged faculty. When Richard was urgently placed into the position with little notice, he had little confidence in his leadership skills and even less in his knowledge of the faculty business and activities. With several million dollars bleeding from the faculty each year, strong change leadership was needed. But this was a faculty that had resisted change and blamed the leader for their misfortune. Fortunately, he had a core of good people who would be working with him, but that was not overly helpful in addressing his limited leadership capabilities. As luck would have it, discussions had begun with the previous dean and OSDS to provide some targeted support. He had agreed to a retreat for senior academic leaders to encourage greater engagement. The change of leadership two days before the programme led to some rapid meetings and discussions as to how the event could best assis Richard in moving into his new leadership role. It was decided to focus on building leadership commitment across the group and providing an avenue for Richard to get to know his community. During the two day programme discussions as to the difficult context and the need for change were held. The group was challenged by the facilitator to move from high avoidance behaviours to more active engagement with the change agenda. The new dean was coached throughout, and assisted in speaking publicly and persuasively on the challenges to be addressed.

Since that time Richard has continued to work closely with the OSDS staff – he has attended leadership programmes, enjoyed coaching and feedback on his skills, learned to speak with more confidence, and built strong ownership of his change agenda. He has established a strong team of supporters and in a recent strategic planning day, brought the group further along toward a sustainable management of the faculty. Throughout the process, he has been assisted by the developers. They have met him regularly to discuss strategy, guided him on long-term change strategies and provided him with quick feedback on various leadership initiatives on request. While he is still moving toward his ultimate goal of being a confident, assured leader, he has quickly established his reputation for courage, intelligent leadership and authenticity. He has been brought into contact with other senior leaders and now has a mentor who is a highly successful dean. His faculty note the respect they hold for him and their willingness to support his vision for the community. This is a major step forward for this recalcitrant group.

Matt – The Law Of Magnetism

The establishment of a major new research institute can be a big challenge – particularly when the university has very high expectations for the outcomes of the unit. As the inaugural director of the institute, Matt faced considerable problems. He was a leader who liked quick wins and did not enjoy tasks that required long perseverance. He also found it difficult to give honest feedback or address issues that were undermining the group's formation. The process of building this new community was made more difficult by Matt's sponsor's prior assignation of key leadership roles to a range of researchers. He had come into the role with many of the structures set up and pre-determined. He subsequently discovered that there was little engagement with the model. Further, the senior researchers who were identified as "champions" in the model were only marginally engaged – they remained attached to their substantive work groups and were expected to affiliate with the Institute as voluntary contributors. Matt found it hard to get the senior researchers, his champions, energized and involved. They were supportive, but any meetings were poorly attended, and they were largely absent from this new community. The strategy that he had put together lacked ownership from anyone other than he and his manager.

In discussions with OSDS, it became clear that he was, in fact, beginning to irritate his senior researchers. They were being pressured to belong and were retreating from the institute rather than embracing it. OSDS developers worked with Matt to build a new strategy: Matt would open discussions about the structure of the institute and invite people to join him in building a leadership model that better reflected the likely needs of the community. Those who wished to be part of this exciting initiative would need to demonstrate their commitment – particularly in attending a two day leadership retreat with other leaders and aspirant leaders. Matt also scheduled individual meetings with each potential leader to more fully engage them in the institute's future. In conjunction, Matt needed to develop his own leadership skills by recognising he was high on passion and charisma, but low on follow-through. His manager helped him focus on maintaining a consistent leadership approach. This partnership, along with the growing alliance with OSDS, provided Matt with the necessary insights into his own leadership strategies to commence an effective change process for his research institute.

What The Cases Show Us

While the three cases are drawn from a higher education context, they also apply to many other organizational settings. Leaders come in all shapes and sizes – ranging from hugely capable to very tentative. They have the potential to destroy whole communities and the lives of individuals if they employ destructive or defensive strategies from their positions of power. Unfortunately, these styles are often employed by leaders who are less confident of their skills. While these vignettes describe three leaders who moved late into senior leadership roles, many leaders receive little guidance or education in thinking about leadership of change before confronting the harsh reality of moving their community to a new reality. When financial or competitive pressures are also evident, the resistance and fear from the community must also be managed. In these contexts it is easy to feel afraid and revert to learned or traditional leadership models. The challenge for organizations is to guide leaders toward best practice. Organizational research has clearly shown the impact of poor leadership on productivity, morale, turnover and workplace well-being. In times of change, these impacts become even more pronounced. The profiled leaders faced considerable challenges in harnessing the collective will to change. If left to their own devices, they would have experienced difficulties in achieving engagement and in seeing the issues with some necessary perspective. The use of an external developer encouraged a more balanced view of the context and ensured the leaders retained an optimistic view of the likely outcomes.

The Role Of Coaches And Developers

The vignettes highlight the different roles that a developer might assume. One role is to be a mirror: to assist the leader in building greater self-awareness of their leadership style and its impact. Diagnostic tools, peer feedback, interviews and observation can all assist in gaining a picture of how the leader is operating. In some instances, the support role may include guidance on image management and communication skills. Coaching can then assist in moving behaviours toward more constructive leadership styles. This process can take considerable time. The developer also acts as a telescope, focusing the leader's attention on the main priorities that need to be addressed. In this capacity, the developer can facilitate consultations, work with leadership teams to help build a common vision, draw out the difficult conversations and guide them toward constructive outcomes, help to build a team's focus and commitment, and protect the leader while "robust" discussions take place. This work is high end facilitation, requiring careful management of individual and group learning, goal setting, communication and interaction, and ensuring the direction of the discussions remains constructive and fruitful. Finally, the developer can also operate as a futurist: providing the leader with reassurance and guidance on potential futures and the paths that can be taken to reach them. The importance of building a positive approach to leadership and community development has been well argued by Sekerka and Frederickson (2008). These insights can be very important to new or inexperienced leaders as they learn to envision the consequences of their leadership decisions and to assess risks and opportunities.

The Ultimate Goal Of Leadership Coaching And Development

The ultimate goal of leadership coaching and development is to help leaders learn, grow, and build healthy, high performance organizations. The partnership process allows the leader to assume control as they see the outcomes of the various activities that assist their change agendas. A further role for these developers is to host the various leadership networks that operate across the university. Our academic heads are strongly supported by their colleagues – through networking, mentoring, and via more formal presentations about the strategies and lessons that have been gained through their leadership journeys (Debowski & Blake, 2007). The developers' role as knowledge diffusers and leadership guides also enables cross-fertilization of ideas, models and templates, leading to the development of a strong leadership support base.

Conclusion

These three vignettes offer some successful stories of leaders who have strengthened their leadership through their partnerships with organization development coaches. The concept of change transitions is now being employed to emphasise that change is a series of incremental steps that requires ongoing consultation, review and recasting of the strategy. This encourages leaders to maintain contact with their organizational developer throughout the ongoing journey. Despite our systemic influence, it can be difficult to show the impact of this supportive work. We can show numerous resilient, successful leaders who are taking our organization forward – and many have been assisted through their development journey. But of course, as they become independent, confident leaders, there is little recognition of any support that may have enabled their reaching that point. They are seen as heroic champions of change who reached this stage by themselves!

The charismatic change leader does exist. But for every individual who operates successfully in this manner, there are probably another ten who just get by. Major organizational transitions can have disastrous consequences for leaders and others if they are left to sink or swim on their own leadership capabilities. These vignettes demonstrate the role organizational developers might play in taking leaders to a higher plane of leadership. They offer a realistic preview of how leaders who need more than personal charisma can make change work. Good leaders can be greatly assisted by good partnerships with their OD professionals and peers.

Discussion Questions:

1. What are the advantages of leaders having coaches and especially help from organization development professionals who are knowledgeable about how to build healthy, high performance organizations and successfully manage change?

2. What help did each of the three leaders receive from the Organizational and Staff Development Services (OSDS) group?

3. Discuss the primary lessons you think each leader learned from partnering with the OSDS group?

4. Discuss the three roles coaches and developers might assume and other roles they could play.

5. What would you look for in selecting a coach and developer and what are some cautions leaders should be aware of in partnering in a coaching and development process? What are some cautions leaders and developers should look for in their relationship with leaders?

Key Leadership Lessons:

1. Leaders need to see their progressive development of capabilities and skills as an ongoing journey – one that can be assisted by peers, expert professionals, coaches, mentors and many other sources of support.

2. Leaders are sure to have blind spots and gaps in their development that can usually be dealt with if they have ways of becoming aware, particularly through working with coaches and developers.

3. Organizations can benefit from recognizing the challenges of leading and building healthy, high performance organizations and providing the necessary support and infrastructure for leaders.

4. While change takes many forms, leadership authenticity and a genuine concern for gaining stakeholder engagement lies at the heart of successful change and cultural shifts.

References

Burke, W.W., Lake, D.G. & Paine, J. W. (2008). *Organization change: A comprehensive reader.* Jossey Bass.

Debowski, S. & Blake, V. (2007). Collective capacity building of academic leaders: a university model of leadership and learning in context. *International Journal of Learning and Change, vol.2, no. 3,* 307 - 324.

Kotter, J. (2007). Leading change: Why transformation efforts fail. *Harvard Business Review,* Available at: http://www.harvardmacy.org/Upload/pdf/Kotter%20article.pdf

Kotter, J. & Cohen, D. S. (2002). *The Heart of Change: Real-life stories of how people change their organizations.* Harvard Business Review Press.

Latta, G. (2009). A Process Model of Organizational Change in Cultural Context (OC3 Model) *Journal of Leadership & Organizational Studies,* 16(1), 19-37

Sekerka, L. E. & Frederickson, B. L. (2008) Establishing positive emotional climates to advance organizational transformation. Available at: http://sekerkaethicsinaction.com/docs/pdfs/Sekerka-Fredrickson%20Climate%20Chapter%20Web%209-07.pdf

Swanson, R.A. & Holten, E. F. (2009). *Foundations of Human Resource Development.* Berrett-Koehler Publishers.

BIOGRAPHY

Professor Shelda Debowski is internationally regarded for her work in higher education development. She has a long history of leading work groups, projects and communities through change and development. Shelda has published widely in the areas of knowledge management, higher education leadership and organizational development. She currently works with many different academic communities and leaders at the University of Western Australia and has played a major role in building a strong leadership culture across the university. She also operates as a leadership consultant to educational communities working through large-scale change processes. Shelda has received national recognition for her work in organizational development and regularly speaks on these matters at conferences and other forums.

Professor Shelda Debowski, PhD
Professor (Higher Education Development) and Director, Organizational
and Staff Development Services University of Western Australia
35 Stirling Hwy, Crawley WA Australia 6009
Tel. 61 8 64883845 · Fax: 618 64881156
Email: Shelda.Debowski@uwa.edu.au

2

Training Leaders To Lead Change

John Adams, Ph.D.

Major Focus

An apparently universal shortcoming in leading change is the absence of consistent and persistent attention to the intangibles represented by the people who are going through the change. Societal culture, organizational culture, and ingrained individual mindsets are all focused on maintaining the status quo. When the people being asked to change are overlooked in the process, the goals of the change are almost universally unmet. This case presents a set of people-based success factors for leading a complex organizational change process.

Nineteen factors were identified from the author's research, and from others' research, that appear to be essential to successful change implementation. The selected change factors were allocated across Lewin's rudimentary model of "Unfreezing, Moving, and Refreezing." A few of the factors were identified as being essential generally throughout the change process.

The list of 19 factors was originally assembled at the request of the Vice-Chancellor of a small university in southern India for his use in initiating and leading significant system-wide changes. Since the university is committed to expressing the human values of "truth, right action, peace, love and nonviolence" in all aspects of its operations, the human factors of change are of utmost importance. These factors are suggested for use as an on-going checklist for leaders of any organizational complex change effort.

Introduction

For many years, I have visited southern India once or twice a year. Since 2003, I have been fortunate enough to be invited to teach in a university MBA program, and also to join Ph.D. in Management Science dissertation committees, during these visits. Each visit, one of my first activities has been to visit the Vice-Chancellor of the university to gain his "permission" to teach during the present visit. Each of these meetings essentially amounted to a catching up with each other's activities since the previous visit.

During the spring of 2007, the Vice-Chancellor requested my assistance in improving his ability to implement university-wide changes that he had determined were needed (e.g. improving the use of IT capabilities in the educational process, improving the students' abilities to speak "global English" rather than "village English," generating more faculty publications in international peer-reviewed journals, etc.). The Vice-Chancellor's concern was that the faculty had very long tenures, while V-Cs are appointed to serve only for a few years each. Bringing about the fundamental changes he felt was needed was proving to be a very challenging endeavor!

I have long been concerned about the high world-wide rate of organizational change effort failures, in spite of all the guides and models that have been developed over the past few decades – ranging from a few simple pointers (Kotter, 1996) that can be summarized in eight brief paragraphs, to fully developed systemic and systematic models that take two full volumes to describe (Ackerman Anderson and Anderson, 2001 and Anderson and Ackerman Anderson, 2001). I had also carried out some of my own research on successful and unsuccessful change cases, on both the individual and the organizational levels, and in the process, identified 12 intangible people oriented success factors (Adams, 2003). So the V-C's request was very exciting to me, and I agreed to create a template for him to use in preparing for, implementing, and leading change processes during the remainder of his tenure. When I returned to the USA, I dug into the literature and pulled together what seemed to me to be a very comprehensive and yet simple list of qualities for the VC to follow in implementing his change agenda at the university.

I used Lewin's three stages of change – unfreezing, moving, refreezing – as the organizing principle, and also found that some of the qualities I found in my literature review seemed to be general and would be needed across all three stages of change. Overall, since I would not be present when these guidelines were put to use by the VC, I endeavored to keep the list short, simple and transparently logical. Since the VC would be operating alone in most of the instances in which he wished to bring about change, I also endeavored to keep each item on the list focused on people factors and system dynamics factors. The VC had previously served in senior management positions in Indian industry, and did not need to be taught about management and leadership in general.

Preparing For Change

In preparing for change leaders need to evaluate how the organization they lead is presently governed and ideally should be governed. Governance is made up of the formal and informal processes for making decisions, communicating information, and distributing resources (Doppelt, 2003). If decision making, information flow, and resource distribution is not rearranged to reflect the desired new state, the old state will most likely prevail.

In changing how the organization is governed, leaders need to accomplish seven things (Meadows, 1997):

1. Change business as usual by changing the mind-set or mental models of how to do things from supporting the old ways to supporting the new desired ways.
2. Rearrange key parts of the organization by creating transition teams to make needed changes.
3. Engage the transition teams in crafting a clear and inspiring vision and set of guiding principles for decision making henceforth.
4. Alter the rules of engagement by developing both the operational and the governance strategies to reflect the new goals and principles.
5. Communicate the new state relentlessly through the newly altered information flow channels.
6. Encourage and reward innovation and learning towards the new state.
7. Integrate the new state in the systems, structures, and standard operating procedures.

The Change Leader Checklist

Given these seven tasks that have to do with fundamentally changing the governance to the new order of things, I have returned to the research literature on change leadership and I have found **19 qualities** that receive wide recognition for the various research studies I consulted including my own research. Leading change requires special leadership skills. Change leaders must keep the organization focused on achieving its new mission while simultaneously carrying out the requirements of the existing operating system. They must also guide the process of creating a compelling vision, identify targets for change, guide the development of a plan for becoming a fundamentally different social system, build a sense of urgency for action, and ensure that the governance system is arranged to support the needed changes. With this in mind, here is the Change Leader Checklist:

General Qualities (Useful at all times)

1. Able to engage in productive conflict with ideas and not to attack people
2. Never stops improving relationships
3. Has a systematic and comprehensive approach to implementing the changes
4. Continues to learn on the go and invites others to learn

Initiation of Change ("Unfreezing" the status quo)

5. Courage to question present conditions, willingness to generate uncertainty, and to search without knowing
6. Able to generate an understanding, acceptance, and sense of urgency in relation to the need for change
7. Able to build the belief that the change is both desirable and possible
8. Establishes new mindsets that hold the desired state as essential and the status quo as unacceptable

Diffusion of Change ("Moving" to the desired new state)

9. Always tells the truth and forms "until further notice" expectations
10. Naturally generates a passionate commitment to the desired outcomes (perhaps through metaphor rich stories)
11. Articulates specific deliverables and ensures that all key people know what to do next
12. Deliberately uses new governance processes and parts arrangements to ensure that the desired state is top priority in people's minds, and that action is taken
13. Able to work with intervention processes that bring the whole system into the room
14. Ensures that the governance process rewards movement towards the desired state and removes rewards from maintenance of the status quo
15. Remembers to constantly scan the "boundaries of the change" for potential problems, resources and new agreements
16. Builds critical masses of alignment (Getting early adopters into alignment and giving them things to do) around each essential component of the change vision through engaging and mobilizing agreement

Integration of the New State ("Refreezing" – stabilizing the change)

17. Maintains an appreciative stance of encouraging and rewarding what is already working in the newly emerging change process
18. Demonstrates patience and perseverance in supporting all in moving forward
19. Visible, vocal, consistent and persistent with the "story" of the change

On my next visit to India, the VC announced that the list was most helpful and that he had referred to it repeatedly. Indeed, many new practices had been implemented in the six months following my sending the above list to him.

Discussion

1. A high percent of change efforts fail altogether or fail to achieve the desired results primarily because leaders are not trained how to successfully lead change. What are typical mistakes made by leaders in leading changes?

2. What did you learn about things leaders should be prepared to do in leading change?

3. What are some insights you gained about leading change that you found in the Change Leader Checklist?

4. Are there any items you would add or remove from the checklist?

5. What would be some alternatives for how organizations could create and utilize their own Change Leader Checklist?

Leadership Lessons

1. It is very important for leaders to be trained in how to successfully lead change. There are serious consequences to organizations and the people in them when leaders ineffectively lead change.

2. Leadership is more than a position – it requires a future focused state of mind, a commitment to building something special, and the courage to make needed changes.

3. Change efforts are unlikely to be successful if governance processes (at least including how decisions are made, how information is disseminated and how resources are allocated) are not changed to reflect the desired state.

4. Visible, vocal, consistent and persistent leadership is necessary to keep the organization focused on achieving the desired changes while simultaneously carrying out the requirements of the existing operating system.

References

Ackerman Anderson, L. S. and Anderson, D. (2010). *The change leader's roadmap: How to navigate your organization's transformation* (2nd Edition). San Francisco: Pfeiffer.

Anderson, D. and Ackerman Anderson, L. S. (2010). *Beyond change management: Advanced strategies for today's transformational leaders* (2nd Edition). San Francisco: Pfeiffer.

Adams, J. (2003). Successful change: Paying attention to the intangibles." *OD Practitioner.* Winter 35(4).

Holt, D.T., Armenakis, A.A., Feild, H.S. & Harris, S.G. (2007). Readiness for Organizational Change: The Systematic Development of a Scale. *Journal of Applied Behavioral* Science. 43(232 – 255).

Doppelt, J. (2003). *Leading change toward sustainability.* Sheffield, UK: Greenleaf Publishing Limited.

Kotter, J. (1996). *Leading change.* Cambridge, MA: Harvard Business School Press.

Meadows, D. (1997). Places to intervene in a system. Whole Earth. *Winter, 1997:* 78-85.

BIOGRAPHY

John D. Adams, Ph.D. – Emeritus Professor, speaker, author, consultant, and seminar leader – has been at the forefront of the Organization Development and Transformation profession for over 40 years. John served as the Chair of the Organizational Systems Ph.D. Program at the Saybrook University (San Francisco) for 10 years, and also as a guest faculty member at The Bainbridge Island Graduate Institute in the MBA in Sustainability program. He is currently Director of Education for Foothill Collaborative for Sustainability (FoCuS) and administrative director for Prevention International: No Cervical Cancer in India (PINCC-India).

His latest book (2000), *Thinking Today as if Tomorrow Mattered: The Rise of a Sustainable Consciousness,* is the culmination of several years' research, speaking, and writing. John is also founder of Eartheart Enterprises, an international speaking, publishing, and consulting business. John has previously served as a manager in executive education and workplace effectiveness at Sun Microsystems; Director of Professional Development at the NTL Institute; and as a Visiting Lecturer at The University of Leeds (U.K.). He has written prolifically in the areas of health and stress management, personal effectiveness at work, and change. John's earlier books, *Transforming Work* and *Transforming Leadership,* are widely held as defining a new role for the Organization Development profession in a rapidly transforming world.

John D. Adams, Ph.D.
Emeritus Professor, Organizational Systems Program
Saybrook University
San Francisco, CA, USA
PO Box 4387, Camp Connell, CA 95223-4387 USA
Tel. (209) 795-6672 · Email: JAdams2212@comcast.net
www.eartheart-ent.com · www.saybrook.edu

3

Leadership Lessons In
Whole System Transformation™

Susan Donnan, William J. Rothwell, Roland Sullivan & Tom Dick

Major Focus Of The Case

This case describes how the Whole System Transformation (WST) methodology was used to exceed the expectations of internal customers by engaging the critical mass of a world-renowned Information Technology and Communication (ICT) function to (1) transform the executive leadership team; (2) transform the critical mass of people in ICT; (3) transfer WST technology to the internal change agent; and (4) ensure the organization sustains a "built-to-change" capability.

One important lesson learned in the case was that, to succeed with change, the top management team of any organization must first "walk the talk." The top team members must experience transformation first before engaging others. While 60 to 70 percent of all change management cases in today's organizations fail, 98 percent of WST cases succeed. One reason most change efforts fail is that executive teams dictate what they want others to do and be rather than, to paraphrase Gandhi, be the change they wish to see in the world. Secondly, leadership pushes down the change rather then engages the system in the change journey.

The entry phase of this case aligned a transformed leadership team as it learned to lead organization transformation so that overall performance would be enhanced. A special transformation network was established to represent the whole function. The network performed courageously in moving the system forward in a truly dramatic fashion. A key to the success was experienced, qualified and competent internal change agent leadership.

The Organizational Context

This case describes what happened in an anonymous global corporation, a large manufacturer with 55,000 employees worldwide. A new Chief Information Office (CIO) was appointed. He inherited a function with 1,200 staff. The function had been integrated, split, and reorganized numerous times over a seven year period. Within the context of the global financial and economic crisis, the CIO also faced challenges resulting from a decreasing budget, growing business demands, a changing business model, and increasingly disenchanted internal customers. To do more and better with less, his function could not afford the baby steps of incremental change management. The organization needed to make a quantum leap to change. Transformational change was thus essential if the company was to remain the world leader in its industry.

In the CIO's first year, he worked with his new executive leadership team and a core group of middle managers to define a new vision, mission, and customer-facing transnational organization. However, he knew that these changes were only the beginning. It could take months, or even years, to formulate and implement the necessary change. But the company's COO was impatient and demanded immediate results.

At the recommendation of an internal change consultant, the WST methodology was selected to accelerate a paradigm shift in the function. (See Figure 1.)

Figure 1:

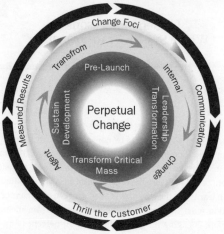

THE WHOLE SYSTEM TRANSFORMATION MODEL

The CIO wanted a self-sustaining change process that would have a positive ripple effect. An experienced external change consultant was engaged to help make that happen. Since the internal change agent had pursued graduate work in WST and other large group interactive events, she was successful in selling the methodology effectively to her internal clients.

The Whole System Transformation Model

The whole system transformation journey is a dynamic "holistic" process designed to help leaders engage a critical mass of the organization in reinventing itself and creating a future of aligned and committed action.

At the core, the process begins with transforming the leader and his or her team so they're aligned both intellectually and emotionally around a compelling and new vision.

Once leadership is aligned, then and only then can the process move into transforming the critical mass. This is accomplished through the design and execution of a powerful large-group interactive event where enough people within the system participate to drive a significant shift for the organization. These people go through a process that fully and safely engages them in a dialog addressing the most significant issues. They come away feeling valued. They know they have made an important contribution to moving the organization forward. They are now aligned with the leadership; all are "one brain and one heart".

Throughout the journey, it is critical that there is at least one internal change agent participating in and learning this process. Their role is to carry the shift forward as the organization navigates its way through perpetual change in the future.

The Transformation Journey

Transform The Executive Leadership Team The start up phase of the intervention, in this case, was a 3-day leadership retreat for the CIO and his direct reports. Its aim was to improve the effectiveness and align the efforts of the ICT executive leadership team. As a result of the retreat, the team members became more cohesive and learned to speak as one voice.

Transform A Microcosm Of The Critical Mass: Designing The Summit

Immediately following the retreat, twelve people – representing all units, levels, and locations – were nominated to work together to design a 300-person transformation summit. This group originally named the design team, eventually re-named themselves as the *transformation agent network*.

The internal and external change consultants jointly facilitated three 2- or 3-day design team sessions over a three-month period. These sessions followed a customized agenda allowing open conversations around what was not working, what was working and what needed to happen in a large meeting to reshape the organization. This democratic and engaging approach is distinctly different from a typical change management program where an external consulting firm essentially drives the process and controls the change agenda.

People resist what others try to sell them but usually support changes that they have been authentically involved in. The CIO and his direct reports took turns participating in the design sessions, giving both their support and their input. During this time, the twelve strangers, who were initially skeptical and confused, became transformed into a high-performing team. They worked together to design a 3-day summit that would transform a critical mass of people into a unified team with a unified spirit.

Transform The Critical Mass: The Summit

The 300 participants were a carefully selected microcosm of ICT. They represented all units, levels, and locations. For the first time in their history with the company, the participants found themselves sitting face-to-face with their colleagues, middle managers and senior managers. They worked together as equals. The deep-seated feelings of some participants lingered, resulting from the devastation their parents experienced with each other in World War II. As they rallied, they realized a oneness that dissipated past feelings and current work tensions.

The summit exceeded participant expectations. By focusing on strengths, the participants felt good about their action plans. The participants expressed their appreciation by standing ovations during the event, generally not part of the group's behavioral norm. One highlight of the session: of the 40 or so robust group activities during the summit, the CIO and his direct reports openly and transparently answered anonymously-submitted "elephant in the room" questions. They answered the questions frankly – much to the joy of all. Another highlight of the session: after listening intensely to the business intelligence generated by all, the executive leadership team made personal commitments and action plans that would transfigure the function on stage in front of all. The plans were on target. They created a great deal of excitement because they were influenced by the key business intelligence generated by the 300. **The participants left the summit with a clear understanding of the rationale for change, vivid pictures of what success would look like, and clear first steps at the individual, unit, and system-wide levels.**

The CIO reported in his interview for this chapter that the "ripple effect (of the large meeting) was unbelievable." "A miracle had been promised and a miracle was deliered." Since the summit, the twelve design team members have continued to drive change as transformation agents. Initially they were to be a temporary team. But, at their request, they have become a standing team to govern the change effort.

The Payoffs And Sustaining Transformation After The Summit

The internal change agent regularly reviews progress with the transformation agent network, the CIO, and his direct reports. Early indicators of success include the immediate engagement of the entire organization, the translation of actions and commitments from the summit into projects

BIOGRAPHY

initiatives, will

Susan Donnan was initiated into the world of OD with Pat William's MSOD program at Pepperdine University in 1997.
She has 30 years of diverse business experience, facilitating complex change in large organizations. She consults cross-culturally in global and trans-national settings. She is currently working in Europe as an internal change agent for a global manufacturer.

Susan Donnan
sdonnan@metavolution.com

William J. Rothwell is a Professor on the University Park campus at Penn State University. Author, coauthor, editor or coeditor of over 70 books and 230 articles, he directs a graduate program in learning and performance and also leads his own consulting company known as Rothwell and Associates, Inc. Before arriving at Penn State in 1993, he had 20 years of HR work experience in the public and private sectors.

William J. Rothwell The Pennsylvania State University
Tel. 814-863-2581 · www.rothwell-associates.com

Roland Sullivan was initiated into the world of OD with a Charlie Seashore HR Lab in 1962 at NTL. Roland coined the phrase "Whole System Transformation" in 1974. He is known for "actually" transforming large systems. He has been involved in OD change efforts with over 1,000 organizations in 30 countries. With Rothwell and Pareek, he co-founded the Asian OD Network.

Roland Sullivan Sullivan Transformation Agents Pte. Ltd.
Tel. 952-818-4744 · Email: R@rolandsullivan.com

Tom Dick has over 22 years of experience working as an internal and external change consultant in a broad set of industries.
He has performed numerous strategic and change implementation engagements with a diverse set of organizations ranging from startups to fortune 50 corporations.

Tom DickSolutia Consulting
Tel. 651-439-6505 · Email: Tom_Dick@msn.com